Practice*Planners*

Homework Planners feature dozens of behaviorally based, ready-to-use assignments that are designed for use between sessions, as well as a disk or CD-ROM (Microsoft Word) containing all of the assignments—allowing you to customize them to suit your unique client needs.

- ❑ Brief Couples Therapy Homework Planner ....978-0-471-29511-2 / $55.00
- ❑ Child Psychotherapy Homework Planner, Second Edition..........................978-0-471-78534-7 / $55.00
- ❑ Child Therapy Activity and Homework Planner ....978-0-471-25684-7 / $55.00
- ❑ Adolescent Psychotherapy Homework Planner, Second Edition ....978-0-471-78537-8 / $55.00
- ❑ Addiction Treatment Homework Planner, Third Edition...............................978-0-471-77461-7 / $55.00
- ❑ Brief Employee Assistance Homework Planner ....978-0-471-38088-7 / $55.00
- ❑ Brief Family Therapy Homework Planner...978-0-471-38512-7 / $55.00
- ❑ Grief Counseling Homework Planner ....978-0-471-43318-7 / $55.00
- ❑ Divorce Counseling Homework Planner...978-0-471-43319-4 / $55.00
- ❑ Group Therapy Homework Planner ....978-0-471-41822-1 / $55.00
- ❑ School Counseling and School Social Work Homework Planner ....978-0-471-09114-1 / $55.00
- ❑ Adolescent Psychotherapy Homework Planner II ....978-0-471-27493-3 / $55.00
- ❑ Adult Psychotherapy Homework Planner, Second Edition ....978-0-471-76343-7 / $55.00
- ❑ Parenting Skills Homework Planner..978-0-471-48182-9 / $55.00

Progress Notes Planners contain complete prewritten progress notes for each presenting problem in the companion Treatment Planners.

- ❑ The Adult Psychotherapy Progress Notes Planner.....................................978-0-471-76344-4 / $55.00
- ❑ The Adolescent Psychotherapy Progress Notes Planner ....978-0-471-78538-5 / $55.00
- ❑ The Severe and Persistent Mental Illness Progress Notes Planner ....978-0-470-18014-3 / $55.00
- ❑ The Child Psychotherapy Progress Notes Planner......................................978-0-471-78536-1 / $55.00
- ❑ The Addiction Progress Notes Planner...978-0-471-73253-2 / $55.00
- ❑ The Couples Psychotherapy Progress Notes Planner ....978-0-471-27460-5 / $55.00
- ❑ The Family Therapy Progress Notes Planner ....978-0-471-48443-1 / $55.00

Client Education Handout Planners contain elegantly designed handouts that can be printed out from the enclosed CD-ROM and provide information on a wide range of psychological and emotional disorders and life skills issues. Use as patient literature, handouts at presentations, and aids for promoting your mental health practice.

- ❑ Adult Client Education Handout Planner ....978-0-471-20232-5 / $55.00
- ❑ Child and Adolescent Client Education Handout Planner...........................978-0-471-20233-2 / $55.00
- ❑ Couples and Family Client Education Handout Planner ....978-0-471-20234-9 / $55.00

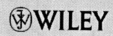

TheraScribe®

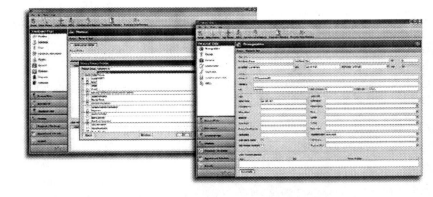

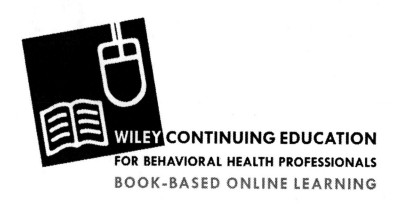

The Severe and Persistent Mental Illness Treatment Planner, Second Edition

Practice*Planners*® Series

Treatment Planners

The Complete Adult Psychotherapy Treatment Planner, Fourth Edition
The Child Psychotherapy Treatment Planner, Fourth Edition
The Adolescent Psychotherapy Treatment Planner, Fourth Edition
The Addiction Treatment Planner, Third Edition
The Continuum of Care Treatment Planner
The Couples Psychotherapy Treatment Planner
The Employee Assistance Treatment Planner
The Pastoral Counseling Treatment Planner
The Older Adult Psychotherapy Treatment Planner
The Behavioral Medicine Treatment Planner
The Group Therapy Treatment Planner
The Gay and Lesbian Psychotherapy Treatment Planner
The Family Therapy Treatment Planner
The Severe and Persistent Mental Illness Treatment Planner, Second Edition
The Mental Retardation and Developmental Disability Treatment Planner
The Social Work and Human Services Treatment Planner
The Crisis Counseling and Traumatic Events Treatment Planner
The Personality Disorders Treatment Planner
The Rehabilitation Psychology Treatment Planner
The Special Education Treatment Planner
The Juvenile Justice and Residential Care Treatment Planner
The School Counseling and School Social Work Treatment Planner
The Sexual Abuse Victim and Sexual Offender Treatment Planner
The Probation and Parole Treatment Planner
The Psychopharmacology Treatment Planner
The Speech-Language Pathology Treatment Planner
The Suicide and Homicide Treatment Planner
The College Student Counseling Treatment Planner
The Parenting Skills Treatment Planner
The Early Childhood Intervention Treatment Planner
The Co-Occurring Disorders Treatment Planner
The Complete Women's Psychotherapy Treatment Planner

Progress Notes Planners

The Child Psychotherapy Progress Notes Planner, Third Edition
The Adolescent Psychotherapy Progress Notes Planner, Third Edition
The Adult Psychotherapy Progress Notes Planner, Third Edition
The Addiction Progress Notes Planner, Second Edition
The Severe and Persistent Mental Illness Progress Notes Planner, Second Edition
The Couples Psychotherapy Progress Notes Planner
The Family Therapy Progress Notes Planner

Homework Planners

Brief Couples Therapy Homework Planner
Brief Employee Assistance Homework Planner
Brief Family Therapy Homework Planner
Grief Counseling Homework Planner
Group Therapy Homework Planner
Divorce Counseling Homework Planner
School Counseling and School Social Work Homework Planner
Child Therapy Activity and Homework Planner
Addiction Treatment Homework Planner, Third Edition
Adolescent Psychotherapy Homework Planner II
Adolescent Psychotherapy Homework Planner, Second Edition
Adult Psychotherapy Homework Planner, Second Edition
Child Psychotherapy Homework Planner, Second Edition
Parenting Skills Homework Planner

Client Education Handout Planners

Adult Client Education Handout Planner
Child and Adolescent Client Education Handout Planner
Couples and Family Client Education Handout Planner

Complete Planners

The Complete Depression Treatment and Homework Planner
The Complete Anxiety Treatment and Homework Planner

PracticePlanners®

Arthur E. Jongsma, Jr., Series Editor

The Severe and Persistent Mental Illness Treatment Planner, Second Edition

David J. Berghuis

Arthur E. Jongsma, Jr.

Timothy J. Bruce, Contributing Editor

WILEY

JOHN WILEY & SONS, INC.

Published by John Wiley & Sons, Inc., Hoboken, New Jersey.
Published simultaneously in Canada.

For general information on our other products and services please contact our Customer Care Department within the U.S. at (800) 762-2974, outside the United States at (317) 572-3993 or fax (317) 572-4002.

Wiley also publishes its books in a variety of electronic formats. Some content that appears in print may not be available in electronic books. For more information about Wiley products, visit our web site at www.wiley.com.

Library of Congress Cataloging-in-Publication Data

Berghuis, David J.
    The severe and persistent mental illness treatment planner / David J. Berghuis, Arthur E. Jongsma Jr. — 2nd ed.
       p. ; cm. — (Practice planners series)
    Includes bibliographical references and index.
    ISBN 978-0-470-18013-6 (pbk. : alk. paper)
    1. Mental illness—Treatment—Planning—Handbooks, manuals, etc. 2. Chronic illness—Treatment—Planning—Handbooks, manuals, etc. 3. Psychiatric records—Handbooks, manuals, etc. I. Jongsma, Arthur E., 1943- II. Title. III. Series: Practice planners.
    [DNLM: 1. Mental Disorders—therapy—Handbooks. 2. Chronic Disease—therapy—Handbooks. 3. Patient Care Planning—Handbooks. 4. Psychotherapy—methods—Handbooks. WM 34 B497s 2008]
    RC480.53.B47 2008
    616.89'14—dc22
                                                                                2008027403

10 9 8 7 6 5 4 3

To my wife, Barbara, for whom my love grows every day, and to my children, Katherine and Michael, who make me proud.

—David J. Berghuis

To Tom Van Wylen and Mary Boll, two friends who have stepped forward to show their support for those who work with clients struggling with severe and persistent mental illness. Thank you and God bless you.

—Arthur E. Jongsma, Jr.

To all of those individuals who struggle with severe mental problems and to all of the individuals who dedicate their lives to helping them.

—Timothy J. Bruce

CONTENTS

▽ indicates that the Objective/Intervention is consistent with those found in evidence-based treatments.

PRACTICE*PLANNERS*® SERIES PREFACE

Accountability is an important dimension of the practice of psychotherapy. Treatment programs, public agencies, clinics, and practitioners must justify and document their treatment plans to outside review entities in order to be reimbursed for services. The books and software in the Practice*Planners*® series are designed to help practitioners fulfill these documentation requirements efficiently and professionally.

The Practice*Planners*® series includes a wide array of treatment-planning books, including not only the original *Complete Adult Psychotherapy Treatment Planner, Child Psychotherapy Treatment Planner,* and *Adolescent Psychotherapy Treatment Planner*, all now in their fourth editions, but also *Treatment Planners* targeted to a wide range of specialty areas of practice, including:

- Addictions
- Behavioral medicine
- College students
- Co-occurring disorders
- Couples therapy
- Crisis counseling
- Early childhood education
- Employee assistance
- Family therapy
- Gays and lesbians
- Group therapy
- Juvenile justice and residential care
- Mental retardation and developmental disability
- Neuropsychology
- Older adults
- Parenting skills
- Pastoral counseling

- Personality disorders
- Probation and parole
- Psychopharmacology
- School counseling
- Severe and persistent mental illness
- Sexual abuse victims and offenders
- Special education
- Suicide and homicide risk assessment
- Women's issues

In addition, there are three branches of companion books that can be used in conjunction with the *Treatment Planners,* or on their own:

- *Progress Notes Planners* provide a menu of progress statements that elaborate on the client's symptom presentation and the provider's therapeutic intervention. Each *Progress Notes Planner* statement is directly integrated with the behavioral definitions and therapeutic interventions from its companion *Treatment Planner.*

- *Homework Planners* include homework assignments designed around each presenting problem (e.g., anxiety, depression, chemical dependence, anger management, eating disorders, or panic disorder) that is the focus of a chapter in its corresponding *Treatment Planner.*

- *Client Education Handout Planners* provide brochures and handouts to help educate and inform clients on presenting problems and mental health issues, as well as life skills techniques. The handouts are included on CD-ROMs for easy printing from your computer and are ideal for use in waiting rooms, at presentations, as newsletters, or as information for clients struggling with mental illness issues. The topics covered by these handouts correspond to the presenting problems in the *Treatment Planners.*

The series also includes:

- **Thera***Scribe*®, the best-selling treatment-planning and clinical record-keeping software system for mental health professionals. Thera*Scribe*® allows the user to import the data from any of the *Treatment Planner, Progress Notes Planner,* or *Homework Planner* books into the software's expandable database to simply point and click to create a detailed, organized, individualized, and customized treatment plan along with optional integrated progress notes and homework assignments.

Adjunctive books, such as *The Psychotherapy Documentation Primer* and *The Clinical Documentation Sourcebook* contain forms and resources to aid the clinician in mental health practice management.

The goal of our series is to provide practitioners with the resources they need in order to provide high-quality care in the era of accountability. To put it simply: We seek to help you spend more time on patients and less time on paperwork.

ARTHUR E. JONGSMA JR.
Grand Rapids, Michigan

ACKNOWLEDGMENTS

A variety of people should be acknowledged for their assistance in developing this *Planner*. First, the clients who have been willing to share their lives and troubles have taught us more than can be written. Several staff members of the Community Mental Health Centers in Ionia County and Newaygo County (both in Michigan) have either knowingly or unknowingly provided feedback and ideas throughout the unfolding of this project. While developing the first edition of this *Planner*, the authors were also involved in the writing of *The Mental Retardation and Developmental Disability Treatment Planner*, with Kellye Slaggert. Many ideas developed for that *Planner* were adapted for this one. Barbara Berghuis, wife of the primary author, and a case manager herself, was instrumental in developing and critiquing the manuscript throughout the process. The library staff of Calvin College and Seminary were invaluable in their assistance while researching material for this project.

This second edition has been improved beyond measure by the guidance and contribution of Dr. Tim Bruce. He has been our well-informed expert on the evidence-based content that exists in the professional literature. Thank you, Tim.

Sue Rhoda, our manuscript manager, has been a wonderful assistant who has very efficiently kept all the details organized, allowing us to submit a final product that has been polished by her professional hand. Thank you, Sue.

No project this large gets completed without other priorities being rearranged. The willingness of our families to allow us to take the time to bring this idea to fruition is very much appreciated. It is their support and guidance that have allowed us to help others. The editorial staff at John Wiley & Sons has consistently provided us with supremely competent encouragement and guidance for which we are grateful.

A. E. J.
D. J. B.

The Severe and Persistent Mental Illness Treatment Planner, Second Edition

INTRODUCTION

ABOUT PRACTICE*PLANNERS*® TREATMENT PLANNERS

Pressure from third-party payors, accrediting agencies, and other outside parties has increased the need for clinicians to quickly produce effective, high-quality treatment plans. *Treatment Planners* provide all the elements necessary to quickly and easily develop formal treatment plans that satisfy the needs of most third-party payors and state and federal review agencies.

Each *Treatment Planner:*

- Saves you hours of time-consuming paperwork.
- Offers the freedom to develop customized treatment plans.
- Includes over 1,000 clear statements describing the behavioral manifestations of each relational problem, and includes long-term goals, short-term objectives, and clinically tested treatment options.
- Has an easy-to-use reference format that helps locate treatment plan components by behavioral problem or *DSM-IV* diagnosis.

As with the rest of the books in the Practice*Planners*® series, our aim is to clarify, simplify, and accelerate the treatment planning process, so you spend less time on paperwork, and more time with your clients.

ABOUT THE SEVERE AND PERSISTENT MENTAL ILLNESS TREATMENT PLANNER

The field of treatment for the severely and persistently mentally ill is at a pivotal point in its evolution. New medications have provided stability to people who have been chronically unstable in the past. What started with deinstitutionalization and the growth of community mental health centers has gradually transformed into a myriad of agencies and clinicians who provide treatment in a variety of settings. Many changes have also occurred for the agencies serving this population. In many areas, the service providers have been compelled to become more efficient and competitive for their clientele. Most agencies are required to obtain accreditation from outside auditors, such as the Joint Commission on the Accreditation of Health Organizations (JCAHO), Council on Accreditation (COA), or the Commission on Accreditation of Rehabilitation Facilities (CARF). Payors often demand documentation of positive outcomes for clients whom we serve. With these many changes in the field, the need for better organization, treatment techniques, and documentation becomes self-evident.

To fill this need, we have developed *The Severe and Persistent Mental Illness Treatment Planner.* This *Planner* suggests thousands of prewritten behavioral definitions, objectives, goals, and interventions for a variety of problem areas experienced by the men and women who suffer from chronic mental illness. This book will be useful to any clinician working with this population, but care has been taken to write from the perspective of the clinician who manages the client's entire treatment, whether he or she be called a case manager, supports coordinator, social worker, or some other name. Goals and interventions are written for a variety of types and levels of intensity of severe and persistent mental illnesses. It is our hope that this *Planner* will allow clinicians to quickly and accurately develop and implement helpful treatment plans for their clients. In this second edition, we have made the chapters more focused and, in many cases, shorter. We have also added a few new chapters. But the most significant change for this edition is the addition of evidence-based Objectives and Interventions to those chapters where research data is available to inform the content.

INCORPORATING EVIDENCE-BASED TREATMENT (EBT)

Evidence-based treatment (that is, treatment that is scientifically shown in research trials to be efficacious) is rapidly becoming critically important to the mental health community because insurance companies are beginning to offer preferential pay to organizations using it. In fact, the APA Division 12 (Society of Clinical Psychology) lists of empirically supported treatments have been referenced by a number of local, state, and federal funding agencies, which are beginning to restrict reimbursement to these treatments, as are some managed care and insurance companies.

In this second edition of *The Severe and Persistent Mental Illness Treatment Planner,* we have made an effort to empirically inform some chapters by highlighting short-term objectives (STOs) and therapeutic interventions (TIs) that are consistent with psychological treatments or therapeutic programs that have demonstrated some level of efficacy through empirical study. Watch for this icon ▼ as an indication that an Objective/Intervention is consistent with those found in evidence-based treatments.

References to their empirical support have been included in Appendix B. For information related to the identification of evidence-based practices (EBPs), including the benefits and limitations of the effort, we suggest Bruce and Sanderson (2005); Chambless et. al. (1996, 1998); Chambless and Ollendick (2001); Drake, Merrens, and Lynde (2005); Hofmann and Tompson (2002); Nathan and Gorman (2002); and Stout and Hayes (2005).

In this *Planner*, we have included STOs and TIs consistent with EBPs that are more programmatic than psychotherapeutic in nature and that have been found efficacious for problems common to those struggling with severe and persistent mental illnesses (SPMIs). Examples include supported employment and family psychoeducation. We have also included STOs and TIs reflective of psychotherapeutic approaches that have shown efficacy for disorders typically subsumed under the SPMI rubric (e.g., interpersonal therapy for depression, cognitive behavior therapy for psychotic features). In addition, we included STOs and TIs reflective of treatments that been found efficacious for problems not commonly characterized as SPMIs (e.g., obsessive compulsive disorder, panic disorder, social anxiety), but that nonetheless present clinically on occasion, have an evidence base within the populations studied, and that therapists may adapt for use with clients who struggle with these problems. Beyond references to the empirical studies supporting these interventions, we have provided references to therapist- and client-oriented books and treatment manuals that describe the use of identified EBPs or treatments consistent with their objectives and interventions. Recognizing that there are STOs and TIs that practicing clinicians have found useful but that have not yet received empirical scrutiny, we have included those that reflect common best practice among experienced clinicians. The goal is to provide a range of treatment plan options, some studied empirically, others reflecting common clinical practice, so the users can construct what they believe to be the best plan for a particular client.

In some instances, the EBPs referenced are short-term, problem-oriented treatments that focus on improving current specific problems or symptoms related to a client's current distress and disability. For those, STOs and TIs reflective of the EBP have been placed earlier in the sequence of STO and TI options. In addition, some STOs and TIs reflect core components of the EBP approach that are always delivered (e.g., exposure to feared objects and situations for a phobic disorders; behavioral activation for depression). Others reflect adjuncts to treatment that may or may not be used all the time (e.g., social and other communication skills, stress management skills). For the EBPs that are more programmatic in nature, such as supported employment, the STOs and TIs are consistent with the types of competencies in which professionals who deliver these inventions are trained. Most of the STOs and TIs associated with the EBPs are described at a level of detail that permits flexibility and adaptability in their specific application. As with all *Planners* in this series, each chapter includes the option to add STOs and TIs at the therapist's discretion.

Criteria for Inclusion of Evidence-Based Therapies

The EBPs from which STOs and TIs were taken have different levels of empirical work supporting them. Some have been well established as efficacious for the changes they target (e.g., supported employment). Others have less support, but nonetheless have demonstrated efficacy. The EBPs for disorders not typically classified as SPMIs, such as panic disorder and other anxiety disorders, have very strong empirical support for their efficacy, but have established that support through studies whose participants carried a primary diagnosis of an anxiety disorder, not a SPMI. These approaches have been included in this edition because some clients who struggle with SPMIs and also struggle with these other disorders may benefit from these EBP approaches. With that in mind, however, we have included EBPs for which the empirical support has either been well established or demonstrated at more than a preliminary level as defined by those authors who have undertaken the task of identifying them, such as Drake and colleagues (2003, 2005), Chambless and colleagues (1996, 1998), and Nathan and Gorman (1998, 2002).

At minimum, efficacy needed to be demonstrated through a clinical trial or large clinical replication series with features reflecting good experimental design (e.g., random assignment, blind assignments, reliable and valid measurement, clear inclusion and exclusion criteria, state-of-the-art diagnostic methods, and adequate sample size or replications). Well-established EBPs typically have more than one of these types of studies demonstrating their efficacy, as well as other desirable features such as demonstration of efficacy by independent research groups and specification of client characteristics for which the treatment was effective.

Because treatment literatures for various problems develop at different rates, treatment STOs and TIs that have been included may have the most empirical support for their problem area, but less than that found in more heavily studied areas. For example, Dialectical Behavioral Therapy (DBT) has the highest level of empirical support of tested psychotherapies for borderline personality disorder (BPD), but that level of evidence is lower than that supporting, for example, supported employment or exposure-based therapy for phobic fear and avoidance. The latter two have simply been studied more extensively, so there are more trials, replications, and the like. Nonetheless, within the psychotherapy outcome literature for BPD, DBT clearly has the highest level of evidence supporting its efficacy and usefulness. Accordingly, STOs and TIs consistent with DBT have been included in this edition. Last, all interventions, empirically supported or not, must be adapted to the particular client in light of his/her personal circumstances, strengths, and vulnerabilities. The STOs and TIs included in this *Planner* are written in a manner to suggest and allow this adaptability.

Summary of Required and Preferred SPMI EBT Inclusion Criteria

Required
- Demonstration of efficacy through at least one randomized controlled trial with good experimental design, or
- Demonstration of efficacy through a large, well-designed clinical replication series.

Preferred
- Efficacy has been shown by more than one study.
- Efficacy has been demonstrated by independent research groups.
- Client characteristics for which the treatment was effective were specified.
- A clear description of the treatment was available.

HOW TO USE THIS TREATMENT PLANNER

Use this *Treatment Planner* to write treatment plans according to the following six-step progression:

1. **Problem Selection.** Although the client may discuss a variety of issues during the assessment, the clinician must determine the most significant problems on which to focus the treatment process. Usually a primary problem will surface, and secondary problems may also be evident. Some other problems may have to be set aside as not urgent enough to require treatment at this time. An effective treatment plan can only deal with a few selected problems or treatment will lose its direction. Choose the problem within this *Planner* that most accurately represents your client's presenting issues.

2. **Problem Definition.** Each client presents with unique nuances as to how a problem behaviorally reveals itself in his or her life. Therefore, each problem that is selected for treatment focus requires a specific definition about how it is evidenced in the particular client. The symptom pattern should be associated with diagnostic criteria and codes such as those found in the *DSM-IV* or the *International Classification of Diseases*. This *Planner* offers such behaviorally specific definition statements to choose from or to serve as a model for your own personally crafted statements.

3. **Goal Development.** The next step in developing your treatment plan is to set broad goals for the resolution of the target problem. These statements need not be crafted in measurable terms but can be global, long-term goals that indicate a desired positive outcome to the treatment procedures. This *Planner* provides several possible goal statements for each problem, but one statement is all that is required in a treatment plan.

4. **Objective Construction.** In contrast to long-term goals, objectives must be stated in behaviorally measurable language so that it is clear to review agencies, health maintenance organizations, and managed care organizations when the client has achieved the established objectives. The objectives presented in this *Planner* are designed to meet this demand for accountability. Numerous alternatives are presented to allow construction of a variety of treatment plan possibilities for the same presenting problem.

5. **Intervention Creation.** Interventions are the actions of the clinician designed to help the client complete the objectives. There should be at least one intervention for every objective. If the client does not accomplish the objective after the initial intervention, new interventions should be added to the plan. Interventions should be selected on the basis of the client's needs and the treatment provider's full therapeutic repertoire. This *Planner* contains interventions from a broad range of therapeutic approaches, and we encourage the provider to write other interventions reflecting his or her own training and experience.

    Some suggested interventions listed in the *Planner* refer to specific books that can be assigned to the client for adjunctive bibliotherapy. Appendix A contains a full bibliographic reference list of these materials. For further information about self-help books, mental health professionals may wish to consult *The Authoritative Guide to Self-Help Resources in Mental Health, Revised Edition* (New York: Guilford Press, 2003) by Norcross et al.

6. **Diagnosis Determination.** The determination of an appropriate diagnosis is based on an evaluation of the client's complete clinical presentation. The clinician must compare the behavioral, cognitive, emotional, and interpersonal symptoms that the client presents with the criteria for diagnosis of a mental illness condition as described in *DSM-IV*. Despite arguments made against diagnosing clients in this manner, diagnosis is a reality that exists in the world of mental health care, and it is a necessity for third-party reimbursement. It is the clinician's thorough knowledge of *DSM-IV* criteria and a complete understanding of the client assessment data that contribute to the most reliable, valid diagnosis.

Congratulations! After completing these six steps, you should have a comprehensive and individualized treatment plan ready for immediate implementation and presentation to the client. A sample treatment plan for Medication Management is provided at the end of this introduction.

A FINAL NOTE ON TAILORING THE TREATMENT PLAN TO THE CLIENT

One important aspect of effective treatment planning is that each plan should be tailored to the individual client's problems and needs. Treatment plans should not be mass-produced, even if clients have similar problems. The individual's strengths and weaknesses, unique stressors, social network, family circumstances, and symptom patterns must be considered in developing a treatment strategy. Drawing on our years of clinical experience, we have put together a variety of treatment choices. These statements can be combined in thousands of permutations to develop detailed treatment plans. Relying on their own good judgment, clinicians can easily select the statements that are appropriate for the individuals whom they are treating. In addition, we encourage readers to add their own definitions, goals, objects, and interventions to the existing samples. As with all of the books in the *Treatment Planners* series, it is our hope that this book will help promote effective, creative treatment planning—a process that will ultimately benefit the client, clinicians, and mental health community.

REFERENCES

Bruce, T. J., and Sanderson, W. C. (2005). Evidence-based psychosocial practices: Past, present, and future. In C. Stout and R, Hayes (Eds.), *The Handbook of Evidence-Based Practice in Behavioral Healthcare: Applications and New Directions*. Hoboken, NJ: Wiley.

Chambless, D. L., Baker, M. J., Baucom, D., Beutler, L. E., Calhoun, K. S., Crits-Christoph, P., et al. (1998). Update on empirically validated therapies: II. *Clinical Psychologist, 51*(1), 3–16.

Chambless, D. L., and Ollendick, T. H. (2001). Empirically supported psychological interventions: Controversies and evidence. *Annual Review of Psychology, 52,* 685–716.

Chambless, D. L., Sanderson, W. C., Shoham, V., Johnson, S. B., Pope, K. S., Crits-Christoph, P., et al. (1996). An update on empirically validated therapies. *Clinical Psychologist, 49*(2), 5–18.

Drake, R. E., and Goldman, H. (2003). *Evidence-Based Practices in Mental Health Care.* Washington, DC: American Psychiatric Association.

Drake, R. E., Merrens, M. R., and Lynde, D. W. (2005). *Evidence-Based Mental Health Practice: A Textbook.* New York: Norton.

Hofmann, S. G., and Tompson, M. G. (2002). *Treating Chronic and Severe Mental Disorders: A Handbook of Empirically Supported Interventions.* New York: Guilford Press.

Nathan, P. E., and Gorman, J. M. (Eds.). (1998). *A Guide to Treatments That Work.* New York: Oxford University Press.

Nathan, P. E., and Gorman, J. M. (Eds.). (2002). *A Guide to Treatments That Work, Vol. II.* New York: Oxford University Press.

Stout, C., and Hayes, R. (2005). *The Evidence-Based Practice: Methods, Models, and Tools for Mental Health Professionals.* Hoboken, NJ: Wiley.

SAMPLE TREATMENT PLAN

MEDICATION MANAGEMENT

Definitions: Fails to consistently take psychotropic medications as prescribed.

Verbalizes fears and dislike related to physical and/or emotional side effects of prescribed medications.

Lacks knowledge of medications' usefulness and potential side effects.

Makes statements of an unwillingness to take prescribed medications.

Goals: Regular, consistent use of psychotropic medications at the prescribed dosage, frequency, and duration.

Increased understanding of the psychotropic medication dosage, the side effects, and the reasons for being prescribed.

Decreased frequency and intensity of psychotic and other severe mental illness symptoms.

OBJECTIVES

1. List all medications that are currently being prescribed and consumed.

▼ 2. Describe thoughts and feelings about medication use and willingness or unwillingness to explore personal use.

INTERVENTIONS

1. Request that the client identify all currently prescribed medications, including names, times administered, and dosage.

2. Request that the client provide an honest, realistic description of his/her medication compliance; compare this with his/her medical chart.

1. Conduct Motivational Interviewing to assess the client's stage of preparation for change; intervene accordingly, moving from building motivation, through strengthening commitment to change, to participation in treatment (see *Motivational Interviewing* by Miller and Rollnick). ▼

▼ indicates that the Objective/Intervention is consistent with those found in evidence-based treatments.

▽ 3. Identify and replace misinformation and mistaken beliefs that support medication noncompliance.

1. Request that the client identify the reason for the use of each medication; correct any misinformation regarding the medication's expected effects, the acceptable dosage levels, and the possible side effects. ▽

2. Request that the client describe fears that he/she may experience regarding the use of the medication; cognitively restructure these fears, correcting myths and misinformation while paying particular attention to the following common biases: underestimating benefits of medication therapy, overestimating the threat posed by side effects, beliefs that medications are not necessary, beliefs that medication is harmful or part of a conspiracy, and beliefs that medication could change his/her personality or make him/her addicted. ▽

3. Reinforce the client's positive, reality-based cognitive messages that enhance medication prescription compliance. ▽

▽ 4. Family members enroll in a multi-family group educational program for families of the mentally ill.

1. Refer the family to a multi-family group psychoeducational program (see *Multi-family Groups in the Treatment of Severe Psychiatric Disorders* by McFarlane) to increase understanding of severe and persistent mental illness and the need for medication. ▽

▽ 5. The client and family participate in a family-focused therapy.

1. Conduct or refer the client and family to a therapy based on the principles of family-focused treatment (e.g., see *Bipolar Disorder: A Family-Focused Treatment Approach* by Miklowitz and Goldstein). ▽

6. Report the side effects and the effectiveness of the medications to the appropriate professional(s).

1. Review the potential side effects of the medication with the client and the medical staff. ▽

2. Obtain a written release of information from the client to his/her primary physician or other health care providers to allow for informing them of the medications, side effects, and benefit that the client is experiencing. ▽

▽ 7. Verbalize positive feelings about the improvement that is resulting from the medication's effectiveness.

1. Request that the client identify how the reduction in mental illness symptoms has improved his/her social or family system; reinforce functioning and continued medication usage. ▽

DIAGNOSIS

295.10   Schizophrenia, Disorganized Type

ACTIVITIES OF DAILY LIVING (ADL)

BEHAVIORAL DEFINITIONS

1. Demonstrates substandard hygiene and grooming, as evidenced by strong body odor, disheveled hair, or dirty clothing.
2. Fails to use basic hygiene techniques, such as bathing, brushing teeth, or washing clothes.
3. Evidences medical problems due to poor hygiene.
4. Consumes a poor diet due to deficiencies in cooking, meal preparation, or food selection.
5. Impaired reality testing results in bizarre behaviors that compromise ability to perform activities of daily living (ADLs).
6. Demonstrates poor interaction skills as evidenced by limited eye contact, insufficient attending, and awkward social responses.
7. Has a history of others excusing poor performance on ADLs due to factors that are not related to mental illness.
8. Demonstrates inadequate knowledge or functioning in basic skills around the home (e.g., cleaning floors, washing dishes, disposing of garbage, keeping fresh food available).
9. Has a history of loss of relationships, employment, or other social opportunities due to poor hygiene and inadequate attention to grooming.

__. _____
_____
__. _____
_____
__. _____
_____

LONG-TERM GOALS

1. Increase functioning in ADLs in a consistent and responsible manner.
2. Understand the need for good hygiene and implement healthy personal hygiene practices.
3. Learn basic skills for maintaining a clean, sanitary living space.
4. Regularly shower or bathe, shave, brush teeth, care for hair, and use deodorant.
5. Experience increased social acceptance because of improved appearance or functioning in ADLs.
6. Family, friends, and caregivers provide constructive feedback to the client regarding ADLs.

—. _____
_____
_____
—. _____
_____
_____
—. _____
_____

SHORT-TERM OBJECTIVES

1. Describe current functioning in ADLs. (1, 2, 3)

THERAPEUTIC INTERVENTIONS

1. Assist the client in preparing an inventory of his/her positive and negative functioning regarding ADLs.

2. Ask the client to identify a trusted individual from whom he/she can obtain helpful feedback regarding daily hygiene and cleanliness. Coordinate feedback from this individual to the client.

3. Review the client's diet or refer him/her to a dietician for an assessment regarding basic nutritional knowledge and skills, usual diet, and nutritional deficiencies.

2. List the negative effects of not giving enough effort to responsible performance of ADLs. (4, 5, 6)

4. Ask the client to identify two painful experiences in which rejection was experienced (e.g., broken relationships, loss of employment) due to the lack of performance of basic ADLs.

5. Review with the client the medical risks (e.g., dental problems, risk of infection, lice) that are associated with poor hygiene or lack of attention to other ADLs.

6. Assist the client in expressing emotions related to impaired performance in ADLs (e.g., embarrassment, depression, low self-esteem).

3. Verbalize insight into the secondary gain that is associated with decreased ADL functioning. (7)

7. Reflect the possible secondary gain (e.g., less involvement in potentially difficult social situations) that is associated with decreased ADL functioning.

4. Identify any cognitive barriers to ADL success. (8)

8. Refer the client for an assessment of cognitive abilities and deficits.

5. Participate in a remediation program to teach ADL skills. (9)

9. Recommend remediating programs to the client, such as skill-building groups, token economies, or behavior-shaping programs that are focused on removing deficits to ADL performance.

6. Acknowledge ADL deficits as a symptom of mental illness being inadequately controlled or treated. (10)

10. Educate the client about the expected or common symptoms of his/her mental illness (e.g., manic excitement or negative symptoms of schizophrenia), which may negatively impact basic ADL functioning; reflect or interpret poor performance in ADLs as an indicator of psychiatric decompensation.

7. Stabilize, through the use of psychotropic medications, psychotic and other severe and persistent mental illness symptoms that interfere with ADLs.
(11, 12, 13, 14, 15)

11. Arrange for an evaluation of the client by a physician for a prescription for psychotropic medication.

12. Educate the client about the proper use and the expected benefits of psychotropic medication.

13. Monitor the client for compliance with the psychotropic medication that is prescribed and for its effectiveness and possible side effects.

14. Provide the client with a pillbox for organizing and coordinating each dose of medication; teach and quiz the client about the proper use of the medication compliance package/reminder system (see the Medication Management chapter in this *Planner*).

15. Coordinate the family members or caregivers who will regularly dispense and/or monitor the client's medication compliance.

8. Remediate the medical effects that have resulted from a history of a lack of ADL performance.
(16, 17)

16. Arrange for a full physical examination of the client, and encourage the physician to prescribe any necessary ADL remediation behaviors.

17. Refer the client to a dentist to determine dental treatment needs; coordinate ongoing dental treatment.

9. Implement skills that are related to basic personal hygiene on a consistent daily basis.
(18, 19, 20, 21)

18. Provide the client with written or video educational material for basic personal hygiene skills (e.g., *The Complete Guide to Better Dental Care* by Taintor and Taintor, or *The New Wellness Encyclopedia* by the editors of the University of California, Berkeley wellness letter).

19. Refer the client to an agency medical staff for one-to-one training in basic hygiene needs and techniques.

20. Conduct or refer the client to a psychoeducational group for teaching personal hygiene skills. Use the group setting to help teach the client to give and receive feedback about hygiene skill implementation.

21. Encourage and reinforce the client for performing basic hygiene skills on a regular schedule (e.g., at the same time and in the same order each day).

10. Utilize a self-monitoring system to increase the frequency of implementing basic hygiene skills. (22, 23)

22. Refer the client to a behavioral treatment specialist to develop and implement a program to monitor and reward the regular use of ADL techniques or develop a self-monitoring program (e.g., a check-off chart for ADL needs) with the client.

23. Provide the client with regular feedback about progress in his/her use of self-monitoring to improve personal hygiene.

11. Utilize community resources to improve personal hygiene and grooming. (24, 25)

24. Review the use of community resources with the client (e.g., laundromat/dry cleaner, hair salon/barber) that can be used to improve personal appearance.

25. Coordinate for the client to tour community facilities for cleaning and pressing clothes, cutting and styling hair, or purchasing soap and deodorant, with an emphasis on increasing the client's understanding of this service and how it can be used.

12. Terminate substance abuse that interferes with the ability to care for self. (26, 27)

26. Assess the client for substance abuse that exacerbates poor ADL performance.

27. Refer the client to Alcoholics Anonymous (AA), Narcotics Anonymous (NA), or to a more intensive

co-occurring enabled treatment program (see the Chemical Dependence chapter in this *Planner*).

13. Implement basic skills for running and maintaining a home or apartment. (28)

28. Teach the client basic housekeeping skills, utilizing references such as *Mary Ellen's Complete Home Reference Book* (Pinkham and Burg), or *The Cleaning Encyclopedia* (Aslett); facilitate this teaching from the client's natural supports.

14. Report as to the schedule that is adhered to regarding the regular use of housekeeping skills. (22, 29, 30)

22. Refer the client to a behavioral treatment specialist to develop and implement a program to monitor and reward the regular use of ADL techniques or develop a self-monitoring program (e.g., a check-off chart for ADL needs) with the client.

29. Provide the client with feedback about the care of his/her personal area, apartment, or home.

30. Encourage family members and caregivers to provide regular assignment of basic chores around the home.

15. Implement basic cooking skills and eat nutritionally balanced meals daily. (3, 31, 32, 33)

3. Review the client's diet or refer him/her to a dietician for an assessment regarding basic nutritional knowledge and skills, usual diet, and nutritional deficiencies.

31. Educate the client on basic cooking techniques (see portions of *The Good Housekeeping Illustrated Cookbook* by the editors of *Good Housekeeping,* or *How to Cook Everything* by Bittman).

32. Refer the client to or conduct a psychoeducational group regarding cooking skills and dietary needs; monitor changes.

33. Facilitate the client's enrollment in a community education cooking class or seminar.

16. Take steps to increase safety and health in the home setting. (34, 35, 36)

34. Join the client in an inspection of his/her living situation for potential safety hazards; prioritize and ameliorate safety concerns.

35. Assist the client in advocating with the landlord, home provider, or family members to remediate safety hazards, insect infestations, or other problems.

36. Facilitate the client's involvement with programs that assist low-income or special-needs individuals with safety equipment (e.g., free smoke or carbon monoxide detectors).

17. Terminate engagement in high-risk sex or substance abuse behaviors. (37, 38)

37. Teach the client about high-risk sexual behaviors and refer to a free condom program (see the Sexuality Concerns chapter in this *Planner*).

38. Teach the client about the serious risk that is involved with sharing needles for drug abuse; refer the client to needle exchange and substance abuse treatment programs.

18. Sign an intervention action plan that will be implemented when cognitive decompensation begins. (39)

39. Develop a written, signed intervention plan (e.g., call a treatment hotline, contact a therapist or a physician, go to a hospital emergency department) to decrease the potential for injury, poisoning, or other self-care problems during periods of mania, psychosis, or other decompensation.

__. _____
   _____
__. _____
   _____
__. _____
   _____

__. _____
   _____
__. _____
   _____
__. _____
   _____

DIAGNOSTIC SUGGESTIONS

Axis I: 297.1   Delusional Disorder
                 295.xx   Schizophrenia
                 295.10   Schizophrenia, Disorganized Type
                 295.30   Schizophrenia, Paranoid Type
                 295.90   Schizophrenia, Undifferentiated Type
                 295.60   Schizophrenia, Residual Type
                 295.70   Schizoaffective Disorder
                 296.xx   Bipolar I Disorder
                 296.89   Bipolar II Disorder

                 _____   _____

                 _____   _____

AGING

BEHAVIORAL DEFINITIONS

1. Advanced age is debilitating to independent functioning.
2. Is experiencing decreased intensity of severe and persistent mental illness symptoms.
3. Demonstrates cognitive decline, including memory problems, confusion, or an inability to learn new information.
4. Has lost a social support system due to infirmity or death of members of family of origin and friends.
5. Receives little or no interest or support from offspring.
6. Experiences medical problems related to advanced age.
7. Displays physical deficits due to long-term use of psychiatric medications (e.g., tardive dyskinesia).
8. Spiritual confusion leads to uncertainty about the meaning or purpose in life and fears surrounding mortality issues.
9. Demonstrates decreased ability to perform activities of daily living (ADLs) or independent activities of daily living (IADLs).
10. Reports increased depression and suicidal ideation related to feelings of isolation and loss.
11. Is more vulnerable to sexual, physical, and psychological abuse.
12. Displays anger outbursts due to frustration over declining abilities.

__. _____

   _____

__. _____

   _____

__. _____

   _____

LONG-TERM GOALS

1. Stabilize medical status and find meaning to life.
2. Decrease the slope or severity of cognitive decline.
3. Accept the loss of loved ones and other important individuals.
4. Develop additional social/emotional support systems.
5. Decrease the effects of long-term use of medications.
6. Terminate suicidal ideation and increase satisfaction with life.

___. _____

_____

_____

___. _____

_____

_____

___. _____

_____

SHORT-TERM OBJECTIVES

THERAPEUTIC INTERVENTIONS

1. Identify problematic changes that are related to the aging process. (1, 2)

1. Request that the client identify negative situations or fears that have occurred due to aging issues.

2. Provide the client with general information regarding the aging process; recommend books such as *The Practical Guide to Aging* by Cassel, or *Alzheimer's and Dementia: Questions You Have . . . Answers You Need* by Hay.

2. Express emotions regarding the aging process. (3, 4, 5)

3. Assist the client in identifying his/her emotions regarding aging issues (e.g., fear of abandonment, sadness regarding loss of abilities).

4. Teach the client healthy ways to express anger and other emotions, such as writing, drawing, empty-chair techniques, assertiveness, or relaxation techniques (see the Anger Management chapter in this *Planner*).

3. Identify positive aspects of senior citizen status. (6, 7)

4. Cooperate with a medical evaluation and follow through on obtaining treatment for physical health difficulties. (8, 9)

5. Express physical health concerns to medical staff. (10, 11)

6. Verbalize an understanding of physical health difficulties and the recovery process. (12)

5. Coordinate training for the caregivers in physical management and anger diffusion techniques.

6. Assist the client in preparing a list of benefits that are related to the aging process (e.g., decreased work expectations, new residential opportunities).

7. Provide the client with specific information about the aging process and his/her mental illness (e.g., the tendency for severe and persistent mental illness symptoms to decrease in intensity in later years).

8. Refer the client for a complete physical evaluation by a medical professional who is knowledgeable in both geriatric and mental illness concerns.

9. Support and monitor the client in following up on the recommendations from the medical evaluation, such as pursuing specialty evaluations, lab work, medications, or other treatments.

10. Assist the client in expressing physical health needs to the medical staff (e.g., "translate" the client's bizarre descriptions to the medical staff, role-play asking questions of or reporting concerns to the medical staff).

11. Interpret psychiatric decompensation as a possible reaction to medical instability and the stress that is associated with it. Inquire about medical needs when the client has decompensated psychiatrically.

12. After obtaining the necessary confidentiality release from the client or his/her guardian, obtain

information about physical health concerns from the attending physician; review these health concerns and recovery needs with the client on a regular basis.

7. Cooperate with a physician's evaluation as to the need for a change in or initiation of psychotropic medication. (13, 14)

13. Arrange for an evaluation by a physician as to the necessity for a change in or the initiation of a prescription for psychotropic medication.

14. Educate the client about the use, expected benefits, and possible side effects of the medication; monitor the client's medication compliance and side effects, reporting significant changes to the medical staff.

8. Take all medications safely and as medically prescribed. (15, 16)

15. Assess the client's ability to adhere consistently to the prescribed regimen for all medications.

16. Provide the client with assistance in coordinating medications (e.g., a dose-by-dose pillbox). Count the amount of medications that the client currently has available, which should correspond with the amount that remains if the prescription regimen has been followed; review discrepancies with the client and the medical staff.

9. Authorize and encourage all physicians who are prescribing medications to communicate with each other and coordinate their medications. (17)

17. Coordinate authorizations to release confidential information so that multiple physicians can communicate with each other regarding the medications that are prescribed and their chemical interactions; facilitate this exchange of information.

10. Preserve independence by maintaining ADLs and IADLs. (18)

18. Coordinate an evaluation of ADLs and IADLs, identifying strengths, weaknesses, and expected future levels of functioning; develop

supports for maintenance of ADLs/IADLs from family, community, and paid staff (see the Activities of Daily Living [ADL] chapter in this *Planner*).

11. Attend and participate in an auditory and/or vision evaluation. (19, 20)

19. Inquire about hearing or vision needs when the client complains about the increase in auditory and visual hallucinations, particularly when they are not accompanied by other severe and persistent mental illness symptoms.

20. Refer the client for auditory and vision exams.

12. Move to a supervised residential environment that meets psychiatric, physical, and cognitive needs. (21, 22, 23)

21. Refer the client to an appropriate (based on ADL and IADL functioning) supervised residential option (e.g., independent living senior citizens' center, assisted living center, adult foster care, or nursing home).

22. Advocate with age-appropriate housing programs to accept the client and to provide needed adaptations for him/her; train the housing staff about how to assist the mentally ill resident.

23. Acknowledge with the client his/her history of institutionalization. Help him/her to differentiate between previous psychiatric hospitalizations and a move from hard-won independence into a more restrictive residential placement due to aging concerns.

13. Express and report a resolution of grief associated with losses of loved ones, capabilities, freedom, or other attachment. (24, 25, 26)

24. Explore with the client his/her history of significant loss due to death, geographical move, aging, or physical/mental disability; provide the client with support and empathy regarding the losses.

25. Educate the client about the grief process, and how these concerns

may impact his/her severe and persistent mental illness symptoms.

26. Refer the client for individual or group therapy regarding the history of his/her losses.

14. Make at least two social contacts on a daily basis to reduce isolation. (27, 28, 29, 30, 31)

27. Assist the client in developing social skills (see the Social Skills Deficits chapter in this *Planner*).

28. Coordinate or link the client to age-appropriate social activities.

29. Refer the client to a recreational therapist for an evaluation of recreational abilities, needs, and opportunities.

30. Attune the client to the need to self-regulate his/her social involvement depending on his/her needs and symptoms (e.g., increase or decrease frequency and intensity of contacts to modulate stress level).

31. Assist the client in identifying activities in which he/she can now be engaged as psychotic symptoms gradually abate.

15. State a plan that is focused on repairing and restoring lost relationships as functioning improves. (32, 33)

32. Request that the client identify the important relationships that he/she would like to restore.

33. Assist the client in developing a plan for restoring relationships (see the Social Skills Deficits or Family Conflicts chapters in this *Planner*).

16. Caregivers share their frustrations associated with supervising a person with psychosis. (34, 35, 36)

34. Provide the family and the caregiver with adequate information and training relative to the client's mental illness, physical health, and aging concerns (recommend *Surviving Schizophrenia* by Torrey; *Helping Someone with Mental Illness* by Carter and Golant; *Coping with Your Difficult Older Parent* by Lebow,

Kane, and Lebow; or *The Hospice Handbook* by Beresford).

35. Allow the caregiver to vent about difficulties that are related to caring for the client. Listen with empathy, eventually focusing the caregiver toward developing alternative plans for the client's care or committing to continue the care. Do not allow the caregiver to deride the client.

36. Refer the caregiver to a support group for those who care for the chronically mentally ill, the aged, or both.

17. Describe incidents of being physically, emotionally, sexually, or financially abused. (37)

37. Assess the client for the possibility of him/her being a victim of elder abuse in any form; gently probe the client for an emotional reaction to being an abuse victim.

18. Terminate contact with perpetrators of physical, sexual, or emotional abuse. (38, 39, 40)

38. Facilitate the client in making changes of residence, program, or other contacts to terminate the abuse immediately; follow applicable abuse reporting procedures as outlined in local law and agency guidelines.

39. Educate the client and caregivers about definitions of elder abuse, and how to report concerns to the clinician or local adult protective services unit.

40. Advocate for the client to change his/her legal guardian or payee procedures to stem financial abuse.

19. Develop a plan for care prior to age-related decompensation. (41, 42, 43)

41. Talk openly with the client about the specialized needs that he/she will face due to the natural deterioration of physical capabilities that are associated with aging.

42. Coordinate tours and other means of providing information regard-

ing residential or other programs that are available for the client as he/she ages.

43. Assist the client in developing a written plan should he/she become legally unable to make his/her own decisions, including a plan for guardianship, advanced medical directives, and a last will and testament.

___. _____   ___. _____
    _____   _____
___. _____   ___. _____
    _____   _____
___. _____   ___. _____
    _____   _____

DIAGNOSTIC SUGGESTIONS

Axis I:		
	290.xx	Dementia of the Alzheimer's Type
	294.1x	Dementia Due to . . . [*General Medical Condition*]
	297.1	Delusional Disorder
	295.xx	Schizophrenia
	295.10	Schizophrenia, Disorganized Type
	295.30	Schizophrenia, Paranoid Type
	295.90	Schizophrenia, Undifferentiated Type
	295.60	Schizophrenia, Residual Type
	295.70	Schizoaffective Disorder
	296.xx	Bipolar I Disorder
	296.89	Bipolar II Disorder
	780.9	Age-Related Cognitive Decline
	_____	_____
	_____	_____

7. Manage normal life stressors with minimal levels of anxiety.
8. Learn coping techniques to decrease the effects of anxiety.
9. Increase concentration and ability to function on a daily basis.

—· _____
   _____
   _____
—· _____
   _____
   _____
—· _____
   _____

SHORT-TERM OBJECTIVES

1. Describe the history of anxiety symptoms. (1, 2, 3, 4)

THERAPEUTIC INTERVENTIONS

1. Focus on developing a level of trust with the client. Provide support and empathy to encourage the client to feel safe in expressing his/her anxiety symptoms.

2. Assess the client's frequency, intensity, duration, and history of panic symptoms, fear, and avoidance (e.g., *The Anxiety Disorders Interview Schedule for the DSM-IV* by Brown, DiNardo, and Barlow).

3. Utilize a graphic display, such as a time line, to help the client identify the pattern of anxiety symptoms that he/she has experienced (e.g., when they started, how they have varied in intensity or type over time).

4. Coordinate psychological testing to assess the extent and severity of anxiety symptoms, or administer a measure to help assess the nature and degree of the client's worry and anxiety symptoms (e.g., *Behaviour Research and Therapy* by Meyer, Miller, Metzger, and Borkovec).

2. Obtain a complete physical evaluation to rule out medical and substance related etiologies for anxiety symptoms. (5, 6)

5. Refer the client to a general physician for a complete physical examination to evaluate for any organic basis for the anxiety.

6. Assist the client in following up on the recommendations from a physical evaluation, including medications, lab work, or specialty assessments.

3. Identify any foods, alcohol, or street drugs that could be triggering anxiety. (7, 8)

7. Review the client's use of non-prescription medications or psychoactive chemicals (e.g., nicotine, caffeine, alcohol abuse, or street drugs) and their relationship to symptoms.

8. Recommend the termination of consumption of substances that could trigger anxiety; refer for substance abuse evaluation or treatment if indicated.

4. Differentiate between symptoms that are related to anxiety versus those that are related to severe and persistent mental illness. (9, 10, 11, 12)

9. Help the client differentiate symptoms that are a direct effect of his/her severe and persistent mental illness (e.g., a product of delusion), as opposed to a separate diagnosis of an anxiety disorder.

10. Assist the client in differentiating between actual life situations and those that appear real, but are due to hallucinations or delusions.

11. Acknowledge that both real and delusional experiences can cause anxiety, providing support to the client.

12. Utilizing a description of anxiety symptoms such as that found in Bourne's *The Anxiety and Phobia Workbook,* help the client to identify with a specific diagnostic classification.

⩔ 5. Cooperate with a medication evaluation. (13)

⩔ 6. Report a decrease in anxiety symptoms through regular use of psychotropic medications. (14, 15)

⩔ 7. Report the side effects and effectiveness of the medications to the appropriate professional. (16)

⩔ 8. Verbalize an understanding of the cognitive, physiological, and behavioral components of anxiety and its treatment. (17, 18, 19)

13. Refer the client to a physician for an evaluation as to the need for psychotropic medications. ⩔

14. Educate the client about the use and expected benefits of the medication. ⩔

15. Monitor the client's medication compliance and effectiveness; reinforce consistent use of the medication. ⩔

16. Review the effects of the medications with the client and the medical staff to identify possible side effects or confounding influence of polypharmacy. ⩔

17. Discuss how generalized anxiety typically involves excessive worry about unrealistic threats, various bodily expressions of tension, overarousal, and hypervigilance, and avoidance of what is threatening that interacts to maintain the problem (see *Mastery of Your Anxiety and Worry: Therapist Guide* by Zinbarg, Craske, and Barlow). ⩔

18. Discuss how treatment targets worry, anxiety symptoms, and avoidance to help the client manage worry effectively, reduce overarousal, and eliminate unnecessary avoidance. ⩔

19. Assign the client to read psychoeducational sections of books or treatment manuals on worry and generalized anxiety (e.g., *Mastery of Your Anxiety and Worry: Workbook* by Craske and Barlow). ⩔

⩔ indicates that the Objective/Intervention is consistent with those found in evidence-based treatments.

▽ 9. Learn and implement calming skills to reduce overall anxiety and manage anxiety symptoms. (20, 21, 22, 23)

20. Teach the client relaxation skills (e.g., progressive muscle, guided imagery, slow diaphragmatic breathing) and how to discriminate better between relaxation and tension; teach the client how to apply these skills to his/her daily life (e.g., *Progressive Relaxation Training* by Bernstein and Borkovec; *Treating GAD* by Rygh and Sanderson). ▽

21. Assign the client homework each session in which he/she practices relaxation exercises daily; review and reinforce success while providing corrective feedback toward improvement. ▽

22. Assign the client to read about progressive muscle relaxation and other calming strategies in relevant books or treatment manuals (e.g., *Progressive Relaxation Training* by Bernstein and Borkovec; *Mastery of Your Anxiety and Worry: Workbook* by Craske and Barlow). ▽

23. Use biofeedback techniques to facilitate the client's success at learning calming skills. ▽

▽ 10. Identify, challenge, and replace biased, fearful self-talk with positive, realistic, and empowering self-talk. (24, 25, 26, 27)

24. Explore the client's schema and self-talk that mediate his/her fear response, challenge the biases; assist him/her in replacing the distorted messages with reality-based alternatives and positive self-talk that will increase his/her self-confidence in coping with irrational fears. ▽

25. Assign the client a homework exercise in which he/she identifies fearful self-talk and creates reality-based alternatives; review and reinforce success, providing

corrective feedback toward improvement. ▽

26. Teach the client to implement a thought-stopping technique (thinking of a stop sign and then a pleasant scene) for worries that have been addressed but persist (or assign "Making Use of the Thought-Stopping Technique" in *Adult Psychotherapy Homework Planner*, 2nd ed. by Jongsma); monitor and encourage the client's use of the technique in daily life between sessions. ▽

27. Assign the client to read about cognitive restructuring of worry in relevant books or treatment manuals (e.g., *Mastery of Your Anxiety and Worry: Workbook* by Craske and Barlow). ▽

▽ 11. Undergo gradual repeated imaginal exposure to the feared negative consequences predicted by irrational worries and develop reality-based predictions. (28, 29, 30, 31, 32)

28. Assign the client to read about "worry exposure" in books or treatment manuals on the treatment of worry and generalized anxiety (e.g., *Mastery of Your Anxiety and Worry: Workbook* by Craske and Barlow). ▽

29. Direct and assist the client in constructing a hierarchy of two to three spheres of worry for use in exposure (e.g., worry about harm to others, financial difficulties, relationship problems). ▽

30. Select initial exposures that have a high likelihood of being a success experience for the client; develop a plan for managing the negative affect engendered by exposure; mentally rehearse the procedure. ▽

31. Assign the client a homework exercise in which he/she does worry exposures and records

responses (see *Mastery of Your Anxiety and Worry: Workbook* by Craske and Barlow; or *Generalized Anxiety Disorder* by Brown, O'Leary, and Barlow*)*; review, reinforce success, and provide corrective feedback toward improvement. ▽

32. Ask the client to vividly imagine worst-case consequences of worries, holding them in mind until anxiety associated with them weakens (up to 30 minutes); generate reality-based alternatives to that worst case and process them (see *Mastery of Your Anxiety and Worry: Therapist Guide* by Zinbarg, Craske, and Barlow). ▽

▽ 12. Learn and implement problem-solving strategies for realistically addressing worries. (33, 34)

33. Teach problem-solving strategies involving specifically defining a problem, generating options for addressing it, evaluating options, implementing a plan, and re-evaluating and refining the plan. ▽

34. Assign the client a homework exercise in which he/she problem-solves a current problem (see *Mastery of Your Anxiety and Worry: Workbook* by Craske and Barlow; or *Generalized Anxiety Disorder by* Brown, O'Leary, and Barlow*)*; review, reinforce success, and provide corrective feedback toward improvement (or assign "Applying Problem-Solving to Interpersonal Conflict" in *Adult Psychotherapy Homework Planner*, 2nd ed. by Jongsma). ▽

▽ 13. Learn and implement relapse prevention strategies for managing possible future anxiety symptoms. (35, 36, 37)

35. Discuss with the client the distinction between a lapse and relapse, associating a lapse with an initial and reversible return of worry,

anxiety symptoms, or urges to avoid and relapse with the decision to continue the fearful and avoidant patterns. ▽

36. Identify and rehearse with the client the management of future situations or circumstances in which lapses could occur. ▽

37. Instruct the client to routinely use relaxation, cognitive restructuring, exposure, and problem-solving exposures as needed to address emergent worries, building them into his/her life as much as possible. ▽

14. Identify a secondary gain that may be reinforcing anxiety symptoms. (38)

38. Assist the client in identifying a secondary gain that is achieved by the presence of the anxiety symptoms (e.g., lowered expectations from others).

15. Implement a quieter, more routine environment. (39)

39. Encourage the client to develop a routine daily pattern, including waking and resting at the same times, establishing regular mealtimes, and routinely performing daily chores.

16. Include significant others in facilitating implementation of new anxiety reduction techniques. (40)

40. Enlist the help of the client's support system in implementing anxiety reduction techniques.

___. _____
_____
___. _____
_____
___. _____
_____

___. _____
_____
___. _____
_____
___. _____
_____

DIAGNOSTIC SUGGESTIONS

Axis I:	297.1	Delusional Disorder
	295.xx	Schizophrenia
	295.10	Schizophrenia, Disorganized Type
	295.20	Schizophrenia, Catatonic Type
	295.90	Schizophrenia, Undifferentiated Type
	295.30	Schizophrenia, Paranoid Type
	295.70	Schizoaffective Disorder
	296.xx	Bipolar I Disorder
	296.89	Bipolar II Disorder
	298.9	Psychotic Disorder NOS
	300.00	Anxiety Disorder NOS
	300.02	Generalized Anxiety Disorder
	309.24	Adjustment Disorder With Anxiety
	_____	_____
	_____	_____
Axis II:	301.4	Obsessive-Compulsive Personality Disorder
	_____	_____
	_____	_____

BORDERLINE PERSONALITY

BEHAVIORAL DEFINITIONS

1. A minor stress leads to extreme emotional reactivity (anger, anxiety, or depression) that usually lasts from a few hours to a few days.
2. Displays a pattern of intense, chaotic interpersonal relationships.
3. Evidences a marked identity disturbance.
4. Engages in impulsive behaviors that are potentially self-damaging.
5. Engages in recurrent suicidal gestures, threats, or self-mutilating behavior.
6. Experiences chronic feelings of emptiness and boredom.
7. Frequently erupts in intense, inappropriate anger.
8. Easily feels unfairly treated and believes that others cannot be trusted.
9. Analyzes most issues in dichotomous terms (e.g., right/wrong, black/white, trustworthy/deceitful) without regard for extenuating circumstances or complex situations.
10. Becomes very anxious with any hint of perceived abandonment in a relationship.

—. _____

_____

—. _____

_____

—. _____

_____

LONG-TERM GOALS

1. Develop and demonstrate coping skills to deal with mood swings.
2. Develop the ability to control impulsive behavior.
3. Replace dichotomous thinking with the ability to tolerate ambiguity and complexity in people and issues.

4. Develop and demonstrate anger management skills.
5. Learn and practice interpersonal relationship skills.
6. Terminate self-damaging behaviors (such as substance abuse, reckless driving, sexual acting out, binge eating, or suicidal behaviors).

__. _____

_____

__. _____

_____

__. _____

_____

SHORT-TERM OBJECTIVES

1. Discuss openly the history of difficulties that have led to treatment seeking. (1, 2, 3)

EB 2. Verbalize an accurate and reasonable understanding of the process of therapy and what the therapeutic goals are. (4, 5)

THERAPEUTIC INTERVENTIONS

1. Assess the client's experiences of distress and disability, identifying behaviors (e.g., parasuicidal acts, angry outbursts, overattachment), affect (e.g., mood swings, emotional overreactions, painful emptiness), and cognitions (e.g., biases such as dichotomous thinking, overgeneralization, catastrophizing) that will become the targets of therapy.

2. Explore the client's history of abuse and/or abandonment, particularly in childhood years.

3. Validate the client's distress and difficulties as understandable given his/her particular circumstances, thoughts, and feelings.

4. Orient the client to dialectical behavior therapy (DBT), highlighting its multiple facets (e.g., support, collaboration, challenge,

---

EB indicates that the Objective/Intervention is consistent with those found in evidence-based treatments.

problem solving, skill building) and discuss dialectical/biosocial view of borderline personality, emphasizing constitutional and social influences on its features (see *Cognitive-Behavioral Treatment of Borderline Personality* by Linehan). ▽

5. Throughout therapy, ask the client to read selected sections of books or manuals that reinforce therapeutic interventions (e.g., *Skills Training Manual for Treating BPD* by Linehan). ▽

▽ 3. Verbalize a decision to work collaboratively with the therapist toward the therapeutic goals. (6)

6. Solicit from the client an agreement to work collaboratively within the parameters of the DBT approach to overcome the behaviors, emotions, and cognitions that have been identified as causing problems in his/her life. ▽

▽ 4. Verbalize any history of self-mutilative and suicidal urges and behavior. (7, 8, 9, 10)

7. Probe the nature and history of the client's self-mutilating behavior. ▽

8. Assess the client's suicidal gestures as to triggers, frequency, seriousness, secondary gain, and onset. ▽

9. Arrange for hospitalization, as necessary, when the client is judged to be harmful to self. ▽

10. Provide the client with an emergency helpline telephone number that is available 24 hours a day. ▽

▽ 5. Promise to initiate contact with the therapist or helpline if experiencing a strong urge to engage in self-harmful behavior. (11, 12)

11. Interpret the client's self-mutilation as an expression of the rage and helplessness that could not be expressed as a child victim of emotional abandonment or abuse; express the expectation that the client will control the urge for self-mutilation. ▽

12. Elicit a promise (as part of a self-mutilation and suicide prevention contract) from the client that he/she will initiate contact with the therapist or a helpline if a suicidal urge becomes strong and before any self-injurious behavior occurs; throughout the therapy process consistently assess the strength of the client's suicide potential. ▽

▽ 6. Reduce actions that interfere with participating in therapy. (13)

13. Continuously monitor, confront, and problem-solve client actions that threaten to interfere with the continuation of therapy such as missing appointments, noncompliance, and/or abruptly leaving therapy. ▽

▽ 7. Cooperate with an evaluation by a physician for psychotropic medication. (14, 15)

14. Assess the client's need for medication (e.g., selective serotonin reuptake inhibitors) and arrange for prescription, if appropriate. ▽

15. Monitor and evaluate the client's psychotropic medication prescription compliance and the effectiveness of the medication on his/her level of functioning. ▽

▽ 8. Reduce the frequency of maladaptive behaviors, thoughts, and feelings that interfere with attaining a reasonable quality of life. (16)

16. Use validation, dialectical strategies (e.g., metaphor, devil's advocate), and problem-solving strategies (e.g., behavioral and solution analysis, cognitive restructuring, skills training, exposure) to help the client manage, reduce, or stabilize maladaptive behaviors (e.g., angry outbursts, binge drinking, abusive relationships, high-risk sex, uncontrolled spending), thoughts (e.g., all-or-nothing thinking, catastrophizing, personalizing) and feelings (e.g., rage, hopelessness, abandonment; see *Cognitive-Behavioral Treatment of Borderline Personality* by Linehan). ▽

▽ 9. Participate in a group (preferably) or individual personal skills development course. (17, 18)

17. Conduct group or individual skills training tailored to the client's identified problem behavioral patterns (e.g., assertiveness for abusive relationships, cognitive strategies for identifying and controlling financial, sexual, and other impulsivity). ▽

18. Use behavioral strategies to teach identified skills (e.g., instruction, modeling, advising), strengthen them (e.g., role-playing, exposure exercises), and facilitate incorporation into the client's everyday life (e.g., homework assignments). ▽

▽ 10. Verbalize a decreased emotional response to previous or current posttraumatic stress. (19)

19. After adaptive behavioral patterns and emotional regulation skills are evident, work with the client on remembering and accepting the facts of previous trauma, reducing denial and increasing insight into its effects, reducing maladaptive emotional and/or behavioral responses to trauma-related stimuli, and reducing self-blame. ▽

▽ 11. Identify, challenge, and replace biased, fearful self-talk with reality-based, positive self-talk. (20, 21, 22)

20. Explore the client's schema and self-talk that mediate his/her trauma-related and other fears, identify and challenge biases; assist him/her in generating thoughts that correct for the negative biases and build confidence (see *Cognitive Behavioral Therapy for Severe Personality Disorders* by Freeman). ▽

21. Assign the client a homework exercise in which he/she identifies fearful self-talk and creates reality-based alternatives; review and reinforce success, providing corrective feedback for failure (see "Journal and Replace Self-Defeating Thoughts" in *Adult Psychotherapy*

Homework Planner, 2nd ed. by Jongsma; or "Daily Record of Dysfunctional Thoughts" in *Cognitive Therapy of Depression* by Beck, Rush, Shaw, and Emery).▽

22. Reinforce the client's positive, reality-based cognitive messages that enhance self-confidence and increase adaptive action. ▽

▽ 12. Participate in imaginal and/or *in vivo* exposure to trauma-related memories until talking or thinking about the trauma does not cause marked distress. (23, 24, 25)

23. Direct and assist the client in constructing a hierarchy of feared and avoided trauma-related stimuli. ▽

24. Direct imaginal exposure to the trauma in session by having the client describe a chosen traumatic experience at an increasing, but client-chosen, level of detail; integrate cognitive restructuring and repeat until associated anxiety reduces and stabilizes; record the session and have the client listen to it between sessions (see "Share the Painful Memory" in *Adult Psychotherapy Homework Planner,* 2nd ed. by Jongsma; or *Posttraumatic Stress Disorder* by Resick and Calhoun); review and reinforce progress, problem-solve obstacles. ▽

25. Assign the client a homework exercise in which he/she does an exposure exercise and records responses or listens to a recording of an in-session exposure (see *Posttraumatic Stress Disorder* by Resick and Calhoun); review and reinforce progress, problem-solve obstacles. ▽

▽ 13. Verbalize a sense of self-respect that is not dependent on others' opinions. (26)

26. Help the client to value, believe, and trust in his/her evaluations of himself/herself, others, and situations and to examine them non-defensively and independent of others' opinions in a manner that

14. Engage in practices that help enhance a sustained sense of joy. (27)

15. Participate in multiple family group treatment. (28)

builds self-reliance but does not isolate the client from others. ▽

27. Facilitate the client's personal growth by helping him/her choose experiences that strengthen self-awareness, personal values, and appreciation of life (e.g., insight-oriented therapy, spiritual practices, or other relevant life experiences). ▽

28. Refer or enroll client and his/her family in multiple family group treatment (see *Multiple Family Group Treatment for Borderline Personality Disorder* by Whitehurst, Ridolfi, and Gunderson). ▽

___. _____
    _____
___. _____
    _____
___. _____
    _____

___. _____
    _____
___. _____
    _____
___. _____
    _____

DIAGNOSTIC SUGGESTIONS

Axis I: 300.4   Dysthymic Disorder
             296.3x   Major Depressive Disorder, Recurrent

             _____   _____
             _____   _____

Axis II: 301.83   Borderline Personality Disorder
             301.9   Personality Disorder NOS

             _____   _____
             _____   _____

CHEMICAL DEPENDENCE

BEHAVIORAL DEFINITIONS

1. Consistently uses alcohol or other mood-altering substances (not including prescribed medications) until high, intoxicated, or passed out.
2. Exacerbates primary (e.g., hallucinations, delusions, mania) or secondary (e.g., anxiety, unstable affect, disorganization) psychosis symptoms as a result of the use of or withdrawal from mood-altering illicit substances.
3. Unable to stop the use of mood-altering substances once started, despite the verbalized desire to do so or the negative consequences that continued use brings.
4. Blood tests reflect a pattern of heavy substance abuse (for example, elevated liver enzymes).
5. Denies that chemical dependence is a problem, despite direct feedback from family, peers, or treatment staff that the substance use is negatively affecting functioning or relationships.
6. Continues drug and/or alcohol use despite experiencing persistent or recurring physical, legal, vocational, social, or relationship problems that are directly caused by the substance use disorder.
7. Diverts limited financial or personal resources into obtaining the substance, using the substance, or recovering from the effects of the substance.
8. Uses substances despite medical warnings from a physician about the negative interactions of psychotropic medications and illicit substances.
9. Gradually increases the consumption of the mood-altering substance in larger amounts and for longer periods than intended to obtain the desired effect.
10. Experiences physical symptoms, including shaking, seizures, nausea, headaches, sweating, or insomnia, when withdrawing from the substance.
11. Relapses into abuse of mood-altering substances after a substantial period of sobriety.

__. _____
_____
__. _____
_____

—. _____
_____

LONG-TERM GOALS

1. Accept the chemical dependence and begin to actively participate in an integrated, dual-diagnosis recovery program.
2. Withdraw from mood-altering substance; stabilize physically, emotionally, and psychiatrically; and then establish a supportive recovery plan.
3. Gain an understanding of the negative impact of substance use on psychiatric symptoms and the effectiveness of psychotropic medications.
4. Improve the quality of life by maintaining an ongoing abstinence from all illicit mood-altering substances.
5. Establish and maintain total abstinence while increasing knowledge of the disease, the interaction with mental illness concerns, and the process of an integrated recovery.
6. Acquire the necessary skills to maintain a long-term sobriety from all illicit mood-altering substances.
7. Develop an understanding of a personal pattern of relapse to help sustain long-term recovery.

—. _____
_____
—. _____
_____
—. _____
_____

SHORT-TERM OBJECTIVES

1. Achieve a medically safe detoxification from substances.
(1, 2, 3, 4, 5)

THERAPEUTIC INTERVENTIONS

1. Obtain permission from the client to remove available substances from his/her immediate access.

2. Refer the client to an emergency room for immediate medical assessment/care relative to present substance use and intoxication.

3. Assess the client's current level of intoxication by a subjective

means, such as reviewing behavior or speech, and/or by an objective means, such as obtaining a Breathalyzer or blood test.

4. Refer the client to an acute detoxification unit in a substance abuse treatment program.

5. Assess the client's suicide risk, providing for or coordinating intervention, as needed.

2. Improve medical stability relative to the effects of long-term substance abuse. (6)

6. Refer to medical staff, such as an agency nurse or a personal physician, to assess the client's physical/medical needs.

3. Improve nutritional/dietary status relative to the effects of long-term substance abuse. (7, 8)

7. Educate the client about the benefits of maintaining healthy nutrition and help him/her implement appropriate changes in diet.

8. Refer to a dietitian or a nutritionist for an assessment or recommendations regarding the client's dietary needs.

4. Maintain or acquire adequate, safe housing or residential placement. (9, 10)

9. Assist the client in identifying residential needs, obtaining crisis housing, as needed.

10. Facilitate an agreement between the client and the landlord or home provider regarding expectations for the client to remain in a residential situation that has been compromised due to his/her exacerbated psychiatric symptoms and substance abuse.

5. Identify recent experiences of victimization relative to a compromised mental condition due to chronic substance abuse. (11, 12)

11. Ask the client about any recent history of having experienced sexual, physical, or other types of victimization, providing empathetic support regarding possible abuse.

12. Contact adult protective services staff regarding abuse to individuals who are unable to advocate for themselves.

6. Accept the legal consequences of behavior related to substance abuse. (13, 14, 15)

13. With proper release, provide information to police/prosecutor regarding the impact of the client's mental illness on his/her behavior.

14. Urge the client to accept personal responsibility for substance abuse and consequent erratic behavior.

15. Facilitate the client's involvement with legal appointments, court dates, and so forth.

▽ 7. Identify and accept the need for substance abuse treatment. (16, 17)

16. Coordinate family members, friends, and colleagues to confront the client about the negative effects that substance abuse has had on their lives and on their relationships with the client. ▽

17. Conduct Motivational Interviewing to assess the client's stage of preparation for change; intervene accordingly, moving from building motivation, through strengthening commitment to change, to participation in treatment (see *Motivational Interviewing: Preparing People for Change,* 2nd ed. by Miller and Rollnick). ▽

▽ 8. Describe the type, amount, frequency, and history of substance abuse. (18, 19)

18. Gather a complete drug/alcohol history from the client, including the amount and pattern of his/her use, signs and symptoms of use, and negative life consequences (e.g., social, legal, familial, vocational). ▽

19. Request that family, peers, and other treatment staff provide additional information regarding the client's substance use history. ▽

▽ indicates that the Objective/Intervention is consistent with those found in evidence-based treatments.

▽ 9. Complete psychological tests designed to assess the nature and severity of substance use. (20)

▽ 10. Cooperate with an evaluation by a physician for psychotropic medication. (21, 22)

▽ 11. Identify the benefits that have promoted substance abuse, including the effect on mental illness symptoms. (23)

▽ 12. Identify the negative consequences of substance abuse, including the exacerbation of mental illness symptoms. (24, 25)

▽ 13. Make verbal "I" statements that reflect a knowledge and acceptance of chemical dependence. (26)

▽ 14. Verbalize increased knowledge of alcoholism and the process of recovery. (27, 28)

20. Administer to the client an objective test of drug and/or alcohol abuse (e.g., the Alcohol Severity Index, the MAST); process the results with the client. ▽

21. Arrange for an evaluation for a prescription of psychotropic medications (e.g., serotonergic medications). ▽

22. Monitor the client for prescription compliance, side effects, and overall effectiveness of the medication; consult with the prescribing physician at regular intervals. ▽

23. Ask the client to make a list of reasons why substance use is attractive (e.g., self-medication of psychotic and other severe mental illness symptoms, novelty seeking), and process this with him/her. ▽

24. Ask the client to make a list of the ways substance abuse has negatively impacted his/her life, identifying any physical/medical consequences of chemical use; process these with him/her. ▽

25. Assign the client to complete a First Step paper and then to process it with group, sponsor, or therapist to receive feedback. ▽

26. Model and reinforce statements that reflect the client's acceptance of his/her chemical dependence and its destructive consequences for self and others. ▽

27. Require the client to learn more about chemical dependency and the recovery process (e.g., through assignment of didactic lectures, reading, films), asking

the client to identify key points; process with the client. ▽

28. Assign the client to meet with an AA/NA member who has been working the 12-step program for several years and find out specifically how the program has helped him/her to stay sober; afterward, process the meeting. ▽

▽ 15. Identify realistic goals for substance abuse recovery. (29, 30, 31)

29. Request that the client write out basic treatment expectations (e.g., physical changes, social changes, emotional needs) regarding sobriety, and process these with the clinician. ▽

30. Emphasize the goal of substance abuse recovery and the need for sobriety, despite lapses or relapses. ▽

31. Plan for an extended monitoring of the chronic nature and high recidivism of mentally ill substance abusers. ▽

▽ 16. Verbalize a commitment to abstain from the use of mood-altering drugs. (32)

32. Develop an abstinence contract with the client regarding the termination of the use of his/her drug of choice; process the client's feelings related to the commitment. ▽

▽ 17. Attend Alcoholics Anonymous/ Narcotics Anonymous (AA/NA) meetings as frequently as necessary to support sobriety. (33)

33. Recommend that the client attend AA or NA meetings and report on the impact of the meetings; process messages the client is receiving. ▽

▽ 18. Verbalize an understanding of factors, including childhood experiences, which can contribute to development of chemical dependence and pose risks for relapse. (34)

34. Assess and facilitate the client's understanding of his/her genetic and environmental risk factors that led to the development of chemical dependency and serve as risk factors for relapse. ▽

▽ 19. Identify and develop social relationships that will support recovery. (35)

35. Review the negative influence of the client continuing his/her alcohol-related friendships

("drinking buddies") and assist him/her in making a plan to develop new sober relationships including "sobriety buddies;" revisit routinely and facilitate toward development of a new social support system. ▽

▽ 20. Identify projects and other social and recreational activities that sobriety will now afford and that will support sobriety. (36)

36. Assist the client in planning household, work-related, social and recreational activities that are free from association with substance abuse; revisit routinely and facilitate toward development of a new set of activities. ▽

▽ 21. Make arrangements to terminate current living situation and move to a place more conducive to recovery. (37, 38)

37. Evaluate the role of the client's living situation in fostering a pattern of chemical dependence; process with the client toward identifying therapeutic changes. ▽

38. Facilitate development of a plan for the client to change his/her living situation to foster recovery; revisit routinely and facilitate toward accomplishing a positive change in living situation. ▽

▽ 22. Identify the positive impact that sobriety will have on intimate and family relationships. (39)

39. Assist the client in identifying positive changes that will be made in family relationships during recovery. ▽

▽ 23. Agree to make amends to significant others who have been hurt by the life dominated by substance abuse. (40, 41)

40. Discuss the negative effects the client's substance abuse has had on family, friends, and work relationships and encourage a plan to make amends for such hurt. ▽

41. Elicit from the client a verbal commitment to make amends to key individuals. ▽

▽ 24. Participate in behavioral couples therapy to learn and implement ways to improve relations, resolve conflicts, solve problems, and communicate effectively. (42)

42. Refer or provide behavioral couples therapy (see the Intimate Relationship Conflicts chapter in this *Planner*) to the client and his/her partner to resolve conflicts and promote communication. ▽

▼ 25. Learn and implement personal coping strategies to manage urges to lapse back into chemical use. (43)

43. Teach the client coping strategies involving calming techniques (e.g., relaxation, breathing), thought- stopping, positive self-talk, and attentional focusing skills (e.g., distraction from urges, staying focused on behavioral goals of abstinence) to manage urges to use chemical substances. ▼

▼ 26. Identify, challenge, and replace destructive self-talk with positive, strength-building self-talk. (44, 45)

44. Use cognitive therapy approaches to explore the client's schema and self-talk that weaken his/her resolve to remain abstinent, challenging the biases; assist him/her in generating realistic self-talk that corrects for the biases and builds resilience. ▼

45. Rehearse situations in which the client identifies his/her negative self-talk and generates empowering alternatives (or assign "Negative Thoughts Trigger Negative Feelings" in the *Adult Psychotherapy Homework Planner,* 2nd ed., by Jongsma); review and reinforce success. ▼

▼ 27. Participate in gradual repeated exposure to triggers of urges to lapse back into chemical substance use. (46, 47)

46. Direct and assist the client in the construction of a hierarchy of urge-producing cues to use substances. ▼

47. Select initial *in vivo* or role-played cue exposures that have a high likelihood of being a successful experience for the client; facilitate coping and cognitive restructuring within and after the exposure, use behavioral strategies (e.g., modeling, rehearsal, social reinforcement) to facilitate the exposure, review with the client and group members, if done in group. ▼

▼ 28. Learn and implement personal skills to manage common day-to-

48. Assess current skills in managing common everyday stressors

day challenges and build confidence in managing them without the use of substances. (48, 49)

▽ 29. Implement relapse prevention strategies for managing possible future situations with high-risk for relapse. (50, 51, 52, 53)

(e.g., work, social, family role demands); use behavioral techniques (e.g., instruction, modeling, role-playing) to build social and/or communication skills to manage these challenges without the use of substances. ▽

49. Assign the client to read about general social and/or communication skills in books or treatment manuals on building social skills (e.g., *Your Perfect Right* by Alberti and Emmons; *Conversationally Speaking* by Garner). ▽

50. Discuss with the client the distinction between a lapse and relapse, associating a lapse with an initial, temporary, and reversible use of a substance and relapse with the decision to return to a repeated pattern of abuse. ▽

51. Identify and rehearse with the client the management of future situations or circumstances in which lapses could occur; request that the client identify the ways in which family and peer conflicts have contributed to his/her stress level, increasing the likelihood to react with substance abuse. ▽

52. Request that the client identify feelings, behaviors, and situations that place him/her at a higher risk for substance abuse, including symptoms of his/her mental disorder that effect the desire for substances. ▽

53. Instruct the client to routinely use strategies learned in therapy (e.g., using cognitive restructuring, social skills, and exposure) while building social interactions and relationships. ▽

▼ 30. Structure time and increase self-esteem by obtaining employment. (54, 55)

54. Refer the client to a supported employment program. ▼

55. Coach the client on preparing for employment, searching for a job, and maintaining employment (see the Employment Problems chapter in this *Planner*). ▼

31. Ask family, friends, and an AA/NA sponsor to support sobriety. (56, 57)

56. Encourage the client to solicit family support for his/her sober lifestyle.

57. Coordinate a sponsor from a 12-step program, providing additional information to the sponsor regarding mental illness issues.

32. Family members increase support of the client to reduce stress, support sobriety, and decrease exacerbation of the primary symptoms. (58)

58. Refer the family members to a community-based support group for loved ones of a chronically mentally ill substance abuser.

33. Attend a 12-step program consistently to support and maintain sobriety. (59)

59. Encourage and reinforce consistent attendance at 12-step recovery program meetings three or more times per week.

34. Accept the long-term recovery nature of substance abuse problems, mental illness, and the need for ongoing treatment. (60, 61)

60. Assign and review the client's written aftercare plan to ensure it is adequate to maintain sobriety.

61. Coordinate a contact between the client and another mentally ill individual who is further along in substance abuse recovery (e.g., three years or more) to process how he/she has achieved this success.

—. _____

   _____

—. _____

   _____

—. _____

   _____

—. _____

   _____

—. _____

   _____

—. _____

   _____

DIAGNOSTIC SUGGESTIONS

Axis I:	303.90	Alcohol Dependence
	305.00	Alcohol Abuse
	304.30	Cannabis Dependence
	305.20	Cannabis Abuse
	304.20	Cocaine Dependence
	305.60	Cocaine Abuse
	304.80	Polysubstance Dependence
	297.1	Delusional Disorder
	295.xx	Schizophrenia
	295.10	Schizophrenia, Disorganized Type
	295.30	Schizophrenia, Paranoid Type
	295.70	Schizoaffective Disorder
	296.xx	Bipolar I Disorder
	296.89	Bipolar II Disorder
	_____	_____
	_____	_____

DEPRESSION

BEHAVIORAL DEFINITIONS

1. Exhibits a loss of appetite.
2. Reports depressed affect.
3. Demonstrates a diminished interest in or pleasure derived from previously enjoyable activities.
4. Reports experiencing sleeplessness or hypersomnia.
5. Demonstrates decreased energy level.
6. Exhibits psychomotor retardation or agitation.
7. Displays social withdrawal.
8. Expresses chronic feelings of hopelessness, worthlessness, or inappropriate guilt.
9. Experiences hallucinations or delusions secondary to and congruent with depressed mood.
10. Has experienced multiple losses related to severe and persistent mental illness symptoms resulting in sorrow, grief, or despair.
11. Reports suicidal ideation, statements, gestures, or attempts.
12. Verbalizes feelings of low self-esteem.

—. _____
   _____
—. _____
   _____
—. _____
   _____

LONG-TERM GOALS

1. Alleviate depressed mood and return to previous level of effective functioning.

2. Recognize, accept, and cope with feelings of depression.
3. Develop healthy cognitive patterns and beliefs about self and the world that lead to alleviation and help prevent the relapse of depression symptoms.
4. Develop healthy interpersonal relationships that lead to alleviation and help prevent the relapse of depression symptoms.
5. Appropriately grieve the loss in order to normalize mood and to return to previous adaptive level of functioning.
6. Stabilize appetite, sleep pattern, and energy level.
7. Develop increased involvement in personal interests.
8. Express emotions regarding losses that are related to severe and persistent mental illness symptoms.
9. Assure safety regarding suicidal impulses.

—. _____
   _____
—. _____
   _____
—. _____
   _____

SHORT-TERM OBJECTIVES

1. Describe current and past experiences with depression and other mood episodes, including their impact on function and attempts to resolve or treat them. (1, 2)

2. Facilitate an assessment of personal and family history of depression and other mood symptoms, allowing

THERAPEUTIC INTERVENTIONS

1. Assess current and past mood episodes including their features, frequency, intensity, and duration; impact on role functioning; previous treatments; and response to treatments (e.g., clinical interview supplemented by the *Archives of General Psychiatry* by Zimmerman, Coryell, Corenthal, and Wilson).

2. Utilize a graphic display, such as a time line, to help the client identify the pattern of his/her mood symptoms.

3. Ask family, friends, and caregivers about the client's own and the family's history of depression symptoms.

family participation. (3, 4)

3. Share feelings of depression and explore their origins. (5)

4. Identify specific losses that are related to severe and persistent mental illness symptoms. (6)

5. Complete psychological testing to assess the depth of depression, the need for antidepressant medication, and suicide prevention measures. (7)

6. Acknowledge the abuse of alcohol and street drugs and their relationship to depression. (8, 9)

7. Obtain an adequate, stable sleep pattern. (10, 11)

4. Provide the client, family, or caretaker with sleeping, eating, and activity logs on which to document current levels of functioning.

5. Encourage the client to identify and share the feelings of depression to clarify them and gain insight into the causes; provide support and empathy.

6. Inquire about specific losses that severely and persistently mentally ill individuals experience (e.g., loss of independence, income, freedom, dignity or relationships) and how these losses may contribute to depression.

7. Arrange for the administration of an objective assessment instrument for evaluating the client's depression and suicide risk (e.g., Beck Depression Inventory-II and/or *Beck Hopelessness Scale*); evaluate results and give feedback to the client.

8. Review the client's use of stimulants (e.g., nicotine, caffeine, or street drugs), and depressants (e.g., alcohol or barbiturates) and their relationship to symptoms.

9. Conduct or refer the client for substance abuse evaluation/treatment (see the Chemical Dependence chapter in this *Planner*).

10. Assess and address basic sleep hygiene needs (e.g., decrease stimulants in the evening; have a quiet, comfortable place to sleep; spend time winding down; same wake-up time) and behavioral strategies (e.g., staying in bed awake no more than 15 minutes) to reinforce structure to sleep routine.

▽ 8. Cooperate with suicide prevention measures. (12, 13)

11. Refer the client for a sleep disorder evaluation.

12. Coordinate an immediate referral to a crisis residential facility or inpatient psychiatric ward to provide a safe, supervised environment for suicidal client. ▽

13. Develop a structured suicide prevention plan (see the Suicidal Ideation chapter in this *Planner*). ▽

▽ 9. Cooperate with a referral to a physician for a psychotropic medication evaluation and take medications responsibly as prescribed. (14, 15)

14. Refer the client to a physician for an evaluation as to the need for psychotropic medications. ▽

15. Educate the client about the use and expected benefits of medication. ▽

▽ 10. Report the side effects and effectiveness of medications to the appropriate professional. (16, 17)

16. Monitor the client's medication for compliance, effectiveness, and possible side effects. ▽

17. Monitor the client's other severe and persistent mental illness symptoms, which may be exacerbated by the introduction of an antidepressant. ▽

▽ 11. Verbalize an understanding of the development and rationale for treatment of depression. (18)

18. Discuss factors related to the development and maintenance of the client's depression and how treatment will target these factors for change. ▽

▽ 12. Identify and replace cognitive self-talk that supports depression. (19, 20, 21 22)

19. Assist the client in developing an awareness of his/her automatic thoughts that reflect a depressogenic schema. ▽

20. Assign the client to keep a daily journal of automatic thoughts associated with depressive feelings (e.g., "Negative Thoughts Trigger

---

▽ indicates that the Objective/Intervention is consistent with those found in evidence-based treatments.

Negative Feelings" in *Adult Psychotherapy Homework Planner,* 2nd ed. by Jongsma, or "Daily Record of Dysfunctional Thoughts" in *Cognitive Therapy of Depression* by Beck, Rush, Shaw, and Emery); process the journal material to challenge depressive thinking patterns and replace them with reality-based thoughts. ▽

21. Do "behavioral experiments" in which depressive automatic thoughts are treated as hypotheses/predictions, reality-based alternative hypotheses/predictions are generated, and both are tested against the client's past, present, and/or future experiences. ▽

22. Reinforce the client's positive, reality-based cognitive messages that enhance self-confidence and increase adaptive action (see "Positive Self-Talk" in *Adult Psychotherapy Homework Planner,* 2nd ed. by Jongsma). ▽

▽ 13. Learn and use behavioral strategies to overcome depression. (23, 24, 25)

23. Assist the client in developing coping strategies (e.g., more physical exercise, less internal focus, increased social involvement, more assertiveness, greater need sharing, more anger expression) for feelings of depression; reinforce success. ▽

24. Engage the client in "behavioral activation" by scheduling activities that have a high likelihood for pleasure and mastery (see "Identify and Schedule Pleasant Activities" in *Adult Psychotherapy Homework Planner,* 2nd ed. by Jongsma); use rehearsal, role-playing, or role reversal, as needed, to assist adoption

in the client's daily life; reinforce success. ▽

25. Employ self-reliance training in which the client assumes increased responsibility for routine activities (e.g., cleaning, cooking, and shopping); reinforce success. ▽

▽ 14. Identify important people in your life, past and present, and describe the quality, good and bad, of those relationships. (26)

26. Assess the client's "interpersonal inventory" of important past and present relationships and evidence of potentially depressive themes (e.g., grief, interpersonal disputes, role transitions, and interpersonal deficits). ▽

▽ 15. Verbalize any unresolved grief issues that may be contributing to depression. (27)

27. Explore the role of unresolved grief issues as they contribute to the client's current depression (see the Grief and Loss chapter in this *Planner*). ▽

▽ 16. Increase assertive communication. (28)

28. Use modeling and/or role-playing to train the client in assertiveness; if indicated, refer him/her to an assertiveness training class/group for further instruction. ▽

▽ 17. Learn and implement problem-solving and/or conflict resolution skills to resolve interpersonal problems. (29, 30, 31)

29. Teach the client conflict resolution skills (e.g., empathy, active listening, "I messages," respectful communication, assertiveness without aggression, compromise) to help alleviate depression; use modeling, role-playing, and behavior rehearsal to work through several current conflicts. ▽

30. Help the client resolve depression related to interpersonal problems through the use of reassurance and support, clarification of cognitive and affective triggers that ignite conflicts, and active problem-solving (or assign "Applying Problem-Solving to Interpersonal Conflict" in *Adult*

Psychotherapy Homework Planner, 2nd ed. by Jongsma). ▽

31. In conjoint sessions, help the client resolve interpersonal conflicts. ▽

▽ 18. Implement effective decision-making skills. (32, 33)

32. Teach the client a decision-making strategy that involves identifying one problem at a time, breaking the decision down into relevant parts, examining the pros and cons of relevant choices, and coming to a decision based on that procedure. ▽

33. Discourage the client from making major life decisions (when possible) until after his/her mood disorder improves. ▽

▽ 19. Implement a regular exercise regimen as a depression reduction technique. (34, 35)

34. Develop and reinforce a routine of physical exercise for the client. ▽

35. Recommend that the client read and implement an exercise program (e.g., *Exercising Your Way to Better Mental Health* by Leith). ▽

▽ 20. Learn and implement relapse prevention skills. (36)

36. Build the client's relapse prevention skills by helping him/her identify early warning signs of relapse, reviewing skills learned during therapy, and developing a plan for managing challenges. ▽

21. Verbally express an understanding of the relationship between a depressed mood and the repression of feelings (e.g., anger, hurt, and sadness). (37)

37. Explain a connection between previously unexpressed (repressed) feelings, such as hurt, anger, or shame, and the current state of depression.

22. Express previously repressed emotions in a safe, cathartic manner. (38)

38. Teach or model healthy ways in which the client can express repressed emotions, including physical expressions (e.g., beating a pillow), verbal/written expressions (e.g., a letter), or rituals (e.g., writing the emotion down, then tearing it up and tossing it into the wind).

23. Increase the frequency of social contacts and the number of recreational activities that you are involved in. (39)

24. Accept support from family members and a social support system. (40, 41)

25. Agree to monitor symptoms and maintain ongoing treatment. (42, 43)

39. Refer the client to an activity therapist to identify social and recreational skills, and to develop a plan for exercise or social involvement (see the Independent Activities of Daily Living [IADL] or Social Skills Deficits chapters in this *Planner*).

40. Educate the family about mental illness concerns with information (e.g., see *What to Do When Someone You Love Is Depressed: A Practical and Helpful Guide* by Golant and Golant).

41. Teach family members how to support changes made by the client through treatment.

42. Educate the client about the ongoing need for maintenance treatment (e.g., keeping follow-up case manager and physician appointments, taking medication consistently, attending support groups) despite the lack of identifiable symptoms.

43. Request the client to identify a list of symptom triggers and indicators; urge the client to share this information with a support network to assist in monitoring the symptoms.

__. _____

_____

__. _____

_____

__. _____

_____

__. _____

_____

__. _____

_____

__. _____

_____

DIAGNOSTIC SUGGESTIONS

Axis I:

297.1	Delusional Disorder
295.xx	Schizophrenia
295.10	Schizophrenia, Disorganized Type
295.30	Schizophrenia, Paranoid Type
295.70	Schizoaffective Disorder
296.xx	Bipolar I Disorder
296.89	Bipolar II Disorder
296.2x	Major Depressive Disorder, Single Episode
296.3x	Major Depressive Disorder, Recurrent
309.0	Adjustment Disorder With Depressed Mood
V62.82	Bereavement
V62.89	Phase of Life Problem
_____	_____
_____	_____

EMPLOYMENT PROBLEMS

BEHAVIORAL DEFINITIONS

1. Has a history of chronic periods of unemployment or underemployment.
2. Has a history of multiple occupational terminations due to interpersonal conflict or inability to control primary psychosis symptoms (e.g., manic phases, hallucinations, delusions).
3. States a decreased desire to actively seek employment or maintain current position.
4. Lacks formal training or on-the-job experience.
5. Fails to achieve or maintain expected levels of occupational involvement, duration, and success.
6. Rebels against and/or has conflicts with authority figures due to unfounded suspiciousness.
7. Verbalizes feelings of anxiety, depression, or other psychiatric destabilization secondary to being fired or laid off.
8. Verbalizes fears about returning to the workplace due to a history of employment problems and failures.
9. Shares feelings of anxiety or depression that are related to the menial or repetitive nature of job placement.
10. Exacerbation of primary psychosis symptoms due to the anxiety of new employment or increased job tasks/expectations.

—. _____

   _____

—. _____

   _____

—. _____

   _____

LONG-TERM GOALS

1. Learn skills for identifying and resolving problems with coworkers and supervisor.
2. Obtain occupational skills that are necessary to gain entry-level or advanced positions.
3. Control primary psychosis symptoms to manageable levels while in the workplace.
4. Understand how chronic mental illness symptoms impact on employment opportunities.

___. _____

_____

___. _____

_____

___. _____

_____

SHORT-TERM OBJECTIVES

▽ 1. Share personal history of employment. (1)

▽ 2. Identify positive and negative experiences in employment. (2)

▽ 3. Identify the role of mental illness symptoms in employment difficulties. (3, 4)

THERAPEUTIC INTERVENTIONS

1. Assist the client in preparing a chronological outline of previous employment; review and identify patterns of success and failure. ▽

2. Ask the client to describe a few examples of previous successful employment situations and any negative job experiences, listening attentively to the circumstances and emotions. ▽

3. Request that the client identify a few examples of situations in which the primary symptoms of his/her mental illness have negatively affected his/her job performance or social interaction at work. ▽

4. Educate the client about the expected or common symptoms of his/her mental illness which impact

upon his/her employment (e.g., mania, paranoia, or negative symptoms of schizophrenia). ▽

▽ 4. Identify the reasons for not obtaining or maintaining employment. (5)

5. Assist the client in identifying possible reasons for not obtaining employment (e.g., concern about loss of disability payments, fear of increased responsibility or expectations), and process these reasons. ▽

▽ 5. List positive reasons to seek and maintain employment. (6)

6. Assist the client with identifying positive reasons for obtaining or maintaining employment (e.g., sense of accomplishment, increased self-esteem, contributing to society, respect from others). ▽

▽ 6. Attend appointments consistently with a physician for psychotropic medication evaluation. (7)

7. Arrange for a psychiatric evaluation to assess the client's need for antipsychotic or other psychotropic medications, and arrange for filling a prescription, if necessary. ▽

▽ 7. Take antipsychotic medications consistently as prescribed. (8, 9)

8. Encourage the client to take his/her medications consistently. ▽

9. Coordinate the availability of a secure, private area where the client can keep and take medications while at the work site, if necessary. ▽

▽ 8. Report the side effects and effectiveness of medications to an appropriate professional. (10)

10. Monitor the client for medication compliance, effectiveness, and side effects, referring him/her back to the physician as necessary for medication evaluation/adjustment. ▽

▽ 9. Verbalize an understanding of the positive effects of medications on employment skills and functioning. (11, 12)

11. Educate the client about the use of and the expected benefits of psychiatric medications. ▽

12. Educate the client about the expected positive effect of the psychotropic medications on common psychiatric symptoms of his/her mental illness that may have an impact on employment functioning (e.g., paranoia, mania). ▽

▽ 10. Verbalize acceptance of employment as a central goal in the recovery process. (13)

13. Encourage the client to make employment a central goal in recovery, discussing its personal, social, financial, and other relevant benefits. ▽

▽ 11. Enroll in a supported employment program. (14)

14. Refer the client to a supported employment program consistent with an evidence-based model such as the Individual Placement and Support model (see Bond, Drake, Mueser, and Becker for a review). ▽

▽ 12. Identify, learn and implement behaviors that facilitate employment. (15, 16, 17)

15. Assist the client in identifying prosocial behaviors (e.g., eye contact, dress, politeness) that will promote better interpersonal functioning in a work situation. ▽

16. Assist the client in identifying situations in which new prosocial behaviors have been or could be utilized. ▽

17. Use behavioral rehearsal, role-playing, and role reversal to assist the client in practicing targeted interpersonal behavior; urge implementation *in vivo*. ▽

▽ 13. Learn and implement assertiveness and other communication skills that facilitate employment. (18, 19)

18. Teach assertive and other communication skills relevant to functioning effectively in the workplace (e.g., *The Real Solution Assertiveness Workbook* by Pfeiffer; or *Assert Yourself* by Lindenfield). ▽

19. Refer the client to an assertiveness training workshop, which will educate the client and facilitate assertiveness skills via lectures, assignments, and role-playing. ▽

▽ 14. Identify and learn technical skills for possible job placement. (20, 21, 22)

20. Help the client identify marketable skills for which he/she has displayed mastery. ▽

21. Conduct and provide or refer the client to a skill assessment and training program to identify and develop job aptitudes and interests and remediate basic deficits (e.g., community education, technical center, vocational rehabilitation, or occupational therapy). ▽

22. Monitor the client's ongoing attendance, functioning in, and progress in educational or vocational rehabilitation program. ▽

▽ 15. Express a desire for and partici- pate in an assessment process in- tended to identify specific possible job placements. (23, 24)

23. Utilize interest testing (e.g., Strong Vocational Interest Blank) to identify specific types of oc- cupations in which the client has interest. ▽

24. Review interest testing with the client to problem-solve toward the goal of identifying possible occupational placements. ▽

▽ 16. Develop a resume. (25)

25. Assist the client in developing a resume (e.g., use *101 Quick Tips for a Dynamite Resume* by Fein, or *Resumes for the First Time Job Hunter* by the editors of McGraw-Hill). ▽

▽ 17. Obtain letter(s) of reference. (26)

26. Request that the client identify family, friends, teachers, former employers, or other clinicians from whom letters of reference may be requested; assign the pro- curement of these letters. ▽

▽ 18. Conduct a job availability search using available sources. (27)

27. Review available sources of job listings (e.g., classified advertise- ments, job placement services) with the client, requesting that he/she identify two or three jobs that he/she would like to apply for. ▽

▽ 19. Demonstrate job interview skills. (28, 29)

28. Assign the client to read material on job interview skills (e.g., *What Color Is Your Parachute?* by

▽ 20. Successfully complete an interview and obtain a job offer.
(30, 31)

▽ 21. Identify and use consistent
sources of transportation to and
from work. (32)

▽ 22. Cooperate with a job coach to
improve performance skills on
the job. (33)

▽ 23. Allow therapist to share information and work with identified
people at the work setting.
(34, 35, 36)

▽ 24. Dress and groom appropriately
and follow the rules of the
workplace. (37, 38)

Bolles; or *10 Minute Guide to
Job Interviews* by Morgan). ▽

29. Utilize role-playing, behavioral
rehearsal, and role reversal to increase the client's confidence and
skill in the interview process. ▽

30. Assist the client in planning an
interview appointment, coordinating assistance as needed. ▽

31. Process the interview and assist
with the decision-making process
about accepting the job offer. ▽

32. Help the client identify and secure reliable transportation to and
from work. ▽

33. Conduct or arrange for a job coach
to meet regularly with the client in
the job setting to review job needs,
skills, and problem areas. ▽

34. After obtaining the proper confidentiality release, review the client's mental illness symptoms
with the employer. ▽

35. After obtaining the proper confidentiality release, provide
information to the client's fellow
employees about mental illness
concerns; provide sensitivity
training to facilitate the client's
integration into the setting. ▽

36. Develop an agreed-upon intervention plan with the client and
employer to manage possible future crises related to mental disorder symptom exacerbation. ▽

37. Visit the client at the job site often, giving him/her feedback
about hygiene, dress, behavior,
and technical skills. ▽

▽ 25. Maintain a record of good job performance. (39)

38. Review the workplace rules and etiquette regularly with the client. ▽

39. Meet with the client and the employer regularly to review the client's functioning and needs, tapering over time. ▽

__. _____

_____

__. _____

_____

__. _____

_____

__. _____

_____

__. _____

_____

__. _____

_____

DIAGNOSTIC SUGGESTIONS

Axis I:	297.1	Delusional Disorder
	295.xx	Schizophrenia
	295.10	Schizophrenia, Disorganized Type
	295.30	Schizophrenia, Paranoid Type
	295.70	Schizoaffective Disorder
	296.xx	Bipolar I Disorder
	296.89	Bipolar II Disorder
	V62.2	Occupational Problem
	_____	_____
	_____	_____

FAMILY CONFLICTS

BEHAVIORAL DEFINITIONS

1. Has estranged relationships with family members.
2. Exhibits abusive, manipulative, or intimidating behavior toward family members.
3. Functions lower than expected in a variety of areas due to overcontrol of the client's basic needs and decisions by the family.
4. Family members fail to accept the mentally ill individual or his/her diagnosis of a mental illness.
5. Family members have limited knowledge of chronic mental illness symptoms and indicators of decompensation.
6. Family members lack understanding of treatment options.
7. Family members are embarrassed and hide the client because of his/her erratic behaviors related to psychosis or other severe mental illness.

__. _____
   _____
__. _____
   _____
__. _____
   _____

LONG-TERM GOALS

1. Rebuild important family relationships.
2. Experience acceptance from family members.
3. Make personal decisions with minimal or the least restrictive oversight.
4. Behave in a direct, assertive, and loving way toward family members.
5. Family members learn about mental illness symptoms, prodromals, possible causes, and expected duration of illness.

6. Family members gain an understanding of and an involvement in the treatment options that are available to the client.

—. _____

   _____

—. _____

   _____

—. _____

   _____

SHORT-TERM OBJECTIVES

1. Describe the history of family relationships. (1, 2, 3)

2. Describe both negative and positive relationships in the family system. (4, 5, 6)

3. Family members express and clarify their feelings about the client's mental illness and its impact on the family. (7, 8)

THERAPEUTIC INTERVENTIONS

1. Request that the client identify and describe family relationships.

2. Request that the client provide two examples of positive and two examples of negative family experiences.

3. Develop a genogram based on the client's description of the family relationships.

4. Request that the client list and describe the positive and the problematic family relationships.

5. Clarify any patterns to the client's behavior that contribute to positive and negative relationships and interactions.

6. Utilize solution-focused techniques to help the client identify how he/she has facilitated positive interactions in the past.

7. Facilitate the family members in identifying and expressing their emotions regarding the client's mental illness.

8. Use the question, "What would happen in your family if the client did not have any mental ill-

ness symptoms?" to help the family identify the impact of the mental illness symptoms on the family.

▽ 4. Family members enroll in a multigroup educational program for families of the mentally ill. (9)

9. Refer the family to a multigroup family psychoeducational program (see *Multi-family Groups in the Treatment of Severe Psychiatric Disorders* by McFarlane). ▽

▽ 5. The client and family agree to participate in a family-focused therapy. (10)

10. Conduct or refer the client and family to a therapy based on the principles of family-focused treatment (e.g., see *Bipolar Disorder: A Family-Focused Treatment Approach* by Miklowitz and Goldstein). ▽

▽ 6. Family members learn about mental illness symptoms. (11, 12, 13, 14)

11. Refer the client and his/her family to a lending library at the agency or in the community to access books or tapes on severe mental illness. ▽

12. Refer the parents to or conduct didactic sessions on severe and persistent mental illness and its treatment. ▽

13. Teach the client, family, and relevant others, using all modalities necessary, about the signs, symptoms, and relapsing nature of the client's disorder; destigmatize and normalize. ▽

14. Teach the client and family a stress diathesis model of the client's disorder that emphasizes the strong role of a biological predisposition to symptoms that is vulnerable to stresses that are managable. ▽

▽ indicates that the Objective/Intervention is consistent with those found in evidence-based treatments.

▽ 7. Identify and manage sources of stress that increase the risk of relapse. (15, 16)

15. Provide the client with a rationale for treatment involving ongoing medication and psychosocial treatment to recognize, manage, and reduce biological and psychological vulnerabilities that could precipitate relapse. ▽

16. Identify the client's sources of stress/triggers of potential relapse (e.g., negative events, cognitive misinterpretations, aversive communication, poor sleep hygiene, medication noncompliance); use cognitive and behavioral techniques to address these triggers (e.g., *Living with Bipolar Disorder* by Otto, Reilly-Harrington, Knauz, Heinin, Kogan, and Sachs). ▽

▽ 8. Verbalize acceptance of the need to take psychotropic medication and commit to prescription compliance with blood level monitoring. (17, 18, 19)

17. Use motivational interviewing approaches (e.g., *Enhancing Motivation for Treatment and Change* by Yahne and Miller) to enhance the client's engagement in medication use and compliance; teach him/her the risk for relapse when medication is discontinued, and work toward a commitment to prescription adherence. ▽

18. Assess factors (e.g., thoughts, feelings, stressors) that have precipitated the client's prescription noncompliance; develop a plan for recognizing and addressing them. ▽

19. Educate and encourage the client to stay compliant with necessary laboratory tests involved in regulating his/her medication levels. ▽

▽ 9. Develop "crises plans" in which roles, responsibilities, and a course of action is agreed upon

20. Assess potential crises (e.g., threats to self or others, symptom increase); problem-solve, and

in the event of identified potential crises. (20, 21)

develop a plan for managing them upon which all family members agree. ▽

21. Help the client and family draw up a relapse drill detailing roles and responsibilities (e.g., who will call a meeting of the family to problem-solve potential relapse; who will call physician, schedule a serum level to be taken, or contact emergency services, if needed); problem-solve obstacles and work toward a commitment to adherence with the plan. ▽

▽ 10. The client and family commit to replacing aversive communication with positive, honest, and respectful communication. (22, 23, 24)

22. Assess and educate the client and family about the role of aversive communication (e.g., strong expressed emotion) in family distress and risk for the client's relapse. ▽

23. Use behavioral techniques (education, modeling, role-playing, corrective feedback, and positive reinforcement) to teach communication skills including offering positive feedback, active listening, making positive requests of others for behavior change, and giving negative feedback in an honest and respectful manner. ▽

24. Assign the client and family homework exercises to use and record use of newly learned communication skills; process results in session. ▽

▽ 11. Increase awareness of one's behavior and its impact on others. (25, 26)

25. Increase the client's sensitivity to the effects of his/her behavior through the use of role-playing, role reversal, and behavioral rehearsal. ▽

26. Identify and confront unhealthy or impulsive behaviors that occur during contacts with the clinician,

enforcing clear rules and roles in the relationship, as well as immediate, short-term consequences for breaking such boundaries. ▽

▽ 12. The client and family implement a problem-solving approach to address current conflicts. (27, 28, 29)

27. Assist the client and family in identifying conflicts that can be addressed with problem-solving techniques. ▽

28. Use behavioral techniques (education, modeling, role-playing, corrective feedback, and positive reinforcement) to teach the client and family problem-solving skills including defining the problem constructively and specifically, brainstorming options, evaluating options, choosing options and implementing a plan, evaluating the results, and reevaluating the plan. ▽

29. Assign the client and family homework exercises (e.g., "Applying Problem-Solving to Interpersonal Conflict" in the *Adult Psychotherapy Homework Planner*, 2nd ed. by Jongsma) to use and record use of newly learned problem-solving skills; process results in session. ▽

▽ 13. Family identifies and engages in a support network that can reduce the stress of caring for a mentally ill family member. (30, 31, 32, 33)

30. Assess the family's support network (e.g., extended family, neighbors, church friends, social relationships) that provides diversion, emotional support, and/or respite care for the client; brainstorm how this network can be developed and utilized more fully. ▽

31. Refer the family to community-based respite services, coordinating for others to provide supervision or to take responsibility for the client on a short-term basis. ▽

32. Acknowledge the family's frustration and anger regarding not having received services that they desired in the past, attempting now to redirect them to formal resources and informal supports. ▽

33. Refer the parents to a support group for families of the mentally ill. ▽

▽ 14. Participate in periodic "tune-up" sessions. (34)

34. Hold periodic booster sessions within the first few months after therapy to facilitate the client's positive changes; problem-solve obstacles to improvement. ▽

15. List enjoyable leisure activities to which the family can be invited, or in which their participation would be desired. (35, 36)

35. Assist the client in identifying mutually satisfying social activities for himself/herself and his/her family.

36. Refer to an activity or a recreational therapist for assistance in developing leisure skills to share with family members.

16. Family members reduce the frequency of speaking for the client or performing activities that the client is capable of doing independently. (37, 38)

37. Identify roles in the family and behavioral patterns that developed in the family's reaction to mental illness symptoms that have inappropriately limited the client's independent functioning and enabled dependence.

38. Encourage the client (and encourage the family to allow the client) to make all possible choices and demonstrate maximum independence in daily events.

17. Family to develop long-term plans for care and advocacy of the client relative to aging parents or the potential loss of the primary advocate/caregiver. (39, 40)

39. Review the options that will be available should the primary caregiver/advocate be unable to care for the client.

40. Encourage the ongoing involvement of non-mentally ill siblings in treatment and social contact with the client.

18. Maintain involvement in family spiritual practices. (41, 42, 43)

41. Encourage the family members to continue normal involvement of the client in church or other religious behaviors if they are a part of the family's spiritual practice.

42. Monitor mental illness symptoms related to religious themes, and provide feedback to the client about such.

43. With the proper release of information, give the information to the clergy or other church leaders regarding assistance that the client may need in accessing spiritual practices and programs.

19. Family members verbalize resolution of feelings of guilt and responsibility for the client's mental illness. (44)

44. Assist the family members in resolving any unrealistic feelings of responsibility and self-blame for the client's mental illness.

__. _____   __. _____
    _____   _____

__. _____   __. _____
    _____   _____

__. _____   __. _____
    _____   _____

DIAGNOSTIC SUGGESTIONS

Axis I:		
	297.1	Delusional Disorder
	295.xx	Schizophrenia
	295.10	Schizophrenia, Disorganized Type
	295.30	Schizophrenia, Paranoid Type
	295.90	Schizophrenia, Undifferentiated Type
	295.60	Schizophrenia, Residual Type
	295.70	Schizoaffective Disorder
	296.xx	Bipolar I Disorder
	296.89	Bipolar II Disorder

V61.20	Parent-Child Relational Problem
V61.10	Partner Relational Problem
V61.8	Sibling Relational Problem
_____	_____
_____	_____

FINANCIAL NEEDS

BEHAVIORAL DEFINITIONS

1. Lives on low income due to the effects of psychosis and other severe mental illness symptoms.
2. Is chronically homeless or constantly uses supportive transitional living services, such as homeless shelters or adult foster care placements.
3. Lacks consistent, adequate employment that is capable of providing funds for basic needs.
4. Spends money impulsively or excessively due to psychotic or manic episodes.
5. Fails to plan, organize, or budget for basic financial responsibilities.
6. Has a history of not applying for or accessing monetary entitlements or other available welfare benefits.
7. Engages in illegal activity to meet financial needs.
8. Has a poor credit history or an inability to qualify for credit.

—. _____
_____
—. _____
_____
—. _____
_____

LONG-TERM GOALS

1. Establish a stable, permanent, legal income that meets basic financial needs.
2. Find living arrangements that are either government supported, independent, or provided by family, and that are stable, safe, and secure.
3. Find full- or part-time employment at a position that is well suited to abilities and with employer/coworkers who are tolerant of mental illness symptoms.

4. Display budgeting skills as evidenced by adherence to a written budget and paying bills on a timely basis.
5. Utilize or apply for appropriate, available, and necessary entitlements or other benefits.

—. _____

_____

—. _____

_____

—. _____

_____

SHORT-TERM OBJECTIVES

THERAPEUTIC INTERVENTIONS

1. Describe the personal history of financial issues and the details of current financial situation. (1, 2)

1. Request that the client relate his/her history or pattern of financial concerns.

2. Provide the client with support and empathy, focusing on decreasing his/her guilt or blame for financial difficulties.

2. Identify both positive and negative financial practices. (3, 4, 5)

3. Request that the client identify at least two financial practices that he/she uses that are beneficial or that add to stability (e.g., saving, budgeting, comparison shopping).

4. Assist the client in identifying at least two financial practices that have led to difficulty (e.g., unstable work history, impulsive spending, failure to pay on commitments).

5. Process financial successes and failures, focusing on patterns, triggers, and consequences of successes and failures.

3. List current financial needs and obligations. (6, 7)

6. Assist the client in creating a written list of all current financial obligations.

7. Compare the client's list of financial obligations with normally

expected obligations (e.g., see those listed on the budgeting worksheet in *Personal Budget Planner: A Guide for Financial Success* by Gelb); process any discrepancies from normal expectations.

4. Identify how mental illness symptoms affect financial concerns. (8, 9)

8. Educate the client about the typical symptoms that are expected in his/her mental illness.

9. Assist the client in identifying at least two ways in which his/her mental illness has negatively affected financial practices.

5. Obtain a payee or other option to receive welfare benefits and disperse funds. (10, 11)

10. Suggest to the client that he/she voluntarily allow someone else to be his/her payee, or otherwise exercise general control over his/her finances.

11. Assist the client in initiating legal procedures for obtaining a payee to accept benefits and disperse funds.

6. Decrease immediate access to funds to limit erratic, impulsive spending. (12, 13)

12. Coordinate for a cosigner to be necessary for all bank withdrawal transactions.

13. Pursue involuntary legal control over the client's finances through guardianship processes.

7. Use medication to decrease the mental illness symptoms that might affect financial abilities or lead to impulsive, erratic spending. (14, 15, 16)

14. Arrange for the client to have a psychiatric evaluation and coordinate medications, if necessary.

15. Educate the client about the use of and expected benefit from medications.

16. Monitor the client's medication compliance, effectiveness, and side effects; report results to the physician.

8. Establish a stable residence that is not dependent on personal finance management. (17, 18)

17. Coordinate for an adult foster care placement if the client is unable to manage finances even with assistance.

18. Coordinate an arrangement for the client to live with family members or friends.

9. Obtain a more independent residence, and maintain responsible control over finances. (19, 20)

19. Assist the client in developing an independent or semi-independent living situation with necessary supports related to financial and other areas.

20. Regularly review the client's financial needs and money management practices; reinforce success and redirect for failures.

10. Obtain all necessary public welfare benefits to provide funds for general use. (21, 22, 23, 24)

21. Assist the client in obtaining, completing, and filing forms for Social Security Disability benefits or other public aid.

22. Coordinate transportation for the client to necessary appointments related to obtaining benefits.

23. Refer the client to specific material regarding eligibility and procedures or obtaining entitlement funds (e.g., *How to Get Every Penny You're Entitled to from Social Security* by Bosley and Gurwitz, or government pamphlets).

24. Provide an agency address as a possible mail drop to which a homeless client may have his/her government benefit check sent.

11. Secure ancillary public and private benefits or grants for specific financial needs (e.g., heating bills, education, etc.). (25, 26)

25. Compile and provide to the client a list of available and relevant financial assistance resources in his/her area (e.g., home heating assistance, scholarships, housing funds).

26. Assist the client with scheduling, filling out forms, and obtaining transportation to obtain assistance from area programs, as necessary.

12. Obtain public or private insurance to assist with payment for medical and psychiatric services. (27)

27. Coordinate the client's application for appropriate public or private insurance.

13. Write a basic budget that will control spending. (28, 29, 30)

28. Educate the client in basic budgeting skills (e.g., see *Personal Budget Planner: A Guide for Financial Success* by Gelb).

29. Assist the client in developing a basic budget, including income, basic expenses, additional spending, and savings plans (or complete together "Plan a Budget" in the *Adult Psychotherapy Homework Planner*, 2nd ed. by Jongsma).

30. Refer the client to a community education class related to basic finances.

14. Develop a long-term financial plan. (31)

31. Request that the client identify realistic, long-term financial plans, and process these plans with the client.

15. Practice basic banking techniques. (32, 33, 34)

32. Educate the client about typical banking procedures.

33. Coordinate for the client to receive a hands-on tour of a bank, with a focus on him/her becoming more comfortable with the procedures and security measures.

34. Practice banking procedures such as check writing and cashing, using imitation supplies or forms.

16. Obtain identification documents necessary for financial practices. (35)

35. Assist the client in obtaining proper identification (i.e., a state identification card) necessary for banking functions.

__. _____

_____

__. _____

_____

__. _____

_____

__. _____

_____

__. _____

_____

__. _____

_____

DIAGNOSTIC SUGGESTIONS

Axis I:

	297.1	Delusional Disorder
	295.xx	Schizophrenia
	295.10	Schizophrenia, Disorganized Type
	295.30	Schizophrenia, Paranoid Type
	295.90	Schizophrenia, Undifferentiated Type
	295.60	Schizophrenia, Residual Type
	295.70	Schizoaffective Disorder
	296.xx	Bipolar I Disorder
	296.89	Bipolar II Disorder
	V62.2	Occupational Problem
	V62.89	Phase of Life Problem

_____   _____

_____   _____

GRIEF AND LOSS

BEHAVIORAL DEFINITIONS

1. Death of a significant other resulting in depression, confusion, and feelings of insecurity regarding the future.
2. Reports thoughts that are dominated by a loss, culminating in confusion, disorganized behavior, and exacerbation of mental illness symptoms.
3. Exhibits signs and symptoms of depression, including changes in eating or sleeping patterns, thoughts of suicide, crying, or depressed mood.
4. Verbalizes feelings of hopelessness, worthlessness, inappropriate guilt, or a fear of abandonment due to multiple losses.
5. Avoids situations, conversations, or thoughts that recall losses.
6. Loss of abilities, status, or competence due to incapacitating effects of psychotic and other severe mental illness symptoms.
7. Expresses feelings of low self-esteem that are associated with a history of losses.
8. Describes childhood traumas, sexual assault, or abusive parent figures.
9. Demonstrates dissociative phenomena or exacerbations of paranoia.
10. Reports ongoing (nondelusional) spiritual conflicts.
11. Loss of support network due to effects of psychotic and other severe mental illness symptoms.

—. _____
_____
—. _____
_____
—. _____
_____

LONG-TERM GOALS

1. Accept the loss and return to stable level of functioning.
2. Express unresolved emotions regarding losses.
3. Display an understanding of the grief process and how this process may be exacerbated by or may exacerbate mental illness symptoms.
4. Develop an understanding of how avoidance of the grief process may affect functioning in many areas.
5. Develop alternative diversions and other coping mechanisms that are related to loss issues.
6. Resolve spiritual conflict.
7. Redevelop a supportive social system.

—. _____
   _____
   _____
—. _____
   _____
   _____
—. _____
   _____

SHORT-TERM OBJECTIVES	THERAPEUTIC INTERVENTIONS
1. Describe the loss of significant others. (1)	1. Provide the client with direct emotional support through active and empathic listening regarding grief issues.
2. Acknowledge any suicidal thoughts. (2, 3)	2. Assess the client for suicidal intent (see the Suicide chapter in this *Planner*).
	3. Refer the suicidal client to a psychiatric hospital or crisis residential placement to provide him/her 24-hour-per-day monitoring and safety.
3. Identify losses due to relationship difficulties. (4, 5)	4. Request that the client prepare a list of important relationships that have been lost; process factors contributing to the loss.
	5. Assist the client in resolving relationship problems (see the Social Skills Deficits chapter in this *Planner*).

4. Identify losses of occupational and other functional abilities. (6, 7)

6. Request that the client prepare a list of job losses and other related losses due to mental illness symptoms.

7. Assist the client in resolving occupational problems (see the Employment Problems chapter in this *Planner*).

5. Express feelings regarding the experience of the loss. (8)

8. Provide the client with an opportunity to vent emotions that are related to losses, symptoms, or setbacks.

6. Take psychotropic medications as prescribed. (9, 10, 11, 12)

9. Refer the client to a physician for a psychiatric evaluation to assess the need for antidepressant or other psychotropic medication.

10. Educate the client about the dosage, expected benefits, and possible side effects of medications.

11. Monitor the client's compliance with prescription medication, its side effects, and its effectiveness.

12. Urge and reinforce a strict compliance with the medication prescription, assessing for refusal or abuse of medication.

7. Verbalize an understanding of the basic grief process. (13, 14)

13. Assign readings to assist the client in understanding typical grief patterns (e.g., *The Grief Recovery Handbook: The Action Program for Moving Beyond Death* by James and Friedman; or *Getting to the Other Side of Grief* by Zonnebelt-Smeenge and De Vries).

14. Teach the client regarding the grief process and help him/her to understand the stage of the grief process which he/she is currently experiencing.

8. Express an understanding of mental illness symptoms that are related to own diagnosis. (15, 16, 17)

15. Educate the client about the mental illness symptoms that are related to his/her diagnosis.

9. Identify defense mechanisms (e.g., denial, minimalization, or rationalization) that are related to the avoidance of grief. (18, 19)

10. Identify how mental illness symptoms have contributed to a feeing of loss and grief. (20, 21)

11. Identify and express basic emotions. (22, 23, 24)

12. Journal emotions that are related to the losses. (25)

16. Review the client's mental illness symptoms, focusing on the impact that these have had on his/her losses.

17. Refer the client to a support group for individuals with mental illness problems.

18. Educate the client about the use of defense mechanisms and provide specific examples (e.g., some individuals deny problems rather than face the reality of a chronic mental illness).

19. Assist the client in identifying ways in which he/she uses defense mechanisms to delay or avoid grief and loss issues.

20. Assign and process readings from material describing the losses associated with severe mental illness (e.g., *Grieving Mental Illness: A Guide for Patients and Their Caregivers* by Lafond).

21. Request that the client develop a list of ways in which the mental illness symptoms have affected him/her; process with the client.

22. Review a list of basic emotions and discuss the social, verbal, and body language cues that help to identify them.

23. Ask the client to list ways in which he/she identifies and labels specific emotions that are experienced.

24. Help the client learn to identify emotions by probing for clarification of his/her unidentified emotional states.

25. Request that the client write in a journal or record on an audiotape the feelings of grief that he/she experienced with relation to the

losses, and then share these with a
clinician; process the client's
identified grief issues.

13. Verbalize acceptance of losses
without being overwhelmed with
grief, anger, or fear. (26, 27)

26. Request that the client write in a
journal or record on an audiotape
his/her feelings of acceptance of
the losses and share these with a
clinician.

27. Assign and process readings from
material to help the client overcome resentment (e.g., *Forgive
and Forget: Healing the Hurts
We Don't Deserve* by Smedes).

14. Implement rituals that begin to
bring a feeling of closure to the
emotions that are related to the
losses. (28, 29, 30)

28. Encourage and coordinate the
client's utilization of typical
mourning events (e.g., visit the
gravesite of a deceased relative,
write a goodbye letter to someone who is deceased).

29. Assist the client in developing
and safely carrying out meaningful rituals for letting go of a loss
(e.g., tying a journal entry, letter,
or picture to a helium balloon
and letting it go).

30. Assist the client in developing
meaningful activities that assist in
resolving grief issues (e.g., volunteer to help in a support group that
focuses on his/her loss issue).

15. Generate alternative diversions to
losses. (31)

31. Encourage and coordinate the
client's increased involvement in
social activities, hobbies, or volunteer placements.

16. Express spiritual concerns that
are related to losses. (32, 33)

32. Explore the client's spiritual
struggles and, if necessary, refer
him/her to an appropriate clergy-
person to allow for further discussion of these issues.

33. Suggest that the client read grief
material that is suitable to his/her
faith (e.g., *How Can It Be All*

Right When Everything Is All Wrong? by Smedes; or *When Bad Things Happen to Good People* by Kushner).

17. Accept support from loved ones or others who are experiencing similar problems. (34, 35)

34. Coordinate a family therapy session that is focused on the client's history of losses to enhance family members' understanding and support of the client.

35. Facilitate contact and support from nonfamily members or others dealing with similar loss issues.

—. _____

_____

—. _____

_____

—. _____

_____

—. _____

_____

—. _____

_____

—. _____

_____

DIAGNOSTIC SUGGESTIONS

Axis I:	297.1	Delusional Disorder
	295.xx	Schizophrenia
	295.10	Schizophrenia, Disorganized Type
	295.30	Schizophrenia, Paranoid Type
	295.70	Schizoaffective Disorder
	296.xx	Bipolar I Disorder
	296.89	Bipolar II Disorder
	296.3x	Major Depressive Disorder, Recurrent
	309.xx	Adjustment Disorder, Chronic
	V62.82	Bereavement
	V62.89	Phase of Life Problem

_____ _____

_____ _____

HEALTH ISSUES

BEHAVIORAL DEFINITIONS

1. Has been diagnosed with a serious medical condition that needs attention and that has an impact on daily living (e.g., high blood pressure, asthma, seizures, diabetes, heart disease, cancer, or cirrhosis).
2. Is under a physician's care for a medical condition.
3. Has had a positive test for human immunodeficiency virus (HIV) or acquired immune deficiency syndrome (AIDS).
4. Has a limited understanding of medical needs, treatment options, and available medical services.
5. Experiences difficulty gaining access to medical facilities or health care providers.
6. Fails to access medical treatment due to psychotic or other severe and persistent mental illness symptoms.
7. Has poor health habits including poor oral hygiene, infrequent bathing, or unsanitary living conditions.
8. Fails to access or follow through with medical treatment due to financial limitations.
9. Experiences medical complications secondary to substance abuse.

—. _____

_____

—. _____

_____

—. _____

_____

LONG-TERM GOALS

1. Stabilize medical condition.
2. Accept the reality of current medical problems and take responsibility for physical health and well-being.
3. Develop and implement an active, comprehensive plan for treatment of medical problem(s).
4. Establish a trusting relationship with a physician who is knowledgeable about working with mentally ill patients.
5. Maintain good personal hygiene.

—. _____
_____
_____
—. _____
_____
—. _____
_____

SHORT-TERM OBJECTIVES

THERAPEUTIC INTERVENTIONS

1. Determine current medical problems. (1)

1. Arrange for an immediate physical examination to determine physical health needs and any necessary medical testing.

2. Stabilize the crisis with medical problems. (2, 3)

2. Consult with the client's physician about his/her needed medical treatment.

3. Educate the client about his/her current medical problems and the treatment options; assist him/her in making decisions about and arrangements for his/her current medical treatment needs.

3. Verbalize an acceptance of the reality of the current medical difficulties. (4)

4. Assist the client in acknowledging an emotional desire to deny or avoid the truth about his/her medical difficulties; reinforce the client's acceptance of the reality of his/her medical problems.

4. Family, friends, and support network learn about medical problems and needs. (5)

5. After obtaining a proper release of information, provide family, friends, and others with information regarding the client's medical needs, encourage them to provide emotional support and positive reinforcement for the client's adherence to medical treatment.

5. Implement a stable, healthy, and appealing diet. (6, 7, 8, 9)

6. Educate the client about healthy food choices and the effect of diet on long-term medical well-being.

7. Assist the client with access to a grocery store, focusing on increasing his/her comfort level.

8. Educate the client about food shopping choices and how to compare healthy foods with unhealthy.

9. Refer the client to a dietician for an assessment of dietary needs, strengths, and weaknesses.

6. Terminate the abuse of mood-altering substances. (10, 11)

10. Assess or refer the client to a substance abuse evaluator to determine the presence of a co-occurring substance abuse problem; refer the client for substance abuse treatment, if appropriate (see the Chemical Dependence chapter in this *Planner*).

11. Educate the client about the short- and long-term effects of substance abuse, especially as these effects relate to his/her severe and persistent mental illness symptoms.

7. Implement good personal hygiene behaviors. (12, 13, 14)

12. Assess the client's personal hygiene needs; encourage him/her to discuss his/her views of his/her own needs (see the Independent Activities of Daily Living [IADL] chapter in this *Planner*).

13. Refer the client to a training group for basic hygiene needs.

14. Institute a checklist and rein-forcement system for the client regarding hygiene needs.

8. Follow an exercise plan. (15, 16, 17)

15. Teach the client about the regular use of exercise and the health benefits that are related to exercise.

16. Refer the client to an activity thera-pist to assist in the development of an enjoyable, practical exercise program.

17. Refer the client to an agency- or community-sponsored exercise group, or coordinate a free or reduced-cost membership to a local health club.

9. Maintain personal health through regular checkups. (18, 19, 20, 21)

18. Coordinate a referral to a general physician for routine and ongo-ing medical evaluation and care.

19. Schedule an intermittent, planned psychiatric hospitalization to complete all needed medical services in a structured, safe, familiar setting.

20. Facilitate transportation to medi-cal, dental, and other health care appointments. If needed, monitor the client's attendance to these ap-pointments by brokering ap-pointments with a doctor's office (i.e., request that the scheduling receptionist contact the clinician regarding appointment changes so the clinician can guarantee the cli-ent's attendance).

21. Obtain a release of information to share the client's health informa-tion with other health care pro-viders; educate the providers about the client's needs relative to mental illness symptoms.

10. Maintain good oral hygiene. (22, 23)

22. Coordinate semiannual dental checkups and cleanings.

23. Train and encourage regular brushing and flossing; reinforce with positive feedback.

11. Preserve or remediate hearing and vision capabilities. (24)

24. Coordinate hearing and vision evaluations; facilitate the client in following up on recommendations.

12. Obtain the needed resources for payment for ongoing health care. (25, 26)

25. Assist the client in filing for and maintaining public assistance, benefits, and insurance.

26. Refer the client to an agency list of health care providers who accept public insurance or provide services at a reduced cost or at no cost.

13. Decrease medical difficulties related to transience or homelessness by maintaining a stable residence. (27, 28, 29)

27. Assist the client in developing or maintaining his/her stable residence (see the Homelessness chapter in this *Planner*).

28. Refer the client to a personal safety class (e.g., self-defense, precautions for safety).

29. Deliver health care services to the client where he/she is accessible (i.e., in a homeless shelter or on the street through mobile health vans).

14. Take psychotropic medications as prescribed. (30, 31)

30. Arrange for a psychiatric evaluation with a physician who is informed and knowledgeable about the client's medical condition; advocate with a psychiatric evaluator to also provide a physical examination.

31. Educate the client about the use, expected benefits, and possible side effects of his/her psychotropic medications; monitor the client's medication compliance, effectiveness and side effects, identifying a possible confounding influence of polypharmacy or permanent side effects of neuroleptic medications (e.g., tardive dyskinesia, muscle rigidity, dystonia).

15. Decrease the likelihood of HIV infection or other sexually transmitted diseases (STDs) by implementing safer sex practices. (32, 33, 34, 35)

32. Provide education to the client regarding precautions to take to avoid HIV infection and other STDs. Tailor this education to gender, sexual orientation, and specific mental illness groups to help shape his/her perspective of HIV risk.

33. Refer the client to a source for or provide him/her with condoms and clean-needle exchange programs.

34. Involve the client in peer education models to help him/her learn or educate others about HIV and other STD concerns; role-play assertiveness regarding implementing safer sex practices and other defenses for personal safety.

35. Include the client's partner in outreach efforts regarding HIV and STD education.

16. Caretakers verbalize the degree of emotional strain that is related to providing care to the client with a comorbid health concern. (5, 36)

5. After obtaining a proper release of information, provide family, friends, and others with information regarding the client's medical needs; encourage them to provide emotional support and positive reinforcement for the client's adherence to medical treatment.

36. Observe the family and the caregivers for frustrations that may reduce their ability to interact effectively with the client; provide them with opportunities for venting their feelings.

17. Caretakers report reduced stress that is related to providing care to the client with a comorbid health concern. (37, 38, 39)

37. Refer the caregivers to a support group for those who are affected by another's mental illness.

38. Teach the caregivers stress reduction techniques, such as muscle relaxation, abdominal breathing, and safe-place imagery.

39. Refer the client to a respite program to provide a brief rest
from the demands of caring for
a mentally ill patient.

__. _____   __. _____
   _____   _____
__. _____   __. _____
   _____   _____
__. _____   __. _____
   _____   _____

DIAGNOSTIC SUGGESTIONS

Axis I:		
	297.1	Delusional Disorder
	295.xx	Schizophrenia
	295.10	Schizophrenia, Disorganized Type
	295.30	Schizophrenia, Paranoid Type
	295.70	Schizoaffective Disorder
	296.xx	Bipolar I Disorder
	296.89	Bipolar II Disorder
	293.0	Delirium Due to . . . *[General Medical Condition]*
	294.1x	Dementia Due to . . . *[General Medical Condition]*
	294.0	Amnestic Disorder Due to . . . *[General Medical Condition]*
	333.xx	Neuroleptic-Related Syndromes
	316	Psychological Factors Affecting Medical Condition

_____   _____

_____   _____

HOMELESSNESS

BEHAVIORAL DEFINITIONS

1. Has a history of living on the streets on a sporadic or long-term basis.
2. Does not maintain a permanent address for long periods of time.
3. Extensively utilizes shelters for the homeless, transitional housing, or other supported living placements.
4. Fails to make rent, mortgage, or utility payments, leading to a loss of residence.
5. Displays unusual behavior due to psychotic or other severe mental illness symptoms, resulting in eviction from residence.
6. Lacks knowledge regarding the basic skills that are needed to maintain a residence (e.g., cleaning, small repairs, budgeting).

—. _____
   _____
—. _____
   _____
—. _____
   _____

LONG-TERM GOALS

1. Move from living on the street through a continuum of supported residential opportunities to a more stable independent residence.
2. Maintain a personal residence for an extended period of time.
3. Decrease dependence on transitional living programs or shelters for the homeless.
4. Accept and manage financial responsibilities as evidenced by paying bills on time.

5. Decrease unusual behavior through stable medication use and supported by an increased level of motivation to stay healthy.
6. Understand basic residential skills, including budgeting, housecleaning, and social skills.

—. _____
_____
—. _____
_____
—. _____
_____

SHORT-TERM OBJECTIVES

THERAPEUTIC INTERVENTIONS

1. Stabilize the current homelessness crisis. (1, 2, 3)

1. Refer the client to a local shelter for the homeless.
2. Coordinate funds for the client's crisis residential placement (i.e., motel voucher or transitional program placement).
3. Facilitate the client's placement at the home of a family member, friend, or peer.

2. Describe the history of the homelessness. (4)

4. Request that the client describe his/her history of successful and problematic residential situations; utilize a time line of residences, periods of homelessness, and use of transitional housing; process the factors contributing to his/her lifestyle.

3. Verbalize feelings regarding homelessness and the attempts to obtain and maintain residence. (5, 6, 7, 8)

5. Assist the client in identifying feelings associated with the homeless situation; provide the client with support and understanding regarding emotional concerns, acknowledging the natural emotions of frustration, discouragement, and embarrassment.

6. Explore possible fears associated with seeking a permanent residence, including fear of rejection, embarrassment, or failure.

7. Provide the client with realistic feedback regarding his/her paranoia or other irrational delusions.

8. Encourage the client to maintain important relationships at the homeless shelter when he/she moves to a more independent status.

4. Identify and resolve the barriers to maintaining long-term housing. (9, 10, 11)

9. Assist the client in identifying and resolving specific barriers to maintaining housing (e.g., finances, fears, lack of understanding of available alternatives, etc.).

10. Educate the client about the available options regarding the continuum of supports and services that are available, and help the client to develop a list of pros and cons for each of the housing options; give structure for making his/her own decision regarding housing.

11. Assist the client in negotiating the application process for desired housing programs.

5. Consistently use psychotropic medication to stabilize the psychotic and other severe mental illness symptoms that interfere with maintaining a personal residence. (12, 13, 14)

12. Arrange for a psychiatric evaluation and for a prescription for psychotropic medication, if necessary.

13. Educate the client about the use, possible side effects, and expected benefits of medication; monitor the client's medication compliance.

14. Monitor side effects of the medication with the client and inform the medical staff.

6. Establish a mode of access to necessary medications despite the lack of a permanent residence or storage capacity. (15, 16, 17)

15. Store medications for the client in a safe, easily accessible facility.

16. Provide the homeless client with smaller immediate supplies of medication.

17. Rent a secure storage space (e.g., locker or mailbox) in which the client may store necessary medications.

7. Cooperate with behavioral, cognitive, and medical evaluations to assess readiness for independent living. (18, 19, 20)

18. Assess the client for safety to himself/herself and to others.

19. Administer or refer the client for assessment of intellectual abilities as related to basic skills to maintain a home.

20. Arrange for a full medical evaluation to determine the client's physical care needs.

8. Obtain funding for residence. (21, 22)

21. Assist the client with obtaining general entitlements, as well as specific subsidies that are available for assisting mentally ill individuals with housing.

22. Encourage and assist the client with obtaining regular employment to increase income that will defray housing costs (see the Employment Problems chapter in this *Planner*).

9. Implement a budget and banking routine to facilitate the regular payment of rent or mortgage. (23, 24, 25)

23. Assist the client in developing a budget for the payment of rent or mortgage (see the Financial Needs chapter in this *Planner*).

24. Assist the client in obtaining a low-interest, no-fee bank account with a participating bank.

25. Arrange for the client's access to emergency funds for payment of rent, mortgage, or utilities to prevent eviction.

10. Move from a more restrictive to a less restrictive housing setting. (26, 27, 28)

26. Contact a discharge-planning coordinator of a state inpatient or a community psychiatric setting as early as possible in the client's

treatment to coordinate discharge planning regarding housing.

27. Meet regularly with the incarcerated client to develop housing plans for after release.

28. Coordinate ample visitation to a new, less restrictive setting for the client to become acquainted with the setting; be readily available to the client for questions and reassurance.

11. Terminate substance abuse, which interferes with the ability to maintain housing. (29, 30, 31)

29. Refer to AA, NA, or other substance abuse treatment options (see the Chemical Dependence chapter in this *Planner*).

30. Refer the client to a drug-free housing program.

31. Arrange for a referral to a coordinated mental health and substance abuse services (i.e., co-occurring capable) within a residential program or setting.

12. Obtain support from family and peers to maintain housing. (32, 33, 34)

32. Encourage family members and friends to support and teach the client and to monitor his/her progress regarding basic living needs, medication administration, and financial management.

33. Refer the client to a support group for individuals with chronic mental illness.

34. Match the client with a mentor who has already successfully moved from homelessness to a stable living environment.

13. Demonstrate basic skills for running and maintaining a home or apartment. (23, 35, 36, 37)

23. Assist the client in developing a budget for the payment of rent or mortgage (see the Financial Needs chapter in this *Planner*).

35. Teach the client basic housekeeping skills (e.g., see *Mary Ellen's Complete Home Reference Book*

by Pinkham and Burg, *The Cleaning Encyclopedia: Your A to Z Illustrated Guide to Cleaning Like the Pros* by Aslett, or the Activities of Daily Living [ADL] chapter in this *Planner*).

36. Refer the client to a structured program (within a continuum) to obtain hands-on training in basic skills for transitioning to more independent care (see the Independent Activities of Daily Living [IADL] chapter in this *Planner*).

37. Obtain visiting homemaker assistance for the client who is not capable of doing such housekeeping activities.

14. Develop plans to manage crises that could lead to destabilization and threaten residential status. (38, 39)

38. Meet regularly with the housing manager to train about mental illness issues and the client's rights, to mitigate the client's problematic behaviors, and to assist in rent reviews and dwelling inspections; remind the housing manager about how to contact agency staff should emergencies arise.

39. Provide the client with an emergency health information card, including individualized information about who to call when in a crisis situation, including the case manager and physicians.

15. Reestablish residential housing quickly after recovering from decompensation. (26, 40)

26. Contact a discharge-planning coordinator of a state inpatient or a community psychiatric setting as early as possible in the client's treatment to coordinate discharge planning regarding housing.

40. Coordinate funds to maintain a client's residence when he/she is hospitalized or otherwise briefly loses eligibility for SSI benefits.

16. Verbalize an understanding of legal rights that are related to housing for the mentally disabled. (41, 42, 43)

41. Train the client about his/her rights, as related to the Americans with Disabilities Act (ADA), including reasonable accommodations that must be made for him/her.

42. Educate the client about a tenant's rights (e.g., see *Renter's Rights* by Portman and Stewart).

43. Coordinate contact with legal assistance programs if the client's rights continue to be violated.

___. _____   ___. _____
     _____   _____
___. _____   ___. _____
     _____   _____
___. _____   ___. _____
     _____   _____

DIAGNOSTIC SUGGESTIONS

Axis I:	297.1	Delusional Disorder
	295.xx	Schizophrenia
	295.10	Schizophrenia, Disorganized Type
	295.30	Schizophrenia, Paranoid Type
	295.90	Schizophrenia, Undifferentiated Type
	295.60	Schizophrenia, Residual Type
	295.70	Schizoaffective Disorder
	296.xx	Bipolar I Disorder
	296.89	Bipolar II Disorder
	V62.89	Phase of Life Problem
	_____	_____
	_____	_____

INDEPENDENT ACTIVITIES OF DAILY LIVING (IADL)

BEHAVIORAL DEFINITIONS

1. Lacks access to, experience with, or functioning relative to independent activities of daily living (IADLs; e.g., transportation, banking, shopping, use of community services, or other skills that are necessary for living more independently).
2. Reports anxiety regarding increasing IADLs.
3. Lacks knowledge of community resources.
4. Fails to respond appropriately in emergency situations.
5. Paranoia, psychosis, or other severe and persistent mental illness symptoms affects ability to use community resources independently.
6. Lacks familiarity with resources such as banking, stores, and other services.
7. Lacks attention to and organization of personal responsibilities, resulting in unpaid bills and unkept appointments.
8. Fails to access community resources such as worship centers, libraries, recreational areas, or businesses.
9. Experiences external restrictions placed on access to community resources due to bizarre behaviors.
10. Has a history of others taking responsibility for performing IADLs for him/her.

—. _____

_____

—. _____

_____

—. _____

_____

LONG-TERM GOALS

1. Increased knowledge and consistent use of community resources.
2. Timely, appropriate, and safe responses to emergency situations.
3. Positive relationships with community resource providers.
4. Management of severe and persistent mental illness symptoms so as not to disturb others in the community.
5. Increased organization of and attention to daily routines, resulting in personal responsibilities being fulfilled.
6. Takes responsibility for IADLs to level of own potential and develops resources for help from others.

—. _____
   _____
—. _____
   _____
—. _____
   _____

SHORT-TERM OBJECTIVES	THERAPEUTIC INTERVENTIONS
1. Describe current functioning in performing IADLs. (1)	1. Assist the client in preparing an inventory of his/her positive and negative experiences with attempting to perform IADLs.
2. Identify the barriers to increasing IADLs. (2, 3)	2. Examine the problematic IADL areas with the client to identify any patterns of behavior or cognitions that cause the failure at independent functioning.
	3. Acquire the proper permission to release information, and obtain feedback from family members, friends, and caregivers about the client's performance of IADLs.
3. Prioritize IADL areas upon which to focus effort and improve functioning. (4)	4. Ask the client to identify, describe, and prioritize those IADLs that are desired but not present in the current repertoire.

4. Identify any cognitive barriers to IADL success. (5)

5. Participate in a remediation program to teach IADL skills. (6)

6. Increase the frequency and appropriateness of social interaction. (7, 8)

7. Develop and implement a regular schedule for performance of routine IADLs. (9)

8. Acknowledge IADL deficits as a symptom of mental illness being inadequately controlled or treated. (10, 11)

5. Refer the client for an assessment of cognitive abilities and deficits.

6. Recommend remediating programs to the client, such as skill-building groups, token economies, or behavior-shaping programs that are focused on removing deficits to IADL performance.

7. Explore the client's anxiety regarding social contacts and increasing independence.

8. Assist the client in learning the skills that are necessary for appropriate social behavior (see the Social Skills Deficits chapter in this *Planner*); providing positive feedback and encouragement for his/her attempts to increase social interaction.

9. Aid the client in developing a specific schedule for completing IADLs (e.g., arrange finances on Monday morning, go to the grocery store on Tuesday); remind the client about situations in which he/she should break from his/her established routine (e.g., do the banking on a different day due to a holiday, or do the weekly cleaning one day earlier to attend a desired social function).

10. Educate the client about the expected or common symptoms of his/her mental illness (e.g., manic excitement behaviors or negative symptoms of schizophrenia), which may negatively impact basic IADL functioning.

11. Reflect or interpret poor performance in IADLs as an indicator of psychiatric decompensation; share these observations with the client, the caregivers, and the medical staff.

9. Stabilize, through the use of psychotropic medications, psychotic and other severe and persistent mental illness symptoms that interfere with IADLs. (12, 13, 14)

12. Arrange for an evaluation of the client by a physician for a prescription for psychotropic medication.

13. Educate the client about the proper use, expected benefits, and possible side effects of psychotropic medication.

14. Monitor the client for compliance, effectiveness, and possible side effects with psychotropic medication that is prescribed; report any significant developments to the medical staff.

10. Obtain and take prescribed medications on a regular basis. (13, 14, 15, 16, 17)

13. Educate the client about the proper use, expected benefits, and possible side effects of psychotropic medication.

14. Monitor the client for compliance, effectiveness and possible side effects with psychotropic medication that is prescribed; report any significant developments to the medical staff.

15. Review and model procedures for the procurement of medications.

16. Develop an agreement with the client regarding the level of responsibility and independence that he/she must display to trigger a decrease in the clinician's monitoring of medications.

17. Coordinate an agreement between the client, the pharmacist, and the clinician regarding circumstances that would trigger the transfer of medication monitoring back to the clinician (e.g., client's failure to pick up monthly prescription, client trying to refill a prescription too soon).

11. Obtain the necessary transportation to work, medical appoint-

18. Brainstorm possible transportation resources with the client

ments, leisure opportunities, or other desired destinations. (18)

(e.g., public transportation, personal vehicle, agency resources, friends and family, walking, bicycling); encourage and reinforce the client's independent use of these transportation resources.

12. Use public transportation in a safe, socially appropriate, efficient manner. (19, 20, 21)

19. Familiarize the client with available public transportation options through discussion, written schedules, and accompanied use of community services; emphasize typical expectations for using public transportation, including payment, time schedule, and social norms for behavior.

20. Predict possible influences that the client's severe and persistent mental illness symptoms may have on his/her ability to use community services; help the client brainstorm techniques to decrease these symptom effects (e.g., medication compliance, relaxation techniques, escape/avoidance plans, graduated steps to independence).

21. Ride with the client to various destinations on public transportation until he/she is adequately comfortable with doing so alone.

13. Identify, attain, and manage adequate sources of financial income. (22)

22. Assist the client in identifying and attaining adequate sources of income; develop a budget with the client that is based on resources and needs (see the Employment Problems and Financial Needs chapters in this *Planner*).

14. Use banking resources to facilitate financial independence. (20, 23, 24, 25, 26)

20. Predict possible influences that the client's severe and persistent mental illness symptoms may have on his/her ability to use community services; help the client brainstorm techniques to decrease these symptom effects (e.g., medication

compliance, relaxation techniques, escape/avoidance plans, graduated steps to independence).

23. Review the procedures for and the advantages of using the banking system to assist the client with IADLs, including increased security, financial organization, and convenience for paying bills; caution the client about the hazards that are related to banking (e.g., credit debt, overdrawn checking account charges).

24. Coordinate a helping relationship between specific bank staff and the client; with a proper permission to release information, provide information to the bank staff about the client's needs and disabilities.

25. Encourage the client to use a specific staff at a specific bank branch to develop a more personal and understanding relationship.

26. Coordinate an agreement between the client, a specified bank staff, and a clinician regarding the circumstances under which the clinician should be notified (e.g., manic client attempts to withdraw his/her entire savings account).

15. Utilize the services of a choice of retail stores in the community. (27, 28, 29)

27. Familiarize the client with retail store resources that are available in his/her area through a review of newspaper advertisements and a tour of the business districts in the community.

28. Role-play situations that commonly occur while shopping at a store (e.g., asking for assistance, declining a pushy salesperson, returning a defective item); provide the client with

feedback about his/her functioning in these situations.

29. Go with the client to retail businesses at which he/she is uncomfortable or uncertain, gradually decreasing support.

16. Assert self to protect own rights against discriminatory barriers to community resources. (30, 31)

30. Support the client in his/her assertive response to instances of discrimination due to mental illness symptoms; advocate for or with the client, as needed.

31. Link the client to advocacy and support groups that will assist in developing open access for the client to community businesses and services.

17. Identify and process (negative) emotional responses to emergency service professionals. (32)

32. Explore the client's prior contact with emergency response professionals; review any situations in which emergency response staff were required to coerce the client (e.g., a prior involuntary hospitalization), as well as when the client may have manipulated emergency response staff (e.g., threatened harm to himself/herself for some secondary gain such as obtaining food or a place to sleep).

18. Use emergency service professionals effectively. (33, 34, 35)

33. Develop a list of specific emergency response professionals who respond effectively to mentally ill individuals (e.g., a police unit mental health liaison or a specific nurse/orderly at the emergency room); direct the client to seek out that professional when he/she contacts that agency or facility. Maintain regular contact with the identified professionals.

34. Provide 24-hour crisis consultation to all emergency response

professionals to assist in responding to the client's use of emergency systems.

35. Teach the client the appropriate use of specific emergency service professionals, including their responsibilities and limitations; brainstorm alternative resources that are available to the client for use instead of "nuisance" calls to emergency response staff (e.g., contact a crisis line for psychotic symptom development, contact a support group member when lonely instead of going to the emergency room, contact family first if feeling ill).

19. Resolve problems with specific community businesses or service providers who have issued restrictions on access due to past inappropriate behavior. (30, 36)

30. Support the client in his/her assertive response to instances of discrimination due to mental illness symptoms; advocate for or with the client, as needed.

36. Discuss the need for making amends to businesses or service providers who have been affected by the client's past inappropriate behavior; brainstorm with the client about the form of restitution (an apology, a service provided, or financial reimbursement).

20. Request assistance from others when attempting to implement IADLs. (37, 38)

37. Ask the client to identify a list of personal resources that he/she can use for assistance in carrying out IADLs (e.g., family and friends, support group members, neighbors).

38. Role-play how to approach strangers for basic assistance (e.g., asking for directions), providing feedback to the client about his/her approach, personal hygiene or dress, and how appearance and manner affect the

21. Agree to implement a specific plan to use when decompensating or when in crisis, relative to IADLs. (39)

22. Increase involvement in recreational activities. (40, 41, 42, 43)

23. Participate in spiritual activities. (44, 45)

stranger's comfort level (see the Activities of Daily Living [ADL] and Social Skills Deficits chapters in this *Planner*).

39. Assist the client in developing a written plan with telephone numbers of resources and clinical assistance for use when he/she is at risk of decompensation.

40. Refer the client to an activity therapist for an assessment of recreational needs, skills, and opportunities.

41. Assist the client in identifying a variety of recreational activities in which he/she might be interested; provide the client with information that is related to the accessibility of these activities.

42. Shadow the client to provide support while he/she attends chosen activities, allowing him/her to determine how closely the clinician is involved to decrease stigma and to increase independent functioning.

43. Coordinate a mentor program so the client can have an identified individual who assists him/her in becoming comfortable with the recreational/social setting.

44. Explore the client's interest in involvement in spiritual activities, acknowledging the potential for his/her confusion regarding spiritual messages and imagery; assist in differentiating between spiritual concerns and symptoms of mental illness.

45. Coordinate the client's attendance at his/her preferred place of worship.

—. _____   —. _____
   _____   _____
—. _____   —. _____
   _____   _____
—. _____   —. _____
   _____   _____

DIAGNOSTIC SUGGESTIONS

Axis I:	297.1	Delusional Disorder
	295.xx	Schizophrenia
	295.10	Schizophrenia, Disorganized Type
	295.30	Schizophrenia, Paranoid Type
	295.90	Schizophrenia, Undifferentiated Type
	295.60	Schizophrenia, Residual Type
	295.70	Schizoaffective Disorder
	296.xx	Bipolar I Disorder
	296.89	Bipolar II Disorder

_____   _____

_____   _____

INTIMATE RELATIONSHIP CONFLICTS

BEHAVIORAL DEFINITIONS

1. Displays indifference to the emotional needs of the partner.
2. Distrusts partner due to paranoia or other severe and persistent mental illness symptoms.
3. Increased levels of stress in the relationship due to the effects of erratic behavior (e.g., legal problems, impulsive spending, inability to work).
4. Has experienced a pattern of repeated separations and/or divorce or discontinuation of relationships due to personal deficiencies in problem solving, social skills, or assertion.
5. Has a history of impulsive sexual involvement outside of the committed relationship.
6. Increased spousal discontent with the changes in the relationship due to the severe and persistent mental illness symptoms.
7. Has a history of violent or abusive interactions with partners.

—. _____

_____

—. _____

_____

—. _____

_____

LONG-TERM GOALS

1. Decrease the severe and persistent mental illness symptoms that affect the relationship.
2. Develop a more trusting relationship with partner.
3. Develop techniques for reducing stress in the relationship.

4. Preserve fidelity within the relationship by discontinuing impulsive sexual acting out.
5. Process changes in the relationship that have occurred as a result of the chronic mental illness.
6. Resolve problems without verbal or physical abuse.

—. _____

_____

—. _____

_____

—. _____

_____

SHORT-TERM OBJECTIVES	THERAPEUTIC INTERVENTIONS
1. Describe the history of intimate relationship concerns. (1, 2, 3)	1. Explore the client's history of intimate relationships, including positive and negative outcomes.
	2. Use a graphic display, such as a time line, to display the client's history of intimate relationship concerns; help him/her identify additional key portions of the time line, such as the onset of symptoms or treatment.
	3. Obtain feedback from the client's partner and the extended family about the client's history of relationship successes and problems.
2. Identify the status of the current relationship. (3, 4, 5)	3. Obtain feedback from the client's partner and the extended family about the client's history of relationship successes and problems.
	4. Request that the client identify successes and challenges in his/her current relationship.
	5. Coordinate the administration of marital satisfaction surveys (e.g., *The Marital Satisfaction Inventory*

by Snyder or *The Marital Status Inventory* by Weiss and Correto); provide feedback of the survey results.

3. Partner and client acknowledge how the severe and persistent mental illness symptoms affect the relationship. (6, 7)

6. Educate the client and his/her partner about the common symptoms of the client's mental illness; recommend books for further information (e.g., *Schizophrenia: The Facts* by Tsuang and Faraone; or *Bipolar Disorder: A Guide for Patients and Families* by Mondimore). Emphasize the fact that neither the family nor the partner are the cause of the client's mental illness.

7. Request that the client (and partner) identify at least two ways in which the relationship has been affected by the severe and persistent mental illness symptoms.

4. Cooperate with a referral to a physician for a psychotropic medication evaluation. (8)

8. Arrange for an evaluation by a physician for a prescription for psychotropic medication.

5. Report a decrease in mental illness symptoms that affect the relationship through the regular use of psychiatric medications. (9, 10)

9. Educate the client (and his/her significant other) about the use, expected benefits, and possible side effects of the medication.

10. Monitor the client's medication compliance, effectiveness, and side effects, including feedback from the partner; report any significant developments to the medical staff.

6. Enlist and cooperate with partner support in monitoring the medication prescription compliance. (9, 11)

9. Educate the client (and his/her significant other) about the use, expected benefits, and possible side effects of the medication.

11. Coordinate an agreement with the client and his/her partner about the responsibility for administration and monitoring of the medication, including specific plans for the

7. Partner to verbalize an understanding of techniques for coping with severe and persistent
mental illness symptoms in a
loved one. (6, 12, 13)

8. Partner to share his/her feelings
related to the client's mental illness symptoms. (14, 15)

circumstances under which control
of the medication will be returned
to the client (e.g., extended period
of time in remission).

6. Educate the client and his/her
partner about the common symptoms of the client's mental illness;
recommend books for further information (e.g., *Schizophrenia:
The Facts* by Tsuang and Faraone; or *Bipolar Disorder: A
Guide for Patients and Families*
by Mondimore). Emphasize the
fact that neither the family nor
the partner are the cause of the
client's mental illness.

12. Assign the client's partner to read
books on coping with a loved one
who has a severe and persistent
mental illness (e.g., *When Someone You Love Has a Mental Illness*
by Woolis; *Surviving Schizophrenia: A Manual for Families, Consumers, and Providers* by Torrey;
or *Bipolar Puzzle Solution: A
Mental Health Client's Perspective*
by Court and Nelson).

13. Teach the client's partner specific
techniques through didactic opportunities, discussion, and role-
playing to help manage the client
when he/she is agitated, psychotic,
or manic (e.g., maintaining a calm
demeanor, providing basic directives, redirection; see the Psychosis
or Mania/Hypomania chapters in
this *Planner*).

14. Process the partner's emotional
reaction to the client's onset or
recurrence of severe and persistent mental illness.

15. Reassure the client's partner about
how accessible a clinician will be

9. Partner to list relationships, activities, and interests outside of those with the client that provide some diversion, respite, and balance to life. (16)

10. Partner to attend a support group for the family and friends of individuals with severe mental illness. (17)

11. Express feelings about the onset of severe mental illness symptoms. (18)

12. Implement newly acquired communication skills in the relationship. (19, 20)

13. Partner and the client to verbalize increased trust in the relationship. (21, 22, 23)

for consultation, questions, or support, including 24-hour crisis line when the clinician is not available.

16. Emphasize the need for the partner and all family members to have interests outside of the mental illness concerns that the client may present.

17. Refer the client's partner to a support group for the family and friends of the mentally ill.

18. Assist the client in expressing his/her feelings regarding experiencing severe and persistent mental illness symptoms and how these affect the relationship.

19. Facilitate conjoint sessions with the client's partner, focusing on increasing relational communication and learning problem-solving skills.

20. Teach the client and his/her partner specific skills for communication, such as expressing specific positive and negative emotions, making requests, communicating information clearly, giving "I messages," and implementing active listening.

21. Focus the client and his/her partner on identifying trust issues that are attributable to mental illness symptoms such as paranoia or mania; emphasize the nonvolitional aspects of these symptoms.

22. Explore each partner's fears regarding getting too close and feeling vulnerable to hurt, rejection, or abandonment.

23. Request that the client and his/her partner identify specific

areas in which they have experienced increased trust; focus on ways to generalize this trust into other areas.

14. Identify role changes in the relationship that are due to mental illness. (24, 25, 26)

24. Request that the client and his/her partner identify the changes that have occurred in the relationship due to the client's mental illness symptoms.

25. Challenge the couple to identify the ways in which power and control can be shared despite mental illness symptoms (e.g., develop advanced directives regarding treatment expectations, returning responsibilities to the mentally ill partner during periods of stabilization).

26. Legitimize the client's and partner's need to mourn the loss of functioning in the relationship, or the changes that have occurred due to the severe and persistent mental illness symptoms.

15. Terminate substance use or abuse. (27, 28)

27. Explore the role of substance abuse as a potentiating factor for the client's severe and persistent mental illness symptoms, as well as relationship problems.

28. Coordinate providing the client with integrated substance abuse and mental health treatment (see the Chemical Dependence chapter in this *Planner*).

16. Client and partner to identify the level of closeness/distance desired in the relationship, and how this may vary due to symptoms. (22, 29, 30)

22. Explore each partner's fears regarding getting too close and feeling vulnerable to hurt, rejection, or abandonment.

29. Facilitate a discussion of the factors that contribute to the desire for closeness or distance/safety; acknowledge the normal need for the client's partner to have a waiting

period after the client's symptoms have abated prior to resuming normal levels of trust, interaction, sexual activity, and so forth.

30. Emphasize to the client the concept of the sexual relationship being a mirror of the rest of the relationship, and the need for positive emotional interaction prior to sexual involvement.

17. Increase sexual functioning by eliminating physiological problems. (31)

31. Refer the client to a physician for a complete physical examination to rule out or to identify any physiological or medication-related barriers to sexual functioning; coordinate follow-up and provision of information to the treating psychiatrist.

18. Improve personal appearance related to sexual arousal. (32)

32. Focus the client on physical appearance and personal hygiene needs as a sexual arousal issue for his/her partner (see the Activities of Daily Living [ADL] chapter in this *Planner*).

19. Partner and the client gain increased understanding and insight into human sexuality. (33)

33. Direct the client and his/her intimate partner to read books on human sexual functioning (e.g., *The New Joy of Sex* by Comfort and Marcus; or *The Reader's Digest Guide to Love and Sex* by Roberts and Padgett-Yawn) and/or to watch sex educational videos (e.g., *Better Sex Videos* by the Sinclair Institute).

20. Acknowledge a history of sexual acting out and the negative effect it has had on the relationship with this partner. (34, 35)

34. Identify the history of (impulsive) sexual acting out and the effect it has had in the relationship; process the partner's emotions related to the client's history of infidelity.

35. Assist the manic or impulsive client in managing symptoms (see the Mania/Hypomania chapter in this *Planner*).

21. Verbalize an agreement on appropriate sexual, emotional, and social boundaries with others. (36)

22. Implement anger control techniques. (37)

23. Agree to a safety plan to prevent any future abuse of family members. (38)

24. Generate mutually agreeable strategies for parenting. (39, 40, 41)

25. Report a decrease in marital stress due to stabilizing financial concerns. (42, 43)

36. Assist the partners in developing a clear set of boundaries for sexual, emotional, and social contact with others.

37. Teach the client about anger control techniques, including a time-out signal to be used when either partner becomes fearful that abuse may occur to anyone in the family (see the Anger Management chapter in this *Planner*).

38. Develop safety plans, including when public safety officers should be contacted, or how to utilize domestic violence services.

39. Assist the couple in identifying how mental illness symptoms affect the children in the relationship (e.g., confusion, embarrassment, caretaking).

40. Educate the parents about effective child-rearing practices (e.g., see *1-2-3 Magic: Effective Discipline for Children 2–12*, 3rd ed. by Phelan).

41. Facilitate an agreement regarding acceptable parenting practices, which should include issues such as discipline and rewards, or when the partner should become involved (see the Parenting chapter in this *Planner*).

42. Assist the client in obtaining work (see the Employment Problems chapter in this *Planner*) or other sources of income, such as disability payments (see the Financial Needs chapter in this *Planner*).

43. Refer the client and his/her intimate partner for credit counseling or other budgeting assistance.

26. Process emotions regarding the end of a relationship. (44)

44. Encourage the client to express his/her emotions regarding the loss of a relationship; encourage reading such books as *How to Survive the Loss of a Love* by Colgrove, Bloomfield, and McWilliams.

27. Attend a divorce support group. (45)

45. Refer the client to a support group for individuals going through a divorce.

—. _____   —. _____
   _____   _____
—. _____   —. _____
   _____   _____
—. _____   —. _____
   _____   _____

DIAGNOSTIC SUGGESTIONS

Axis I:	297.1	Delusional Disorder
	295.xx	Schizophrenia
	295.10	Schizophrenia, Disorganized Type
	295.30	Schizophrenia, Paranoid Type
	295.90	Schizophrenia, Undifferentiated Type
	295.60	Schizophrenia, Residual Type
	295.70	Schizoaffective Disorder
	296.xx	Bipolar I Disorder
	296.89	Bipolar II Disorder
	V61.10	Partner Relational Problem
	V61.9	Relational Problem Related to a Mental Disorder
	V62.81	Relational Problem NOS

_____   _____

_____   _____

LEGAL CONCERNS

BEHAVIORAL DEFINITIONS

1. Demonstrates a pattern of illegal behavior, including theft, assault, disorderly conduct, or threats to others.
2. Has a history of arrests, convictions, and incarceration due to illegal behaviors.
3. Has current legal involvement, including pending charges, incarceration, or probation/parole oversight.
4. Has difficulty functioning in a corrections setting due to paranoia, mania, or other severe and persistent mental illness symptoms.
5. Is vulnerable to attack or manipulation by others while incarcerated due to mental illness.
6. Has a record of illegal behaviors related to substance use or abuse (e.g., drunk driving, drug possession).
7. Guardianship is dictated by the courts.
8. Clinicians, family members, or others are pursuing the court to name a legal guardian.
9. Presents with an imminent threat of harm to self or others due to mental illness symptoms, resulting in involuntary court-ordered hospitalization.
10. Has a need for legal representation due to arrests, involuntary hospitalization, guardianship procedures, or advocacy.
11. Basic personal rights have been lost due to a lack of advocacy.

__. _____

_____

__. _____

_____

__. _____

_____

LONG-TERM GOALS

1. Terminate illegal behaviors by utilizing legal means to meet needs.
2. Decrease inappropriate arrest or incarceration due to behaviors that are related to mental health symptoms.
3. Accept responsibility for decisions or behaviors that have resulted in arrest, arraignment, or trial.
4. Obtain competent, caring legal representation that is knowledgeable about mental illness issues for criminal, civil, or probate matters.
5. Decrease mental illness symptoms and/or substance abuse, which prompt illegal activity or involuntary hospitalization.
6. Obtain the least restrictive, most appropriate guardianship status.
7. Maintain safety while incarcerated.

—. _____
   _____
—. _____
   _____
—. _____
   _____

SHORT-TERM OBJECTIVES	THERAPEUTIC INTERVENTIONS
1. Describe the behaviors or symptoms that have led to legal involvement. (1, 2, 3, 4)	1. Request that the client identify his/her history of illegal behaviors and the legal system's responses.
	2. Review a copy of the client's guardianship stipulations with him/her, and why they are in place.
	3. Obtain information about the client's criminal charges and history from other sources (e.g., police or attorney reports and court documents); compare the record with his/her disclosed history, inquiring about discrepancies.
	4. Assess the client for a pattern of antisocial behavior.
2. Identify current criminal charges and legal needs. (3, 5)	3. Obtain information about the client's criminal charges and history

from other sources (e.g., police or attorney reports and court documents); compare the record with his/her disclosed history, inquiring about discrepancies.

3. Verbalize an understanding of the legal system as it relates to current legal or criminal charges. (6, 7)

5. Assist the client in making decisions about the need for legal representation; refer the client to an attorney, if necessary.

6. Review the basic legal proceedings and the people who are involved in a court hearing; quiz the client about the role of each person to test his/her understanding.

7. Display the steps in a criminal proceeding graphically, identifying the reason for each step in the process (e.g., investigation, arrest, arraignment, pretrial conferences, trial, and sentencing).

4. Participate in a complete forensic evaluation to assess criminal responsibility/safety. (8)

8. Advocate with the court for and/or arrange for a complete psychological assessment of the client's functioning, including intellectual, cognitive, and personality testing, to assess the client's understanding of criminal behaviors.

5. Present a positive impression in the court setting. (9, 10, 11)

9. Coach the client in preparation for court hearings, such as doing personal grooming, clothing selection, and gathering appropriate documentation.

10. Review normal conventions in a court setting with the client (e.g., referring to the judge as "Your Honor," standing when the judge enters, and waiting for the appropriate time to speak) and instruct the client about how to be a good witness (e.g., tell the truth, only answer the question asked, be prepared for an opposing attorney to try to increase his/her anxiety).

11. Role-play a court hearing, emphasizing the progression of the hearing, typical conventions in the courtroom, and being a witness.

6. Participate in an evaluation by a physician as to the need for medication to treat severe and persistent mental illness symptoms. (12, 13)

12. Refer the client to a physician or a psychiatrist for an evaluation of the need for psychiatric medication.

13. Educate the client about the use and expected benefits of psychotropic medications.

7. Report side effects and effectiveness of psychotropic medications to the appropriate professional. (14, 15)

14. Monitor the client's medication compliance and effectiveness.

15. Review the side effects of the psychotropic medications the client is experiencing and communicate these to the medical staff.

8. Successfully complete jail sentence. (16, 17, 18, 19)

16. With the client's permission, advise the jail staff or a jail mental health liaison about the client's mental illness symptoms; provide the jail staff with information and training regarding how to work with the client.

17. Advocate with the court and the jail system for alternative sentencing/housing options for the client as a mentally ill offender who is unable to cope with the typical jail setting (e.g., tether, a mental health unit of the jail).

18. Assist the client in developing an understanding of how his/her mental illness symptoms may interact with incarceration (e.g., increased paranoia, more acute anxiety, or difficulty managing mania).

19. Monitor the provision of medication in the corrections setting; advise the jail staff of the potential side effects that they should be monitoring, as well as the potential

9. Remain safe while incarcerated. (20, 21)

10. Successfully complete probation or other sentencing requirements that have been set forth by the court. (22, 23, 24)

11. Family and support system assist the client through the legal system. (25, 26)

12. Take responsibility for illegal behaviors. (27, 28)

danger resulting from neglecting the client's medications.

20. Review personal safety considerations with the client while he/she is incarcerated (e.g., how other inmates may treat him/her, how to get help if threatened or assaulted, how to respond to others).

21. Assist the client in identifying assertive, nonviolent responses to potentially hostile individuals in a jail setting.

22. Monitor, facilitate, and encourage the client to keep appointments with the court officers.

23. Attend probation meetings with the client on an intermittent basis to facilitate communication; educate the probation staff about the client's strengths and limitations.

24. Support or facilitate the client's involvement in court-mandated activities to adhere to probation requirements (e.g., mental health treatment, job procurement, stable residence, community service).

25. Educate the client's family, friends, and caregivers about the legal system, including allowing the client to experience the appropriate legal ramification of his/her inappropriate behavior (i.e., incarceration if the client was not actively psychotic and mandatory hospitalization if psychosis is uncontrolled).

26. Challenge the client's support system to remain in contact with the client, despite his/her incarceration.

27. Request that the client identify ways in which his/her illegal behaviors have affected others; help

the client to empathize by identifying his/her own emotional responses to prior experiences of being victimized.

28. Encourage the client to provide restitution to those whom he/she has victimized (e.g., financial reimbursement or community service).

13. Decrease mental illness symptoms that contribute to illegal behavior. (14, 29, 30)

14. Monitor the client's medication compliance and effectiveness.

29. Assist the client in developing an understanding of how his/her mental illness symptoms contribute to illegal behaviors.

30. Refer the client to individual, group, or marital therapy to assist in developing alternatives to acting out when facing stressful circumstances.

14. Terminate substance use or abuse. (31)

31. Coordinate a substance abuse evaluation with an individual/agency that is familiar with chronic mental illness concerns; facilitate coordinated mental health/substance abuse treatment (see the Chemical Dependence chapter in this *Planner*).

15. Participate in a psychological evaluation regarding guardianship. (32)

32. Coordinate a psychological evaluation to facilitate a guardianship hearing, including an assessment of functional decision-making abilities (e.g., regarding treatment, finances).

16. Obtain the least restrictive, legally necessary guardianship. (33, 34, 35)

33. Assist the family members or other parties in obtaining guardianship of the client to increase supervision and monitoring of his/her behavior and treatment.

34. Educate the potential guardian about person-centered planning and the ability of mentally ill people to manage many aspects

of their lives despite serious and persistent symptoms.

35. Advocate for the client against unnecessary or overly restrictive guardianship orders or practices.

17. Execute a treatment order and a last will and testament. (36, 37)

36. Assist the client in developing a written description of his/her wishes for treatment, emergency contact, medication needs, and other issues should he/she decompensate and become unable legally to make such decisions.

37. Discuss the client's wishes for end-of-life issues, including funeral arrangements, estate dispersal, and financial needs.

18. Verbalize an understanding of all legal rights and responsibilities regarding treatment. (38, 39)

38. Focus the client on his/her responsibilities regarding treatment (e.g., attendance at appointments, providing the clinician with accurate information, confidentiality regarding other patients in treatment).

39. Advocate for the client with other clinicians, family members, and legal personnel to adhere to the client's rights.

___. _____   ___. _____

_____   _____

___. _____   ___. _____

_____   _____

___. _____   ___. _____

_____   _____

DIAGNOSTIC SUGGESTIONS

Axis I:		
	297.1	Delusional Disorder
	295.10	Schizophrenia, Disorganized Type
	295.20	Schizophrenia, Catatonic Type
	295.90	Schizophrenia, Undifferentiated Type
	295.30	Schizophrenia, Paranoid Type
	295.70	Schizoaffective Disorder
	296.xx	Bipolar I Disorder
	296.89	Bipolar II Disorder
	304.20	Cocaine Dependence
	303.90	Alcohol Dependence
	312.32	Kleptomania
	V71.01	Adult Antisocial Behavior
	_____	_____
	_____	_____
Axis II:	301.7	Antisocial Personality Disorder
	_____	_____
	_____	_____

MANIA OR HYPOMANIA

BEHAVIORAL DEFINITIONS

1. Demonstrates loquaciousness or pressured speech.
2. Reports flight of ideas or thoughts racing.
3. Verbalizes delusional, grandiose, or persecutory beliefs.
4. Displays a decreased need for sleep.
5. Exhibits psychomotor agitation, restlessness, or agitation.
6. Exacerbated loss of natural inhibitions leads to impulsive, self-gratifying behaviors, regardless of the consequences to self or others (e.g., buying sprees, substance abuse).
7. Exhibits an expansive, variable mood that leads to impatience, irritability, anger, or assaultiveness when thwarted or confronted.
8. Fails to follow through on projects or promises due to an inability to organize activity in a goal-directed manner.
9. Shows a disregard for social mores (e.g., public nudity, erratic driving).
10. Engages in bizarre dress or grooming patterns.

—. _____
   _____
—. _____
   _____
—. _____
   _____

LONG-TERM GOALS

1. Reduce psychological energy and return to normal levels of activity, good judgment, stable mood, and goal-directed behavior.
2. Reduce agitation, impulsivity, and pressured speech while achieving sensitivity to the consequences of behavior and having more realistic expectations.

3. Achieve controlled behavior, moderated mood, and more deliberative speech and thought processes.
4. Achieve a more reality-based orientation.
5. Stabilize sleeping pattern and appetite.
6. Increase goal-directed behaviors.
7. Develop an increased understanding of severe and persistent mental illness symptoms, as well as an understanding of the indicators of and the triggers for decompensation.

—. _____
   _____
   _____
—. _____
   _____
   _____
—. _____
   _____

SHORT-TERM OBJECTIVES

1. Describe mood state, energy level, amount of control over thoughts, and sleeping pattern. (1, 2)

2. Agree to placement in an environment that ensures safety to self and others. (3, 4)

THERAPEUTIC INTERVENTIONS

1. Assess the client for classic signs of mania: pressured speech, impulsive behavior, euphoric mood, flight of ideas, reduced need for sleep, inflated self-esteem, and high energy.

2. Assess the client's level of elation: hypomanic, manic, or psychotic.

3. Perform an assessment of the client's ability to remain safe in the community, including level of manic behavior, impulsivity, natural and programmatic supports, and access to potentially unsafe situations.

4. Arrange for admission into a crisis residential unit or psychiatric hospital if the client is judged to be at imminent risk of harm to himself/herself or to others.

3. Maintain community placement while managing manic episode. (5, 6, 7)

5. Develop a short-term, round-the-clock crisis plan, including multiple caregivers, psychiatric involvement, and crisis assistance, to maintain the client within the community.

6. Remove potentially dangerous items, such as sharp objects, weapons, and access to motor vehicles.

7. Provide the client with a calm setting, including low lighting, decreased stimulation (e.g., soothing music), and a direct, but nonargumentative, approach.

▼ 4. Cooperate with psychiatric evaluation as to the need for medication and/or hospitalization to stabilize mood and energy. (8, 9)

8. Arrange for a psychiatric evaluation of the client for pharmacotherapy (e.g., lithium carbonate, Depakote, Lamictil). ▼

9. Monitor the client's reaction to the psychotropic medication (e.g., compliance, side effects, and effectiveness) and intervene accordingly. ▼

▼ 5. Achieve a level of symptom stability that allows for meaningful participation in psychotherapy. (10)

10. Monitor the client's symptom improvement toward stabilization sufficient to allow participation in psychotherapy. ▼

▼ 6. Participate in family therapy, or individual therapy if family is unavailable. (11)

11. Conduct family-focused treatment with the client and significant others, or adapt the model to individual therapy if family therapy is not possible (see *Bipolar Disorder: A Family-Focused Treatment Approach* by Miklowitz and Goldstein). ▼

▼ 7. Complete psychological testing to assess communication patterns

12. Arrange for the administration of an objective assessment instrument

---

▼ indicates that the Objective/Intervention is consistent with those found in evidence-based treatments.

within the family or with significant others. (12)

for evaluating communication patterns with family/significant others, particularly expressed emotion (e.g., *Perceived Criticism Scale* by Hooley and Teasdale); evaluate results and process feedback with the client and family. ▽

▽ 8. Verbalize an understanding of the causes for, symptoms of, and treatment of manic, hypomanic, mixed, and/or depressive episodes. (13, 14, 15)

13. Teach the client, family, and relevant others, using all modalities necessary, about the signs, symptoms, and phasic relapsing nature of the client's mood episodes; destigmatize and normalize. ▽

14. Teach the client a stress diathesis model of bipolar disorder that emphasizes the strong role of a biological predisposition to mood episodes that is vulnerable to stresses that are manageable. ▽

15. Provide the client with a rationale for treatment involving ongoing medication and psychosocial treatment to recognize, manage, and reduce biological and psychological vulnerabilities that could precipitate relapse. ▽

▽ 9. Identify and manage sources of stress that increase the risk of relapse. (16)

16. Identify the client's sources of stress/triggers of potential relapse (e.g., negative events, cognitive interpretations, aversive communication, poor sleep hygiene, medication noncompliance); use cognitive and behavioral techniques to address as needed (e.g., *Cognitive-Behavioral Therapy for the Management of Bipolar Disorder* by Otto and Reilly-Harrington). ▽

▽ 10. Verbalize acceptance of the need to take psychotropic medication and commit to prescription compliance with blood level monitoring. (17, 18, 19)

17. Use motivational approaches (e.g., *Enhancing Motivation for Change in Substance Abuse* by Miller) to enhance engagement in medication use and compliance;

teach him/her the risk for relapse when medication is discontinued, and work toward a commitment to prescription adherence. ▽

18. Assess factors (e.g., thoughts, feelings, stressors) that have precipitated the client's prescription noncompliance; develop a plan for recognizing and addressing them (or assign "Why I Dislike Taking My Medication" in *Adult Psychotherapy Homework Planner,* 2nd ed. by Jongsma). ▽

19. Educate and encourage the client to stay compliant with necessary labs involved in regulating is/her education levels. ▽

▽ 11. Implement good sleep hygiene. (20)

20. Teach the client about the importance of good sleep hygiene (or assign "Sleep Pattern Record" in *Adult Psychotherapy Homework Planner,* 2nd ed. by Jongsma); assess and intervene accordingly. ▽

▽ 12. Develop a "relapse drill" in which roles, responsibilities, and a course of action is agreed upon in the event that signs of relapse emerge. (21, 22)

21. Educate the client and family about the client's signs and symptoms of pending relapse. ▽

22. Help the client and family draw up a relapse drill detailing roles and responsibilities (e.g., who will call a meeting of the family to problem-solve potential relapse; who will call physician, schedule a serum level to be taken, or emergency services, if needed); problem-solve obstacles and work toward a commitment to adherence with the plan. ▽

▽ 13. Client and family commit to replacing aversive communication with positive, honest, and respectful communication. (23, 24, 25)

23. Assess and educate the client and family about the role of aversive communication (e.g., high expressed emotion) in family distress and risk for the client's manic relapse. ▽

24. Use behavioral techniques (education, modeling, role-playing, corrective feedback, and positive reinforcement) to teach communication skills including offering positive feedback, active listening, making positive requests of others for behavior change, and giving negative feedback in an honest and respectful manner. ▽

25. Assign the client and family homework exercises to use and record use of newly learned communication skills; process results in session. ▽

▽ 14. Maintain a reality-based orientation. (26)

26. Use cognitive therapy approaches to help the client differentiate between real and imagined, actual and exaggerated losses, abilities, expectations, and the like (see *Cognitive-Behavioral Therapy for the Management of Bipolar Disorder* by Otto and Reilly-Harrington). ▽

▽ 15. Terminate self-destructive behaviors such as promiscuity, substance abuse, and the expression of overt hostility or aggression. (27, 28, 29, 30)

27. Confront the client's grandiosity and demandingness gradually, but firmly. ▽

28. Refocus the client consistently onto the effects of his/her actions, emphasizing the impulsive nature of manic/hypomanic episodes and his/her need to identify these symptoms as early as possible. ▽

29. Increase the client's sensitivity to the effects of his/her behavior through the use of role-playing, role reversal, and behavioral rehearsal. ▽

30. Identify and confront unhealthy, impulsive, or manic behaviors that occur during contacts with the clinician, enforcing clear rules and roles in

the relationship, as well as immediate, short-term consequences for breaking such boundaries. ▽

▽ 16. Client and family implement a problem-solving approach to addressing current conflicts. (31, 32, 33)

31. Assist the client and family in identifying conflicts that can be addressed with problem-solving techniques. ▽

32. Use behavioral techniques (education, modeling, role-playing, corrective feedback, and positive reinforcement) to teach the client and family problem-solving skills including defining the problem constructively and specifically, brainstorming options, evaluating options, choosing options and implementing a plan, evaluating the results, and reevaluating the plan. ▽

33. Assign the client and family homework exercises to use and record use of newly learned problem-solving skills (or assign "Plan Before Acting" in *Adult Psychotherapy Homework Planner,* 2nd ed. by Jongsma); process results in session. ▽

▽ 17. Report more control over impulses and thoughts, and a slower thinking process. (34, 35, 36)

34. Verbally reinforce the client's slower speech and more deliberate thought process. ▽

35. Reinforce increased control over hyperactivity and help the client set goals and limits on agitation; model and role-play increased behavioral control (or assign "Plan Before Acting" in *Adult Psychotherapy Homework Planner,* 2nd ed. by Jongsma). ▽

36. Monitor the client's energy level and reinforce increased control over behavior, pressured speech, and expression of ideas. ▽

▼ 18. Participate in periodic booster sessions. (37)

37. Hold periodic "booster sessions" within the first few months after therapy to facilitate the client's positive changes; problem-solve obstacles to improvement. ▼

19. Decrease or ameliorate the direct effects of hostile, promiscuous, or otherwise impulsive manic behaviors. (38, 39)

38. Coordinate testing and follow-up treatment for sexually transmitted diseases or pregnancy (see the Sexuality Concerns chapter in this *Planner*).

39. Assist the client in negotiating the criminal justice system (see the Legal Concerns chapter in this *Planner*).

20. Reestablish relationships that have been broken due to the effects or consequences of severe and persistent mental illness symptoms. (40, 41)

40. Assist the client in developing a list of relationships that have been affected by the client's behavior.

41. Provide feedback to the client about how his/her behaviors or verbal messages have an impact on others, encouraging healthier relationship skills (see the Social Skills Deficits chapter in this *Planner*).

21. Increase understanding of bipolar illness by reading a book on the disorder. (42)

42. Ask the client to read a book on Bipolar Disorder (e.g., *The Bipolar Disorder Survival Guide* by Miklowitz).

—. _____
_____

—. _____
_____

—. _____
_____

—. _____
_____

—. _____
_____

—. _____
_____

DIAGNOSTIC SUGGESTIONS

Axis I:

296.xx	Bipolar I Disorder
298.89	Bipolar II Disorder
301.13	Cyclothymic Disorder
295.70	Schizoaffective Disorder
296.80	Bipolar Disorder NOS
310.1	Personality Change Due to . . . *[General Medical Condition]*
_____	_____
_____	_____

MEDICATION MANAGEMENT

BEHAVIORAL DEFINITIONS

1. Fails to consistently take psychotropic medications as prescribed.
2. Medication interactions are causing negative side effects.
3. Verbalizes fears and dislike related to physical and/or emotional side effects of prescribed medications.
4. Fails to respond as expected to a prescribed medication regimen.
5. Lacks knowledge of medications' usefulness and potential side effects.
6. Makes statements of an unwillingness to take prescribed medications.
7. Consumes alcohol or illicit drugs along with psychotropic medications.

—. _____

_____

—. _____

_____

—. _____

_____

LONG-TERM GOALS

1. Regular, consistent use of psychotropic medications at the prescribed dosage, frequency, and duration.
2. Decreased side effects of psychotropic medication through effective, timely regulation of dosage and type of medication
3. Increased understanding of the psychotropic medication dosage, the side effects, and the reasons for being prescribed.
4. Decreased frequency and intensity of psychotic and other severe mental illness symptoms.
5. Support network of family, clinicians, and caregivers assist in taking prescribed medication.

—. _____

_____

_____

—. _____

_____

—. _____

_____

SHORT-TERM OBJECTIVES

THERAPEUTIC INTERVENTIONS

1. List all medications that are currently being prescribed and consumed. (1, 2, 3)

1. Request that the client identify all currently prescribed medications, including names, times administered, and dosage.

2. Request that the client provide an honest, realistic description of his/her medication compliance; compare this with his/her medical chart.

3. Arrange for the client to obtain blood level tests to assess for medications expected to be present.

▽ 2. Describe thoughts and feelings about medication use and willingness or unwillingness to explore personal use. (4)

4. Conduct motivational interviewing to assess the client's stage of preparation for change; intervene accordingly, moving from building motivation, through strengthening commitment to change, to participation in treatment (see *Motivational Interviewing* by Miller and Rollnick). ▽

▽ 3. Identify and replace misinformation and mistaken beliefs that support medication noncompliance. (5, 6, 7, 8)

5. Request that the client identify the reason for the use of each medication; correct any misinformation regarding the medication's expected effects, the

---

▽ indicates that the Objective/Intervention is consistent with those found in evidence-based treatments.

acceptable dosage levels, and the possible side effects. ▽

6. Request that the client describe fears that he/she may experience regarding the use of the medication; cognitively restructure these fears, correcting myths and misinformation while paying particular attention to the following common biases: underestimating benefits of medication therapy, overestimating the threat posed by side effects, beliefs that medications are not necessary, beliefs that medication is harmful or part of a conspiracy, and beliefs that medication could change his/her personality or make him/her addicted. ▽

7. Do "behavioral experiments" in which biased predictions about medication are tested against the client's past, present, and/or future experience using the medication. ▽

8. Reinforce the client's positive, reality-based cognitive messages that enhance medication prescription compliance. ▽

4. Family members enroll in a multi-family group educational program for families of the mentally ill. (9)

9. Refer the family to a multifamily group psychoeducational program (see *Multifamily Groups in the Treatment of Severe Psychiatric Disorders* by McFarlane) to increase understanding of severe and persistent mental illness and the need for medication. ▽

5. The client and family participate in a family-focused therapy. (10)

10. Conduct or refer the client and family to a therapy based on the principles of family-focused treatment (e.g., see *Bipolar Disorder: A Family-Focused Treatment Approach* by Miklowitz and Goldstein). ▽

▼ 6. Cooperate with a psychiatric evaluation. (11)

▼ 7. Report the side effects and the effectiveness of the medications to the appropriate professional(s). (12, 13)

8. Identify the financial resources for payment for medication. (14, 15)

9. Verbalize any thoughts of suicide. (16, 17, 18)

10. Cooperate with in-depth diagnostic procedures to accurately assess symptoms and medication effectiveness. (19)

11. Arrange for a psychiatric evaluation to assess the client's need for modification to his/her current psychotropic medication regimen. ▼

12. Review the potential side effects of the medication with the client and the medical staff. ▼

13. Obtain a written release of information from the client to his/her primary physician or other health care providers to allow for informing them of the medications, side effects, and benefit that the client is experiencing. ▼

14. Assist the client in obtaining and maintaining employment (see the Employment Problems chapter in this *Planner*) or entitlements (e.g., Medicaid, Social Security Disability).

15. Coordinate the client's access to free or low-cost medication programs through drug manufacturers or other resources, or the use of generic drugs, where appropriate.

16. Assess the client's suicidal ideation, taking into account the extent of ideation, the presence of a primary and a backup plan, past attempts, and family history.

17. Remove potentially lethal medication from the client's immediate access, if necessary.

18. Refer the client to crisis residential placement or to a psychiatric hospital when it is assessed that he/she may not be able to control suicidal intent.

19. Arrange for personality testing for the client or other objective diagnostic evaluations to assist in diagnosis.

11. Modify lifestyle to minimize the negative effects on medication effectiveness and side effects. (20)

12. Develop an increased ownership of the medication regimen. (21)

13. Take the medications as administered by a caregiver or a family member. (22, 23)

14. Take the medications responsibly on a single, day-to-day basis. (22, 24, 25)

15. Take the medications responsibly on a week-to-week basis. (25, 26)

20. Arrange for the client to receive information about lifestyle habits (e.g., tobacco use, diet), that can be modified to decrease the side effects of the medication.

21. Coordinate with the prescribing physician for the dosage to be within a certain range, when possible (e.g., 2 or 3 milligrams per day), to increase the client's authority over his own regimen; encourage client consultation with his/her clinician in adjusting the variable dosages.

22. Assess the client's ability to properly self-administer medications and arrange for supervision, if necessary.

23. After obtaining the proper release of information from the client, request assistance from family members, roommates, peers, or caregivers to administer the medications to the client.

22. Assess the client's ability to properly self-administer medications and arrange for supervision, if necessary.

24. Arrange for daily medication drop-offs to the client, with instructions on which dosages to take at each time of day.

25. Encourage the client to take his/her medications at a specific, consistent place and time every day.

25. Encourage the client to take his/her medications at a specific, consistent place and time every day.

26. Arrange for prescriptions to be distributed in a multidose, compartmentalized daily medication box;

16. Take the medications responsibly on an ongoing, permanent basis. (27, 28)

17. Accept assistance from family members, peers, and others regarding the medication usage. (29, 30, 31)

18. Express social concerns that are related to the medication usage. (32)

19. Obtain a more simplified administration of the medications. (33)

20. Describe the extent of alcohol or illicit drug use. (34)

21. Terminate substance use or abuse. (35, 36)

monitor the client for accurate usage of the pillbox.

27. Monitor the client's use of medications and accurate pill counts in pill bottles, on a sporadic basis.

28. Coordinate for all of the client's prescriptions (including nonpsychiatric medications) to be obtained from the same pharmacy.

29. Coordinate family or couples therapy to promote an understanding of the client's illness and the impact of that illness on the client's and the family's needs.

30. Train family members, peers, and others in the proper use and administration of medications, to encourage or reinforce the client when he/she complies, and to communicate issues to the clinician(s).

31. Coordinate family members in providing the client with transportation to the clinic or pharmacy.

32. Request that the client identify social concerns that he/she may experience regarding medication usage (e.g. stigmatization, loss of independence); process these concerns to resolution.

33. Advocate with a physician for less complicated dosing times for the client's medications, including longer acting or time released.

34. Explore and assess the client's use of alcohol or illicit drugs.

35. Provide the client with information about the negative effects of substance abuse on his/her symptoms and the depotentiating effect of substances on his/her medications.

▼ 22. Verbalize positive feelings about the improvement that is resulting from the medication's effectiveness. (37)

36. Refer the client for substance abuse treatment (see the Chemical Dependence chapter in this *Planner*).

37. Request that the client identify how the reduction in mental illness symptoms has improved his/her social or family system; reinforce functioning and continued medication usage. ▼

___. _____

_____

___. _____

_____

___. _____

_____

___. _____

_____

___. _____

_____

___. _____

_____

DIAGNOSTIC SUGGESTIONS

Axis I:		
	297.1	Delusional Disorder
	295.xx	Schizophrenia
	295.10	Schizophrenia, Disorganized Type
	295.30	Schizophrenia, Paranoid Type
	295.90	Schizophrenia, Undifferentiated Type
	295.60	Schizophrenia, Residual Type
	295.70	Schizoaffective Disorder
	296.xx	Bipolar I Disorder
	296.89	Bipolar II Disorder
	304.80	Polysubstance Dependence
	V15.81	Noncompliance With Treatment
	_____	_____
	_____	_____

OBSESSIVE-COMPULSIVE DISORDER (OCD)

BEHAVIORAL DEFINITIONS

1. Intrusive, recurrent and unwanted thoughts, images, or impulses that distress and/or interfere with the client's daily routine, job performance, or social relationships.
2. Fails attempts to ignore or control these thoughts or impulses or neutralize them with other thoughts and actions.
3. Recognizes that obsessive thoughts are a product of his/her own mind.
4. Repetitive and/or excessive mental or behavioral actions are done to neutralize or prevent discomfort or some dreaded outcome.
5. Acknowledges repetitive behaviors as excessive and unreasonable.

—. _____
   _____
—. _____
   _____
—. _____
   _____

LONG-TERM GOALS

1. Reduce the frequency, intensity, and duration of obsessions.
2. Reduce time involved with or interference from obsessions and compulsions.
3. Function daily at a consistent level with minimal interference from obsessions and compulsions.
4. Resolve key life conflicts and the emotional stress that fuels obsessive-compulsive behavior patterns.
5. Let go of key thoughts, beliefs, and past life events in order to maximize time free from obsessions and compulsions.

—. _____
_____
_____
—. _____
_____
—. _____
_____

SHORT-TERM OBJECTIVES

THERAPEUTIC INTERVENTIONS

1. Describe the history of anxiety symptoms. (1, 2)

1. Focus on developing a level of trust with the client; provide support and empathy to encourage the client to feel safe in expressing his/her OCD symptoms.

2. Assess the client's frequency, intensity, duration, and history of obsessions and compulsions (e.g., *The Anxiety Disorders Interview Schedule for the DSM-IV* by Brown, DiNardo, and Barlow).

2. Complete psychological tests designed to assess and track the nature and severity of obsessions and compulsions. (3)

3. Administer a measure of OCD to further assess its depth and breadth (e.g., *The Yale-Brown Obsessive Compulsive Scale* by Goodman and colleagues).

3. Obtain a complete physical evaluation to rule out medical and substance related etiologies for anxiety symptoms. (4, 5)

4. Refer the client to a general physician for a complete physical examination to evaluate for any organic basis for the anxiety.

5. Assist the client in following up on the recommendations from a physical evaluation, including medications, lab work, or specialty assessments.

4. Identify any foods, alcohol, or street drugs that could be triggering anxiety. (6, 7)

6. Review the client's use of nonprescription medications, psychoactive chemicals (e.g., nicotine, caffeine, alcohol, or street drugs) and their relationship to symptoms;

refer to physician for further review, if indicated.

7. Recommend the termination of
consumption of substances that
could trigger anxiety; refer for
substance abuse evaluation or
treatment, if indicated.

5. Differentiate between symptoms
that are related to anxiety versus
those that are related to severe
and persistent mental illness.
(2, 3, 8, 9, 10)

2. Assess the client's frequency, in-
tensity, duration, and history of
obsessions and compulsions (e.g.,
*The Anxiety Disorders Interview
Schedule for the DSM-IV* by
Brown, DiNardo, and Barlow).

3. Administer a measure of OCD to
further assess its depth and
breadth (e.g., *The Yale-Brown
Obsessive Compulsive Scale* by
Goodman and colleagues).

8. Help the client differentiate
symptoms that are a direct effect
of his/her severe and persistent
mental illness (e.g., a product of
delusion), as opposed to a separate diagnosis of an anxiety
disorder.

9. Acknowledge that both real and
delusional experiences can cause
anxiety, providing support to the
client.

10. Utilizing a description of anxiety
symptoms such as that found in
Bourne's *The Anxiety and Phobia Workbook*, help the client to
identify with a specific diagnostic
classification.

 6. Cooperate with a medication
evaluation. (11)

11. Refer the client to a physician for
an evaluation as to the need for
psychotropic medication. ▽

▽indicates that the Objective/Intervention is consistent with those found in evidence-
based treatments.

▽ 7. Report a decrease in anxiety symptoms through regular use of psychotropic medication. (12, 13)

12. Educate the client about the use and expected benefits of the medication. ▽

13. Monitor the client's medication compliance, adverse events, and effectiveness; reinforce consistent use of effective medication. ▽

▽ 8. Participate in small group expo-sure and ritual prevention ther-apy for obsessions and compulsions. (14)

14. Enroll the client in intensive (e.g., daily) or nonintensive (e.g., weekly) small (closed enroll-ment) group exposure and ritual prevention therapy for OCD (see *Obsessive-Compulsive Disorder* by Foa and Franklin). ▽

▽ 9. Verbalize an understanding of the rationale for treatment of OCD. (15, 16)

15. Assign the client to read psycho-educational chapters of books or treatment manuals on the rationale for exposure and ritual prevention therapy and/or cognitive restruc-turing for OCD (e.g., *Mastery of Obsessive-Compulsive Disorder* by Kozak and Foa; or *Stop Obsessing* by Foa and Wilson.) ▽

16. Discuss how treatment serves as an arena to desensitize learned fear, reality test obsessional fears and underlying beliefs, and build con-fidence in managing fears without compulsions (see *Mastery of Obsessive-Compulsive Disorder* by Kozak and Foa). ▽

▽ 10. Identify and replace biased, fear-ful self-talk and beliefs. (17)

17. Explore the client's schema and self-talk that mediate his/her obses-sional fears and compulsive behav-ior; assist him/her in generating thoughts that correct for the biases; use behavioral experiments to test fearful versus alternative predic-tions (see *Mastery of Obsessive-Compulsive Disorder* by Kozak and Foa; or *Obsessive-Compulsive Dis-order* by Salkovskis and Kirk). ▽

▼ 11. Implement the use of the "thought-stopping" technique in conjunction with other "self-talk" work to reduce the frequency of obsessive thoughts. (18, 19)

18. Teach the client to interrupt obsessive thoughts using the "thought-stopping" technique of shouting STOP to himself/herself silently while picturing a red traffic signal and then thinking about a calming scene. ▼

19. Assign the client to implement the "thought-stopping" technique on a daily basis between sessions (or assign "Making Use of the Thought-Stopping Technique" in *Adult Psychotherapy Homework Planner*, 2nd ed. by Jongsma); review implementation, reinforcing success, and redirecting for failure. ▼

▼ 12. Undergo repeated imaginal exposure to feared external and/or internal cues. (20, 21, 22)

20. Assess the nature of any external cues (e.g., persons, objects, situations) and internal cues (e.g., thoughts, images, impulses) that precipitate the client's obsessions and compulsions. ▼

21. Direct and assist the client in construction of a hierarchy of his/her feared internal and external fear cues. ▼

22. Select initial imaginal exposures to the internal and/or external OCD cues that have a high likelihood of being a successful experience for the client: do cognitive restructuring within and after the exposure (see *Mastery of Obsessive-Compulsive Disorder* by Kozak and Foa; or *Treatment of Obsessive-Compulsive Disorder* by McGinn and Sanderson). ▼

▼ 13. Complete homework assignments involving *in vivo* exposure to feared external and/or internal cues. (23)

23. Assign the client a homework exercise in which he/she repeats the exposure to the internal and/or external OCD cues using restructured cognitions between sessions and

records responses (or assign "Re-
ducing the Strength of Compulsive
Behaviors" in *Adult Psychotherapy
Homework Planner,* 2nd ed. by
Jongsma); review during next ses-
sion, reinforcing success and pro-
viding corrective feedback toward
improvement (see *Mastery of
Obsessive-Compulsive Disorder* by
Kozak and Foa). ▽

▽ 14. Implement relapse prevention
strategies for managing possible
future anxiety symptoms.
(24, 25, 26, 27)

24. Discuss with the client the distinction between a lapse and relapse,
associating a lapse with an initial
and reversible return of symptoms, fear, or urges to avoid and
relapse with the decision to return
to fearful and avoidant patterns. ▽

25. Identify and rehearse with the
client the management of future
situations or circumstances in
which lapses could occur. ▽

26. Instruct the client to routinely use
strategies learned in therapy (e.g.,
continued exposure to previously
feared external or internal cues
that arise) to prevent relapse into
obsessive-compulsive patterns. ▽

27. Schedule periodic maintenance
sessions to help the client maintain therapeutic gains and adjust
to life without OCD (see Hiss,
Foa, and Kozak, [1994] for a description of relapse prevention
strategies for OCD). ▽

15. Include significant others in facilitating implementation of new
anxiety reduction techniques. (28)

28. Enlist the help of the client's support system in implementing and
maintaining their therapeutic gains.

16. Identify key life conflicts that
raise anxiety. (29)

29. Explore the client's life circumstances to help identify key unresolved conflicts.

17. Verbalize and clarify feelings con-
nected to key life conflicts. (30)

30. Encourage, support, and assist
the client in identifying and ex-

18. Implement the Ericksonian task designed to interfere with OCD. (31)

19. Develop and implement a daily ritual that interrupts the current pattern of compulsions. (32)

pressing feelings related to key unresolved life issues.

31. Develop and assign an Ericksonian task (e.g., if obsessed with a loss, give the client the task to visit, send a card, or bring flowers to someone who has lost someone) to the client that is centered on the obsession or compulsion and assess the results with the client.

32. Help the client create and implement a ritual (e.g., find a task that the client finds necessary but very unpleasant, and have him/her do this task each time he/she finds thoughts becoming obsessive); follow up with the client on the outcome of its implementation and make and necessary adjustments.

___. _____   ___. _____
    _____   _____
___. _____   ___. _____
    _____   _____
___. _____   ___. _____
    _____   _____

DIAGNOSTIC SUGGESTIONS

Axis I:	300.3	Obsessive-Compulsive Disorder
	300.00	Anxiety Disorder NOS
	296.xx	Major Depressive Disorder
	_____	_____
	_____	_____
Axis II:	301.4	Obsessive-Compulsive Personality Disorder
	_____	_____
	_____	_____

PANIC/AGORAPHOBIA

BEHAVIORAL DEFINITIONS

1. Complains of unexpected, sudden, debilitating panic symptoms (e.g., shallow breathing, sweating, heart racing or pounding, dizziness, depersonalization or derealization, trembling, chest tightness, fear of dying or losing control, nausea) that have occurred repeatedly resulting in persisting concern about having additional attacks.
2. Demonstrates marked avoidance of activities or environments due to fear of triggering intense panic symptoms, resulting in interference with normal routine.
3. Acknowledges a persistence of fear in spite of the recognition that the fear is unreasonable.
4. Increasingly isolates self due to fear of traveling or leaving a "safe environment" such as home.
5. Avoids public places or environments with large groups of people such as malls or big stores.
6. Displays no evidence of agoraphobia.

__. _____

_____

__. _____

_____

__. _____

_____

LONG-TERM GOALS

1. Reduce the frequency, intensity, and duration of panic attacks.
2. Reduce the fear that panic symptoms will recur without the ability to manage them.

3. Reduce the fear of triggering panic and eliminate avoidance of activities and environments thought to trigger panic.
4. Increase comfort in freely leaving home and being in a public environment.

—. _____
_____
_____

—. _____
_____
_____

—. _____
_____

SHORT-TERM OBJECTIVES

THERAPEUTIC INTERVENTIONS

1. Describe the history of anxiety symptoms. (1, 2, 3)

1. Focus on developing a level of trust with the client; provide support and empathy to encourage the client to feel safe in expressing his/her panic symptoms.

2. Assess the client's frequency, intensity, duration, and history of panic symptoms, fear, and avoidance (e.g., *The Anxiety Disorders Interview Schedule for the DSM-IV* by Brown, DiNardo, and Barlow).

3. Assess the nature of any stimulus, thoughts, or situations that precipitate the client's panic.

2. Complete psychological tests designed to assess the depth of agoraphobia and anxiety sensitivity. (4, 5)

4. Administer a fear survey to further assess the depth and breadth of agoraphobic responses (e.g., *The Mobility Inventory for Agoraphobia* by Chambless, Caputo, Jasin, Gracel, and Williams).

5. Administer a measure of fear of anxiety symptoms to further assess its depth and breadth (e.g., *The Anxiety Sensitivity Index* by Reiss, Peterson, and Gursky).

3. Obtain a complete physical evaluation to rule out medical and substance-related etiologies for anxiety symptoms. (6, 7)

6. Refer the client to a general physician for a complete physical examination to evaluate for any organic basis for the anxiety.

7. Assist the client in following up on the recommendations from a physical evaluation, including medications, lab work, or specialty assessments.

4. Identify any foods, alcohol, or street drugs that could be triggering anxiety. (8, 9)

8. Review the client's use of non-prescription medications, psychoactive chemicals (e.g., nicotine, caffeine, alcohol abuse, street drugs) and their relationship to symptoms.

9. Recommend the termination of consumption of substances that could trigger anxiety; refer for substance abuse evaluation or treatment if indicated.

5. Differentiate between symptoms that are related to anxiety versus those that are related to severe and persistent mental illness. (2, 3, 10, 11, 12)

2. Assess the client's frequency, intensity, duration, and history of panic symptoms, fear, and avoidance (e.g., *The Anxiety Disorders Interview Schedule for the DSM-IV* by Brown, DiNardo, and Barlow).

3. Assess the nature of any stimulus, thoughts, or situations that precipitate the client's panic.

10. Help the client differentiate symptoms that are a direct effect of his/her severe and persistent mental illness (e.g., a product of delusion), as opposed to a separate diagnosis of an anxiety disorder.

11. Acknowledge that both real and delusional experiences can cause anxiety, providing support to the client.

12. Utilizing a description of anxiety symptoms such as that found in Bourne's *The Anxiety and*

6. Cooperate with a medication evaluation. (13)

7. Report a decrease in anxiety symptoms through regular use of psychotropic medications. (14, 15)

8. Verbalize an accurate understanding of panic attacks and agoraphobia. (16, 17)

9. Verbalize an understanding of the rationale for treatment of panic. (18, 19)

Phobia Workbook, help the client to identify with a specific diagnostic classification.

13. Refer the client to a physician for an evaluation as to the need for psychotropic medications. ▽

14. Educate the client about the use and expected benefits of the medication. ▽

15. Monitor the client's medication compliance, adverse events, and effectiveness; reinforce consistent use of effective medication. ▽

16. Discuss how panic attacks are false alarms of danger, not medically dangerous, not a sign of weakness or craziness, common, but often lead to fear and unnecessary avoidance. ▽

17. Assign the client to read psychoeducational chapters of books or treatment manuals on panic disorders and agoraphobia (e.g., *Mastery of Your Anxiety and Panic* by Craske and Barlow; or *Don't Panic: Taking Control of Anxiety Attacks* by Wilson). ▽

18. Educate the client as to how exposure serves as an arena to desensitize learned fear, build confidence, and feel safer by building a new history of success experiences. ▽

19. Assign the client to read about exposure-based therapy in chapters of books or treatment manuals on panic disorders and agoraphobia (e.g., *Mastery of Your Anxiety and*

▽ indicates that the Objective/Intervention is consistent with those found in evidence-based treatments.

⛛ 10. Implement calming and coping strategies to reduce overall anxiety and to manage panic symptoms. (20, 21, 22)

Panic by Craske and Barlow; or *Living with Fear* by Marks). ⛛

20. Teach the client progressive muscle relaxation as a daily exercise for general relaxation and train him/her in the use of coping strategies (e.g., staying focused on behavioral goals, muscular relaxation, evenly paced diaphragmatic breathing, positive self-talk) to manage symptom attacks. ⛛

21. Teach the client to keep focus on external stimuli and behavioral responsibilities during panic rather than being preoccupied with internal focus on physiological changes. ⛛

22. Assign the client to read about progressive muscle relaxation and paced diaphragmatic breathing in books or treatment manuals on panic disorder and agoraphobia (e.g., *Mastery of Your Anxiety and Panic* by Craske and Barlow). ⛛

⛛ 11. Practice positive self-talk that builds confidence in the ability to endure anxiety symptoms without serious consequences. (23, 24)

23. Consistently reassure the client of no connection between panic symptoms and heart attack, loss of control over behavior, or serious mental illness ("going crazy"). ⛛

24. Use modeling and behavioral rehearsal to train the client in positive self-talk that reassures him/her of the ability to endure anxiety symptoms without serious consequences. ⛛

⛛ 12. Identify, challenge, and replace biased, fearful self-talk that exacerbates panic symptoms with reality-based, positive self-talk. (25, 26, 27)

25. Explore the client's schema and self-talk that mediate his/her fear response, challenge the biases; assist him/her in replacing the distorted messages with self-talk that does not overestimate the likelihood of catastrophic out-

comes, nor underestimate the ability to cope with panic symptoms. ▽

26. Assign the client to read about cognitive restructuring in books or treatment manuals on panic disorder and agoraphobia (e.g., *Mastery of Your Anxiety and Panic* by Craske and Barlow). ▽

27. Assign the client a homework exercise in which he/she identifies fearful self-talk and creates reality-based alternatives; review and reinforce success, providing corrective feedback for failure (see *10 Simple Solutions to Panic* by Antony and McCabe; or *Mastery of Your Anxiety and Panic* by Craske and Barlow). ▽

▽ 13. Participate in gradual, repeated exposure to feared physical sensations until they are no longer frightening to experience. (28, 29, 30)

28. Teach the client a sensation exposure technique in which he/she generates feared physical sensations through exercise (e.g., breathes rapidly until slightly lightheaded, spins in chair briefly until slightly dizzy), then uses coping strategies (e.g., staying focused on behavioral goals, muscular relaxation, evenly paced diaphragmatic breathing, positive self-talk) to calm himself/herself down; repeat exercise until anxiety wanes (see *10 Simple Solutions to Panic* by Antony and McCabe; or *Mastery of Your Anxiety and Panic: Therapist Guide* by Craske and Barlow). ▽

29. Assign the client to read about sensation (interoceptive) exposure in books or treatment manuals on panic disorder and agoraphobia (e.g., *Mastery of Your Anxiety and Panic* by Craske and Barlow; *10*

Simple Solutions to Panic by Antony and McCabe). ▽

30. Assign the client a homework exercise in which he/she does sensation exposures and records the experience (e.g., *Mastery of Your Anxiety and Panic* by Craske and Barlow; or *10 Simple Solutions to Panic* by Antony and McCabe); review and reinforce success, providing corrective feedback for failure. ▽

▽ 14. Participate in gradual repeated exposure to feared or avoided situations in which an agoraphobic symptom attack and its negative consequences are feared. (31, 32, 33, 34)

31. Direct and assist the client in construction of a hierarchy of anxiety-producing situations associated with the phobic response. ▽

32. Select initial exposures that have a high likelihood of being a successful experience for the client; develop a plan for managing the symptoms and rehearse the plan in imagination. ▽

33. Assign the client to read about situational (exteroceptive) exposure in books or treatment manuals on panic disorder and agoraphobia (e.g., *Mastery of Your Anxiety and Panic* by Craske and Barlow; or *Living With Fear* by Marks). ▽

34. Assign the client a homework exercise in which he/she does situational exposures and records responses (e.g., *Mastery of Your Anxiety and Panic* by Craske and Barlow; or *10 Simple Solutions to Panic* by Antony and McCabe); review and reinforce success, providing corrective feedback for failure. ▽

▽ 15. Implement relapse prevention strategies for managing possible

35. Discuss with the client the distinction between a lapse and relapse,

future anxiety symptoms.
(35, 36, 37, 38)

associating a lapse with an initial and reversible return of symptoms, fear, or urges to avoid and relapse with the decision to return to fearful and avoidant patterns. ▽

36. Identify and rehearse with the client the management of future situations or circumstances in which lapses could occur. ▽

37. Instruct the client to routinely use strategies learned in therapy (e.g., cognitive restructuring, exposure), building them into his/her life as much as possible. ▽

38. Develop a "coping card" on which coping strategies and other important information (e.g., "pace your breathing," "focus on the task at hand," "you can manage it," "it will go away") are written for the client's later use. ▽

16. Verbalize the costs and benefits of remaining fearful and avoidant. (39)

39. Probe for the presence of secondary gain that reinforces the client's panic symptoms through escape or avoidance mechanisms; challenge the client to remain in feared situations and to use coping skills to endure.

17. Verbalize the separate realities of the irrationally feared object or situation and the emotionally painful experience from the past that has been evoked by the phobic stimulus. (40, 41)

40. Clarify and differentiate between the client's current irrational fear and past emotional pain.

41. Encourage the client's sharing of feelings associated with past traumas through active listening, positive regard, and questioning.

18. Commit self to not allowing panic symptoms to take control of life and lead to a consistent avoidance of normal responsibilities. (42)

42. Support the client in following through with work, family, and social activities rather than escaping or avoiding them to focus on panic.

19. Include significant others in facilitating implementation of new anxiety reduction techniques. (43)

43. Enlist the help of the client's support system in implementing anxiety reduction techniques.

20. Return for a follow-up session to track progress, reinforce gains, and problem-solve barriers. (44)

44. Schedule a booster session for the client one to three months after therapy ends.

__. _____   __. _____
    _____   _____
__. _____   __. _____
    _____   _____
__. _____   __. _____
    _____   _____

DIAGNOSTIC SUGGESTIONS

Axis I: 300.01   Panic Disorder Without Agoraphobia
               300.21   Panic Disorder With Agoraphobia
               300.22   Agoraphobia Without History of Panic Disorder

               _____   _____

               _____   _____

PARANOIA

BEHAVIORAL DEFINITIONS

1. Describes fixed persecutory delusions regarding others, their intentions, and possible harm.
2. Demonstrates extreme and consistent distrust of others without sufficient basis.
3. Verbalizes expectations of being exploited or harmed by others.
4. Misinterprets benign events as having a threatening personal significance.
5. Describes auditory or visual hallucinations suggesting harm, threats to safety, or disloyalty.
6. Avoids others out of fear of being hurt or taken advantage of.
7. Is easily offended, with angry, defensive responses.
8. Is resistant to treatment due to irrational persecutory beliefs (e.g., medication is poison, the clinician is an enemy).
9. Has the potential for being violent as a defensive reaction to delusional or hallucinatory content of some person or agency being a threat to self or others.

__. _____

_____

__. _____

_____

__. _____

_____

LONG-TERM GOALS

1. Reestablish and maintain reality-based orientation that is free from bizarre, suspicious thoughts or beliefs.

2. Show more trust in others by speaking positively of them and reporting comfort in socializing.
3. Develop realistic expectations of safety and risks that are related to inter-action with others.
4. Learn coping skills to reduce effects of hallucinations or delusions.
5. Develop trustful relationships at work, at home, and in the community.
6. Reduce the level of vigilance around others.

—. _____
   _____
   _____
—. _____
   _____
   _____
—. _____
   _____

SHORT-TERM OBJECTIVES

1. Describe the history, nature, and extent of paranoid ideation, possible triggers for it, and coping methods. (1, 2, 3, 4, 5)

THERAPEUTIC INTERVENTIONS

1. Request that the client identify his/her history of persecutory hallucinations, delusions, or other paranoid symptoms.

2. Explore the nature and depth of the client's current feelings or ideas of paranoia.

3. Conduct an Antecedent and Coping Interview (ACI) in which emotional and behavioral reactions, coping strategies, and other relevant consequences are assessed for each symptom related to paranoid ideation (see *The Use of Coping Strategies and Self-Regulation in the Treatment of Psychosis* by Tarrier).

4. Arrange for psychological testing to assess the extent and severity of paranoid symptoms.

5. Obtain information about the client's paranoid statements or behaviors from family members,

2. Stabilize the current acute paranoid episode. (6, 7, 8, 9, 10)

     police, guardian, or others who are familiar with the client.

6. Assess the client's immediate ability to maintain reality orientation and to not be a threat to the safety of himself/herself and others.

7. Provide the client with direct, basic instructions and with firm reassurances of his/her safety, confidentiality, and level of control.

8. Refer the client for immediate evaluation by a psychiatrist regarding psychotic symptoms and the need for psychiatric hospitalization.

9. Coordinate voluntary or involuntary psychiatric hospitalization if the client is so out of touch with reality as to pose a threat to himself/herself or others.

10. Arrange for the client to remain in a stable, supervised situation, including crisis adult foster care (AFC) placement or a friend/family member's home at least until the acute psychotic episode is stabilized.

3. Demonstrate a trusting relationship with a clinician by disclosing feelings and beliefs. (11, 12, 13, 14)

11. Provide the client with empathic listening, displaying respect by accepting him/her, despite his/her angry or delusional presentation, but do not confirm the paranoid delusion.

12. Demonstrate a calm demeanor when the client discloses bizarre or antagonistic beliefs, to decrease his/her fear of rejection.

13. Reflect that the client's presentation, posture, and facial expression indicate intense emotion; show empathy for the client who is experiencing significant distress.

4. Cooperate with a physician's evaluation for medical or organic causes of paranoia. (15, 16, 17)

14. Ask the client open-ended questions about some of his/her delusions or paranoid beliefs; refrain from arguing with the client about the validity of his/her beliefs.

15. Refer the client for a complete physical evaluation to rule out or treat medical or organic causes for the client's paranoia.

16. Refer the client for an assessment of sensory loss (e.g., vision or hearing).

17. Coordinate the client's follow-up on evaluation concerns, such as prescriptions, lab work, or specialized assessments.

5. Comply with a neuropsychological assessment to rule out organic etiology as a basis for paranoid ideation. (18)

18. Refer the client for a neuropsychological assessment to rule out cognitive disorders such as dementia as the cause for paranoia.

6. Describe the frequency and amount of alcohol or street drug use. (19)

19. Assess the client's nature and degree of substance use and the effect that this may have on his/her reality orientation and paranoia.

7. Consent to treatment for substance abuse. (20)

20. Refer or treat the client for substance abuse (see the Chemical Dependence chapter in this *Planner*).

▽ 8. Agree to participate in a medication treatment for paranoid thinking. (21)

21. Gently work to help the client understand that his/her delusional persecutory beliefs are based in a mental illness, not in reality; educate the client about the potential benefit of medication treatment for his/her mental illness. ▽

▽ 9. Cooperate with a referral to a psychiatrist for an evaluation and

22. Refer the client to a physician or a psychiatrist for an evaluation of

---

▽ indicates that the Objective/Intervention is consistent with those found in evidence-based treatments.

take medication as prescribed. (22, 23, 24)

the need for psychiatric medication; facilitate the prescription being filled. ▽

23. Educate the client about the use and expected benefits of the medication; take time to assure the client of the medication's level of safety. ▽

24. Monitor the client's medication compliance and its effectiveness. ▽

▽ 10. Report on the side effects and effectiveness of the medications. (25, 26)

25. Arrange for direct, supervised administration of the medication and the use of liquid forms of medication to ensure regular adherence to the medication regimen. ▽

26. Review the side effects of the medications with the client and the medical staff to identify possible tardive dyskinesia or other negative side effects. ▽

▽ 11. Report a decrease in tardive dyskinesia symptoms. (27, 28)

27. Advocate with a physician/ psychiatrist for an adjustment in the medications to reduce or to eliminate tardive dyskinesia. ▽

28. Arrange for a regular assessment of the client's tardive symptoms, using the client, the staff, or a personal observation and/or an objective measurement scale (e.g., the *Abnormal Involuntary Movement Scale [AIMS]*). ▽

▽ 12. Verbalize a willingness to participate in a therapy exploring paranoid thinking. (29, 30)

29. Refer or provide cognitive behavioral therapy to the client involving education, skills training, cognitive restructuring, and behavioral experiments (see *Treating Complex Cases* by Tarrier, Wells, and Haddock). ▽

30. Teach the client how cognitive restructuring and behavioral experiments are used as a means to reality-test delusional thoughts,

decrease fears, develop personal skills, and build confidence. ▽

▽ 13. Identify and challenge delusional beliefs and generate reality-based alternatives. (31, 32)

31. Explore the client's schema and self-talk that mediate his/her paranoid thoughts, help him/her challenge the biases; assist him/her in generating alternative appraisals that correct for the biases and that are testable predictions. ▽

32. Assign the client a homework exercise (e.g., "Check Suspicions Against Reality" in *Adult Psychotherapy Homework Planner*, 2nd ed. by Jongsma) in which he/she identifies a few biased beliefs and creates reality-based alternatives; review and reinforce success, providing corrective feedback toward improving this skill. ▽

▽ 14. Participate in exercises designed to test predictions made regarding paranoid beliefs both within therapy sessions and outside them. (33, 34)

33. Identify activities the client could engage in to test his/her paranoid predictions against reality-based alternatives. ▽

34. Select initial behavioral experiments that have a high likelihood of being a successful experience for the client; do cognitive restructuring within and after the exercise, reinforcing successes and problem-solving obstacles. ▽

▽ 15. Learn and implement calming and coping strategies to manage anxiety during times when beliefs may be challenged or tested. (35)

35. Teach the client relaxation and calming skills (e.g., attentional focusing skills, muscular relaxation, evenly paced diaphragmatic breathing) to manage anxiety symptoms. ▽

▽ 16. Learn and implement social skills to reduce anxiety and build confidence in social interactions. (36, 37, 38, 39, 40)

36. Use instruction, modeling, and role-playing to build the client's general social and/or communication skills, as needed. ▽

37. Assign the client to read about general social and/or communication skills in books or treatment manuals on building social skills (e.g., *Your Perfect Right* by Alberti and Emmons; *Conversationally Speaking* by Garner). ▽

38. Coordinate the client's gradual involvement in community activities, volunteering, and other externally focused activities. ▽

39. Encourage the client to increase his/her involvement in social relationships; reinforce the client's attempts in this area. ▽

40. Attend social/recreational events with the client, allowing him/her to have control over the level of contact or support from the clinician during the outing (see the Social Skills Deficits or Recreational Deficits chapters in this *Planner*). ▽

▽ 17. Family, friends, and caregivers respond calmly and firmly to the client's psychotic behaviors. (41, 42)

41. Educate the client's family, friends, and caregivers about the symptoms of mental illness, emphasizing the nonvolitional aspects of the symptoms. ▽

42. Utilize modeling and role-playing to teach the family, friends, and caregivers how to give calm, assertive responses to paranoid behaviors, cautioning against challenging too vigorously, and supporting reality-based beliefs. ▽

▽ 18. Report a decrease in the stress level as a contributing factor to paranoid ideation. (43, 44, 45)

43. Probe for recent and future stressors that may trigger a psychotic episode; explore the feelings surrounding the stressor that triggered the psychotic episode. ▽

44. Teach or refer the client for training in stress management skills, such as utilizing assertiveness, problem-

solving, and relaxation-inducing techniques (see the Social Skills Deficits chapter in this *Planner*). ▽

45. Assist the client in reducing threat in the environment (e.g., finding a safer place to live, arranging for regular visits from the caseworker, arranging for family members to call more frequently). ▽

▽ 19. Attend a support group for individuals with severe and persistent mental illness. (46)

46. Refer the client to a support group for individuals with severe and persistent mental illness. ▽

___. _____   ___. _____
_____   _____
___. _____   ___. _____
_____   _____
___. _____   ___. _____
_____   _____

DIAGNOSTIC SUGGESTIONS

Axis I:	295.30	Schizophrenia, Paranoid Type
	295.70	Schizoaffective Disorder
	296.xx	Bipolar I Disorder
	296.89	Bipolar II Disorder
	298.9	Psychotic Disorder NOS
	300.01	Panic Disorder Without Agoraphobia
	300.21	Panic Disorder With Agoraphobia
	300.3	Obsessive-Compulsive Disorder
	309.81	Posttraumatic Stress Disorder
	_____	_____
	_____	_____
Axis II:	301.0	Paranoid Personality Disorder
	301.22	Schizotypal Personality Disorder
	_____	_____
	_____	_____

PARENTING

BEHAVIORAL DEFINITIONS

1. Severe and persistent mental illness symptoms affect interactions with the child.
2. Loss of custody of the child due to safety concerns or inability to care for the child.
3. Lacks interest in the child's activities.
4. Has difficulty coping with the day-to-day stressors of parenting.
5. Disagrees with spouse or significant other regarding child-rearing practices.
6. Interference by the extended family due to concerns about the child's welfare.
7. The child takes advantage of the parent's ineffectiveness, which is related to severe and persistent mental illness symptoms.
8. The child experiences shame, embarrassment, or confusion due to the parent's mental illness symptoms.

—. _____
_____
_____
—. _____
_____
_____
—. _____
_____

LONG-TERM GOALS

1. Decrease the intensity, the frequency, and the duration of severe and persistent mental illness symptoms and their impact on parenting responsibilities.
2. Obtain the least restrictive, but safe and healthy, custody arrangement for the child.
3. Increase interest and involvement in the day-to-day activities of the child.

4. Develop the skills that are needed to cope with the natural stressors of parenting.
5. Negotiate an agreement with the spouse regarding the implementation of joint parenting strategies.
6. Develop a supportive connection with the extended family as an aid to parenting.
7. Child accepts and expresses his/her feelings about the parent's mental illness.

—. _____

_____

—. _____

_____

—. _____

_____

SHORT-TERM OBJECTIVE

THERAPEUTIC INTERVENTIONS

1. Describe the history of parenting conflicts. (1, 2, 3)

1. Explore the client's history of parenting concerns.

2. Develop a genogram or family tree to graphically display the various patterns and relationships within the family.

3. Develop a time line of important events regarding parenting (e.g., births, relationships beginning or ending, loss or return of custody/ visitation). Compare these events with milestones that are related to the illness (e.g., onset of symptoms, hospitalizations). Process with the client.

2. Describe the current challenges and successes regarding parenting. (4, 5)

4. Ask the client (and his/her partner) to review current concerns and successes regarding parenting, including the child's challenging behaviors, the approach taken with the child, and legal concerns (e.g., custody/ visitation issues or Children's Protective Services involvement).

3. Verbalize an understanding of the connection between the mental illness symptoms and the struggles of parenting. (6, 7, 8)

5. Refer the client for psychological testing to evaluate his/her ability to bond emotionally with the child with appropriate boundaries.

6. Educate the client (and his/her family/support system) about the symptoms of his/her mental illness by describing the specific disorder(s) and symptoms. Answer questions that the client and his/her family may have.

7. Refer the client and his/her family to books that provide information regarding the etiology, symptoms, and treatment of severe and persistent mental illness (e.g., *Schizophrenia: The Facts* by Tsuang and Faraone; or *Bipolar Disorder: A Guide for Patients and Families* by Mondimore).

8. Discuss the client's personal experience of severe and persistent mental illness symptoms and how these have affected his/her ability to parent effectively.

4. Cooperate with a physician evaluation for psychotropic medication. (9)

9. Arrange for an evaluation by a physician for a prescription for psychotropic medication.

5. Report a decrease in mental illness symptoms through the regular use of psychotropic medications. (10, 11)

10. Educate the client about and monitor the use and expected benefits of the medication.

11. Assist in obtaining day care for the client's children during his/her appointments for mental illness treatment.

6. Report the side effects and effectiveness of the medications to the appropriate professional. (12)

12. Review the side effects of the medications with the client and the medical staff to identify possible side effects or the confounding influence of polypharmacy.

7. Attend classes that are focused on teaching effective parenting techniques. (13)

8. Implement new skills for parenting. (14, 15)

13. Refer the client to a parenting class.

14. Assign the client readings from books that provide guidance on effective parenting methods (e.g., *1-2-3 Magic: Effective Discipline for Children 2–12,* 2nd ed. by Phelan, *Parenting Teens with Love and Logic: Preparing Adolescents for Responsible Adulthood* by Cline and Fay, or *Positive Parenting From A to Z* by Joslin).

15. Use role-playing, modeling, and behavioral rehearsal to help the client practice implementation of the client's most important parenting skills.

9. Develop and implement a mutually agreeable plan for parenting with the partner. (16, 17)

16. Coordinate a conjoint session with the client's spouse/significant other to develop mutually acceptable plans for parenting of the child. Focus this meeting on the types of approaches to be used with the child.

17. Define intervals with the client at which to review the parenting plan that has been developed.

10. Identify the impact of the mental illness symptoms on parenting interactions with the child. (18, 19)

18. Explore with the client (and his/her significant other) those areas in which the client's mental illness symptoms may affect interactions with the child (e.g., transporting the child when manic, or meeting with the child's teacher when paranoia is not well controlled). Confront the client's denial of mental illness symptoms.

19. Assist the client (and his/her significant other) in developing contingency plans for areas in which the client's mental illness

symptoms may affect interactions with the child (e.g., the partner confiscates the car keys when he/she believes that the client is becoming manic).

11. Develop relief plans for stressful parenting situations or for periods of increased symptomology. (20, 21, 22)

20. Direct the client (and his/her significant other) to develop a listing of family members and other individuals who can provide short-term supervision to the client's child when the client is feeling overwhelmed by his/her parenting responsibilities.

21. Enlist the assistance of the extended family in providing long-term supervision and parenting to the child during acute phases of the client's mental illness.

22. Coordinate access to funds that are available for respite services to provide the client with short- or long-term periods of relief from the additional stress of parenting, or to spend time alone with one child.

12. Identify specific ways of displaying an increased interest in the child's needs and activities. (23)

23. Suggest to the client that he/she set specific times to spend alone with each child. Encourage the client to treat this as a priority while still being flexible enough to reschedule if his/her mental illness symptoms are more acute.

13. Implement relaxation techniques and other stress relievers to decrease the normal strain of parenting and homemaking. (24, 25)

24. Teach the client deep muscle relaxation and deep breathing techniques (e.g., see *The Relaxation and Stress Reduction Workbook*, 6th ed. by Davis, Eshelman, and McKay).

25. Help the client brainstorm diversionary activities (e.g., going for a walk, calling a friend, a hobby) that can relieve parenting stress.

14. Child verbalizes an increased understanding of the parent's

26. Coordinate individual and conjoint sessions for the child to ask

mental illness.
(26, 27, 28)

       questions that are related to the client's mental illness symptoms. Respond to the child's questions at an age-appropriate level.

27. Provide the child with age-appropriate written information about his/her parent's mental illness (e.g., *When Parents Have Problems: A Book for Teens and Older Children with an Abusive, Alcoholic, or Mentally Ill Parent* by Miller).

28. Coach the client about how to discuss his/her mental illness concerns in a manner in which the child can understand.

15. Child expresses feelings about and accepts the parent's mental illness, without rejection of the parent. (28, 29, 30)

28. Coach the client about how to discuss his/her mental illness concerns in a manner in which the child can understand.

29. Explore with the child his/her feelings that are associated with the client's mental illness; explore those times when the symptoms have had a painful impact on the child's life.

30. Reinforce the need for the client to accept, without judgment, the feelings that the child experiences; reassure the client that these feelings are not a personal attack.

16. Child attends an age-appropriate support group for family members of an individual with a severe mental illness. (31)

31. Refer the child to either a multi-family support group or an age-appropriate support group for family members of an individual with a mental illness.

17. Child identifies accommodations that he/she can make that are due to the parent's mental illness. (32)

32. Assist the client and the child in identifying mild accommodations that can be made to increase functioning in the relationship (e.g., the adolescent will get ready for school

on his/her own when the client's sleep pattern is erratic).

18. Child identifies healthy ways of reacting to peer teasing regarding the parent's mental illness. (33)

33. Brainstorm with the client's child about how to respond to teasing or other interference from peers that is relative to the parent's mental illness symptoms (e.g., ignoring teasing, report problems to an adult).

19. Identify decompensation signs, which indicate an inability to parent effectively. (34, 35)

34. Enlist the client's assistance in developing a description of the level of decompensation at which he/she would see himself/herself as temporarily unable to function as a parent.

35. Assist the client in understanding the general guidelines under which the court or Children's Protective Services unit will operate (whether he/she agrees or disagrees with these guidelines).

20. Obtain the least restrictive custody and visitation arrangement while considering the child's safety and emotional needs. (36, 37)

36. Assist the client in understanding and working through the multiple, intricate steps that occur during a custody or protective services case. Attend hearings as is necessary to provide emotional support to the client.

37. Refer the client to an attorney as is necessary.

21. Develop a working relationship with the estranged former partner/parent of the child. (38, 39)

38. Explore the degree of cooperative parenting that occurs with the client's former spouse; emphasize the need for this relationship to be a "working" relationship, focusing on the mutual job of raising the child. Friendship or other emotional needs should be sought elsewhere if this confounds working together in the best interests of the children.

39. With a proper release of information, keep the estranged spouse informed of the client's general level of functioning, as it relates to his/her ability to care for the child.

22. Make and implement decisions regarding whether to voluntarily give up full or partial custody of the child. (40, 41, 42)

40. Discourage the client from making any long-term, major life decisions during an acute phase of his/her illness.

41. Help the client identify the pros and cons of giving up custody. Be sure not to endorse one choice or another, but listen empathically as the client talks about issues in this area. Acknowledge the severe pain that making this decision may evoke.

42. Refer the client for grief counseling if he/she should decide to give up custody of the child.

23. Make informed decisions about having children. (43)

43. Focus the client and his/her intimate partner onto the pros and cons of the choice to have children.

__. _____   __. _____
   _____   _____
__. _____   __. _____
   _____   _____
__. _____   __. _____
   _____   _____

DIAGNOSTIC SUGGESTIONS

Axis I:	297.1	Delusional Disorder
	295.xx	Schizophrenia
	295.10	Schizophrenia, Disorganized Type
	295.30	Schizophrenia, Paranoid Type
	295.90	Schizophrenia, Undifferentiated Type

295.60	Schizophrenia, Residual Type
295.70	Schizoaffective Disorder
296.xx	Bipolar I Disorder
296.89	Bipolar II Disorder
V61.21	Physical Abuse or Neglect of a Child
V61.20	Parent-Child Relational Problem
_____	_____
_____	_____

POSTTRAUMATIC STRESS
DISORDER (PTSD)

BEHAVIORAL DEFINITIONS

1. Exposure to actual or threatened death or serious injury that resulted in an intense emotional response of fear, helplessness, or horror.
2. Intrusive, distressing thoughts or images that recall the traumatic event.
3. Disturbing dreams associated with the traumatic event.
4. A sense that the event is reoccurring, as in illusions or flashbacks.
5. Intense distress when exposed to reminders of the traumatic event.
6. Physiological reactivity when exposed to internal or external cues that symbolize the traumatic event.
7. Avoidance of thoughts, feelings, or conversations about the traumatic event.
8. Avoidance of activity, places, or people associated with the traumatic event.
9. Inability to recall some important aspect of the traumatic event.
10. Lack of interest and participation in significant activities.
11. A sense of detachment from others.
12. Inability to experience the full range of emotions, including love.
13. A pessimistic, fatalistic attitude regarding the future.
14. Sleep disturbance.
15. Irritability.
16. Lack of concentration.
17. Hypervigilance.
18. Exaggerated startle response.
19. Sad or guilty affect and other signs of depression.
20. Alcohol and/or drug abuse.
21. Suicidal thoughts.
22. A pattern of interpersonal conflict, especially in intimate relationships.
23. Verbally and/or physically violent threats of behavior.
24. Inability to maintain employment due to supervisor/coworker conflict or anxiety symptoms.
25. Symptoms have been present for more than one month.

___. _____

_____

___. _____

_____

___. _____

_____

LONG-TERM GOALS

1. Reduce the negative impact that the traumatic event has had on many aspects of life and return to the pretrauma level of functioning.
2. Develop and implement effective coping skills to carry out normal responsibilities and participate constructively in relationships.
3. Recall the traumatic event without becoming overwhelmed with negative thoughts, feelings, or urges.
4. Terminate the destructive behaviors that serve to maintain escape and denial while implementing behaviors that promote healing, acceptance of the past events, and responsible living.

___. _____

_____

___. _____

_____

___. _____

_____

SHORT-TERM OBJECTIVES

1. Describe the history and nature of PTSD symptoms. (1, 2)

THERAPEUTIC INTERVENTIONS

1. Establish rapport with the client toward building a therapeutic alliance.

2. Assess the client's frequency, intensity, duration, and history of PTSD symptoms and their impact on functioning (e.g., *The Anxiety Disorders Interview Schedule for the DSM-IV* by Brown, DiNardo, and Barlow).

2. Complete psychological tests designed to assess and/or track the nature and severity of PTSD symptoms. (3)

3. Administer or refer the client for administration of psychological testing to assess for the presence and strength of PTSD symptoms (e.g., MMPI-2, Impact of Events Scale, PTSD Symptom Scale, or Mississippi Scale for Combat-Related PTSD).

3. Differentiate between symptoms that are related to anxiety versus those that are related to severe and persistent mental illness. (2, 4, 5, 6, 7)

2. Assess the client's frequency, intensity, duration, and history of PTSD symptoms and their impact on functioning (e.g., *The Anxiety Disorders Interview Schedule for the DSM-IV* by Brown, DiNardo, and Barlow).

4. Assess the nature of any stimulus, thoughts, or situations that precipitate the client's specific fears and avoidance.

5. Help the client differentiate symptoms that are a direct effect of his/her severe and persistent mental illness (e.g., a product of delusion), as opposed to a separate diagnosis of an anxiety disorder.

6. Acknowledge that both real and delusional experiences can cause anxiety, providing support to the client.

7. Utilizing a description of PTSD, such as that found in *Overcoming Post-Traumatic Stress Disorder* by Smyth, help the client to identify with recovery from trauma.

4. Describe the traumatic event in as much detail as possible. (8)

8. Gently and sensitively explore the client's recollection of the facts of the traumatic incident(s) and his/her cognitive, behavioral, and emotional reactions at the time.

5. Verbalize the symptoms of depression, including any suicidal ideation. (9)

9. Assess the client's depth of depression and suicide potential and treat appropriately, taking the

necessary safety precautions as indicated (see the Depression and Suicidal Ideation chapters in this *Planner*).

6. Describe the amount, frequency, and history of substance abuse. (10, 11, 12)

10. Gather a complete drug/alcohol use history, including the amount and pattern of use.

11. Request that family, peers, and other treatment staff provide additional information regarding the client's substance use history.

12. Administer the Alcohol Severity Index and process the findings with the client.

7. Verbalize a recognition that mood-altering chemicals were used as the primary coping mechanism to escape from stress or pain, and that their use resulted in negative consequences. (13, 14)

13. Use the biopsychosocial history to help the client understand the familial, emotional, and social factors that contributed to the development of chemical dependence.

14. Refer the client for treatment for chemical dependence (see the Chemical Dependence chapter in this *Planner*).

▼ 8. Cooperate with an evaluation by a physician for psychotropic medication. (15, 16)

15. Assess the client's need for medication (e.g., selective serotonin reuptake inhibitors) and arrange for prescription, if appropriate. ▼

16. Monitor and evaluate the client's psychotropic medication prescription compliance and the effectiveness of the medication on his/her level of functioning. ▼

▼ 9. Verbalize an accurate understanding of PTSD and how it develops. (17, 18)

17. Educate about how PTSD results from exposure to trauma, and results in intrusive recollection, unwarranted fears, anxiety, and a vulnerability to others negative emotions such as shame, anger, and guilt. ▼

18. Assign the client to read psychoeducational chapters of books or

---

▼ indicates that the Objective/Intervention is consistent with those found in evidence-based treatments.

treatment manuals on PTSD that explain its features, development, and treatment (e.g., *Finding Life Beyond Trauma* by Follette and Pistorello). ▽

▽ 10. Verbalize an understanding of the rationale for treatment of PTSD. (18, 19)

18. Assign the client to read psycho-educational chapters of books or treatment manuals on PTSD that explain its features, development, and treatment (e.g., *Finding Life Beyond Trauma* by Follette and Pistorello). ▽

19. Educate about how coping skills, cognitive restructuring and exposure help build confidence, desensitize and overcome fears, and facilitate seeing one's self, others, and the world in a less fearful and/or depressing way. ▽

▽ 11. Learn and implement calming and coping strategies to manage challenging situations related to trauma. (20, 21)

20. Assign the client to read about stress inoculation, cognitive restructuring, and/or exposure-based therapy in chapters of books or treatment manuals on PTSD (e.g., *Overcoming Post-Traumatic Stress Disorder* by Smyth). ▽

21. Teach the client strategies from Stress Inoculation Training such as relaxation, breathing control, covert modeling (e.g., imagining the successful use of the strategies), and/or role-playing (e.g., with therapist or trusted other) for managing fears until a sense of mastery is evident (see *Clinical Handbook/ Practical Therapist Manual for Assessing and Treating Adults with PTSD* by Meichenbaum). ▽

▽ 12. Acknowledge the need to implement anger control techniques; learn and implement

22. Assess the client for instances of poor anger management that have led to threats or actual

anger management techniques. (22, 23)

violence that caused damage to property and/or injury to people. ▽

23. Teach the client anger management techniques (see the Anger Management chapter in this *Planner*). ▽

▽ 13. Implement a regular exercise regimen as a stress release technique. (24, 25)

24. Develop and encourage a routine of physical exercise for the client. ▽

25. Recommend that the client read and implement programs from *Exercising Your Way to Better Mental Health* (Leith). ▽

▽ 14. Sleep without being disturbed by dreams of the trauma. (26)

26. Monitor the client's sleep pattern and encourage use of relaxation, positive imagery, and sleep hygiene as aids to sleep. ▽

▽ 15. Identify, challenge, and replace biased, fearful self-talk with reality-based, positive self-talk. (27, 28, 29)

27. Explore the client's schema and self-talk that mediate his/her trauma-related fears; identify and challenge biases; assist him/her in generating appraisals that correct for the biases and build confidence. ▽

28. Assign the client to read about cognitive restructuring and exposure therapy in books or treatment manuals on PTSD anxiety (e.g., *Overcoming Post-Traumatic Stress Disorder* by Smyth). ▽

29. Assign the client a homework exercise in which he/she identifies fearful self-talk and creates reality-based alternatives; review and reinforce success, providing corrective feedback for failure (e.g., *Overcoming Post-Traumatic Stress Disorder* by Smyth). ▽

▽ 16. Participate in imaginal and *in vivo* exposure to trauma-related memories until talking or thinking about the trauma does not cause marked distress. (30, 31, 32, 33)

30. Direct and assist the client in constructing a hierarchy of feared and avoided trauma-related stimuli. ▽

31. Assign the client a homework exercise in which he/she does an exposure exercise and records responses (see *Overcoming Post-Traumatic Stress Disorder* by Smyth; or *Posttraumatic Stress Disorder* by Resick and Calhoun); review and reinforce progress, problem-solve obstacles. ▽

32. Have the client undergo imaginal exposure to the trauma by having him/her describe a traumatic experience at an increasing, but client-chosen level of detail; repeat until associated anxiety reduces and stabilizes; record the session; have the client listen to it between sessions (see *Overcoming Post-Traumatic Stress Disorder* by Smyth; or *Posttraumatic Stress Disorder* by Resick and Calhoun); review and reinforce progress, problem-solve obstacles. ▽

33. Assign the client to read about exposure in books or treatment manuals on PTSD (e.g., see *Overcoming Post-Traumatic Stress Disorder* by Smyth or *Reclaiming Your Life After Rape* by Rothbaum and Foa). ▽

▽ 17. Learn and implement "thought-stopping" to manage intrusive unwanted thoughts. (34)

34. Teach the client "thought-stopping" in which he/she internally voices the word STOP and/or imagines something representing the concept of stopping (e.g., a stop sign or light) immediately upon noticing unwanted trauma or otherwise negative unwanted thoughts. ▽

▼ 18. Learn and implement guided self-dialogue to manage thoughts, feelings, and urges brought on by encounters with trauma-related stimuli. (35)

35. Teach the client a guided self-dialogue procedure in which he/she learns to recognize mal-adaptive self-talk, challenges its biases, copes with engendered feelings, overcomes avoidance, and reinforces his/her accomplishments (see *Posttraumatic Stress Disorder* by Resick and Calhoun); review and reinforce progress, problem-solve obstacles. ▼

▼ 19. Cooperate with eye movement desensitization and reprocessing (EMDR) technique to reduce emotional reaction to the traumatic event. (36)

36. Utilize EMDR technique to reduce the client's emotional reactivity to the traumatic event. ▼

▼ 20. Implement relapse prevention strategies for managing possible future trauma-related symptoms. (37, 38, 39, 40)

37. Educate the client about the distinction between a lapse and relapse, associating a lapse with an initial and reversible return of symptoms, fear, or urges to avoid and relapse with the decision to return to fearful and avoidant patterns. ▼

38. Identify and rehearse with the client the management of future situations or circumstances in which lapses could occur. ▼

39. Instruct the client to routinely use strategies learned in therapy (e.g., using cognitive restructuring, social skills, exposure) while building social interactions and relationships. ▼

40. Develop a "coping card" or other reminder on which coping strategies and other important information (e.g., "pace your breathing," "focus on the task at hand," "you can manage it," "it will go away") are recorded for the client's later use. ▼

21. Participate in conjoint and/or family therapy sessions. (41)

41. Conduct family and conjoint sessions to facilitate healing of hurt

22. Participate in group therapy sessions focused on PTSD. (42)

23. Verbalize hopeful and positive statements regarding the future. (43)

42. caused by the client's symptoms of PTSD.

42. Refer the client to or conduct group therapy where the focus is on sharing traumatic events and their effects with other PTSD survivors toward the goal of recovery.

43. Reinforce the client's positive, reality-based cognitive messages that enhance self-confidence and increase adaptive action.

—. _____
   _____
—. _____
   _____
—. _____
   _____

—. _____
   _____
—. _____
   _____
—. _____
   _____

DIAGNOSTIC SUGGESTIONS

Axis I:	309.81	Posttraumatic Stress Disorder
	300.14	Dissociative Identity Disorder
	300.6	Depersonalization Disorder
	300.15	Dissociative Disorder NOS
	995.54	Physical Abuse of Child, Victim
	995.81	Physical Abuse of Adult, Victim
	995.53	Sexual Abuse of Child, Victim
	995.83	Sexual Abuse of Adult, Victim
	308.3	Acute Stress Disorder
	304.80	Polysubstance Dependence
	305.00	Alcohol Abuse
	303.90	Alcohol Dependence
	304.30	Cannabis Dependence
	304.20	Cocaine Dependence
	304.00	Opioid Dependence
	296.xx	Major Depressive Disorder

_____   _____
_____   _____

Axis II: 301.83   Borderline Personality Disorder
                 301.9   Personality Disorder NOS

_____   _____

_____   _____

PSYCHOSIS

BEHAVIORAL DEFINITIONS

1. Verbalizes bizarre content of thought (delusions of grandeur, persecution, reference, influence, control, somatic sensations, or infidelity).
2. Demonstrates abnormal speech patterns including tangential replies, incoherence, perseveration, and moving quickly from subject to subject.
3. Describes perceptual disturbance or hallucinations (auditory, visual, tactile, or olfactory).
4. Exhibits disorganized behavior, such as confusion, severe lack of goal direction, impulsiveness, or repetitive behaviors.
5. Expresses paranoid thoughts and exhibits paranoid reactions, including extreme distrust, fear, and apprehension.
6. Exhibits psychomotor abnormalities such as a marked decrease in reactivity to environment; catatonic patterns such as stupor, rigidity, excitement, posturing, or negativism as well as unusual mannerisms or grimacing.
7. Displays extreme agitation, including a high degree of irritability, anger, unpredictability, or impulsive physical acting out.
8. Exhibits bizarre dress or grooming.
9. Demonstrates disturbed affect (blunted, none, flattened, or inappropriate).
10. Demonstrates relationship withdrawal (withdrawal from involvement with the external world and preoccupation with egocentric ideas and fantasies, feelings of alienation).

—. _____
_____
_____
—. _____
_____
—. _____
_____

LONG-TERM GOALS

1. Control or eliminate active psychotic symptoms so that supervised functioning is positive and medication is taken consistently.
2. Increase goal-directed behaviors.
3. Focus thoughts on reality.
4. Normalize speech patterns, which can be evidenced by coherent statements, attentions to social cues, and remaining on task.
5. Interact with others without defensiveness or anger.

—. _____
_____

—. _____
_____

—. _____
_____

SHORT-TERM OBJECTIVES

THERAPEUTIC INTERVENTIONS

1. Describe the history and the current status of psychotic symptoms. (1, 2, 3, 4, 5)

1. Approach an acutely psychotic client in a calm, confident, open, direct, yet soothing manner (e.g., approach slowly, face toward the client with open body language, speak slowly and clearly).

2. Request that the client identify his/her history of hallucinations, delusions, or other psychotic symptoms.

3. Ask the client about his/her current psychotic symptoms.

4. Coordinate psychological testing to assess the extent and the severity of the client's psychotic symptoms.

5. Request that a family member provide information about the client's history of psychotic behaviors.

2. Cooperate with services focused on stabilizing the current acute psychotic episode. (6, 7, 8, 9)

6. Refer the client for an immediate evaluation by a psychiatrist regarding his/her psychotic symptoms

and a possible prescription for antipsychotic medication. ▽

7. Coordinate voluntary or involuntary psychiatric hospitalization if the client is a threat to himself/herself or others and/or is unable to provide for his/her own basic needs.

8. Arrange for the client to remain in a stable, supervised situation (e.g., crisis adult foster care [AFC] placement or a friend/family member's home).

9. Coordinate mobile crisis response services (e.g., physical exam, psychiatric evaluation, medication access, triage to inpatient care) in the client's home environment (including jail, personal residence, homeless shelter, or street setting).

3. Decrease the suicide risk or the potential thereof. (7, 10, 11)

7. Coordinate voluntary or involuntary psychiatric hospitalization if the client is a threat to himself/herself or others and/or is unable to provide for his/her own basic needs.

10. Perform a suicide assessment and take all necessary precautionary steps, if necessary.

11. Remove potentially hazardous materials, such as firearms or excess medication, if indicated.

4. Obtain immediate, temporary support or supervision from friends, peers, or family members. (8, 12 13)

8. Arrange for the client to remain in a stable, supervised situation (e.g., crisis adult foster care [AFC] placement or a friend's/family member's home).

12. Develop a crisis plan to provide supervision and support to the client on an intensive basis.

13. Coordinate access to round-the-clock, professional consultation (e.g., a 24-hour professionally

staffed crisis line) to caregivers and the client.

5. Reorient self to place and time. (14, 15, 16, 17)

14. Provide both visual and verbal cues to focus on reality (e.g., write the date, time, and place in a clearly visible area).

15. Place a wristband on the client's arm with the date, place, and name.

16. Focus on real events in basic, concrete terms.

17. Reinforce the appropriate focus on reality, gradually returning the client to a less restrictive environment and decreased supervision.

▽ 6. Report a decrease in psychotic symptoms through the consistent use of psychotropic medications. (6, 18, 19, 20)

6. Refer the client for an immediate evaluation by a psychiatrist regarding his/her psychotic symptoms and a possible prescription for antipsychotic medication. ▽

18. Consult with the treating physician regarding sleep-inducing medications to provide the client and the caregivers time to re-group, relative to the current psychotic episode. ▽

19. Educate the client about the use and expected benefits of psychotropic medications. ▽

20. Monitor the client's medication compliance and effectiveness. ▽

▽ 7. Report on the side effects and the effectiveness of the medications. (21, 22)

21. Review the side effects of the medications with both the client and the medical staff to identify the possible confounding influence of polypharmacy. ▽

22. Monitor the client for side effects of long-term use of neuroleptic

---

▽ indicates that the Objective/Intervention is consistent with those found in evidence-based treatments.

medications (e.g., tardive dyskinesia, muscle rigidity, dystonia, metabolic effects such as weight gain). ▽

▽ 8. Family, friends, and caregivers demonstrate techniques to cope with the client's psychotic behaviors. (23, 24, 25)

23. Educate the client's family, friends, and caregivers about the symptoms of mental illness, particularly the nonvolitional aspects of the symptoms and methods for addressing them. ▽

24. Role-play calm, adaptive responses to psychotic behaviors with the client's family, friends, and caregivers; train support persons to provide direct, nonreactive, calm responses to the client's psychotic behaviors rather than arguing about reality. ▽

25. Refer the family to a single- or multigroup family psychoeducational program (see *Multifamily Groups in the Treatment of Severe Psychiatric Disorders* by McFarlane). ▽

▽ 9. Identify and understand the role of internal and environmental triggers of psychotic symptoms. (26, 27)

26. Help the client identify specific behaviors, situations, and feelings that serve as a context for symptom exacerbations. ▽

27. Help the client identify his/her emotional reactions and other consequences of psychotic symptoms toward the goal increasing his/her understanding of factors that may be maintaining symptoms (e.g., withdrawal leading to isolation and loneliness; paranoid accusations leading to negative reactions of others that falsely support the delusion). ▽

▽ 10. Identify current strategies used to cope with symptoms (28)

28. Assess adaptive and maladaptive strategies, including deficit

▼ 11. Learn and implement cognitive behavioral strategies that increase resistance to subsequent psychotic episodes. (29, 30, 31, 32, 33)

strategies, that the client is using to cope with psychotic symptoms. ▼

29. Provide or refer the client to a therapy that tailors cognitive behavioral strategies to help the client learn coping and compensation strategies for managing psychotic symptoms (see *Treating Complex Cases: The Cognitive Behavioral Therapy Approach* by Tarrier, Wells, and Haddock). ▼

30. Desensitize the client's fear of his/her hallucinations by allowing or encouraging him/her to talk about them, their frequency, their intensity, and their meaning (or assign "What Do You Hear and See?" in *Adult Psychotherapy Homework Planner*, 2nd ed. by Jongsma). ▼

31. Use education, modeling, role-play, reinforcement, and other cognitive behavioral strategies to teach the client coping and compensation strategies for managing psychotic symptoms (e.g., calming techniques; attention switching and narrowing; realistic self-talk; realistic attribution of the source of the symptom; and increased adaptive personal and social activity). ▼

32. Teach the client adaptive communication and social skills (see the Social Skills Deficits chapter in this *Planner*). ▼

33. Prescribe in-session and homework assignments that allow the client to practice new skills, reality test and challenge his/her maladaptive beliefs, and consolidate a new approach to managing symptoms; process the exercises in session. ▼

▽ 12. Verbalize an understanding of how personal stress can lead to decompensation, how to identify it, and how to manage it. (34, 35, 36, 37)

34. Help the client identify emotional indicators of stress (e.g., anxiousness, uncertainty, anger), and how they affect his/her symptoms and functioning. ▽

35. Help the client identify physical indicators of stress (e.g., tense muscles, headaches, psychomotor agitation) and how they affect his/her symptoms and functioning. ▽

36. Teach the client stress management strategies such as relaxation, positive self-talk, problem solving, communication skills, and lifestyle management considerations to help manage stress. ▽

37. Refer the client to an activity therapist for stress reduction activities (e.g., exercise programs, hobbies, or social clubs). ▽

▽ 13. Identify the early warning signs of symptom exacerbation and decompensation. (38, 39)

38. Request that the client identify symptoms that indicate that he/she is decompensating (e.g., confused thoughts, hallucinations, delusions, irrational fear, withdrawal). ▽

39. Train the family, friends, and caregivers about the client's list of decompensation indicators so they can take appropriate action to get professional services for the client. ▽

▽ 14. Decrease substance abuse as a precipitating trigger. (40, 41)

40. Encourage the client to discontinue substance use, including drugs, alcohol, nicotine, and caffeine (see the Chemical Dependence chapter in this *Planner*). ▽

41. Refer the client to a substance abuse treatment program. ▽

▽ 15. Caregivers, friends, and family members report reduced stress regarding the client's behavior. (42)

42. Teach problem solving, respite care, and assertiveness skills to assist caregivers in meeting their own

▼ 16. Verbalize the acceptance of mental illness and decreased feelings of stigmatization. (43, 44)

43. Encourage the client to express his/her feelings related to acceptance of the mental illness. ▼

needs when they feel overly stressed by the client's psychosis. ▼

44. Explain the nature of the psychotic process, its biochemical component, and its confusing effect on rational thought. ▼

▼ 17. Attend a support group for others with severe mental illness. (45)

45. Refer the client to a support group for individuals with a mental illness with the goal of helping consolidate his/her new approach to recovery. ▼

—. _____

—. _____

—. _____

_____

—. _____

—. _____

—. _____

_____

DIAGNOSTIC SUGGESTIONS

Axis I:	297.1	Delusional Disorder
	295.xx	Schizophrenia
	295.10	Schizophrenia, Disorganized Type
	295.20	Schizophrenia, Catatonic Type
	295.90	Schizophrenia, Undifferentiated Type
	295.30	Schizophrenia, Paranoid Type
	295.70	Schizoaffective Disorder
	296.xx	Bipolar I Disorder
	296.89	Bipolar II Disorder
	293.xx	Psychotic Disorder Due to . . . *[General Medical Condition]*
	298.9	Psychotic Disorder NOS

_____ _____

_____ _____

RECREATIONAL DEFICITS

BEHAVIORAL DEFINITIONS

1. Lacks involvement in recreational activities.
2. Lacks interest in leisure activities.
3. Has limited knowledge of recreational opportunities due to inexperience.
4. Embarrassment, frustration, or agitation act as a barrier to involvement in recreational activities.
5. Mental illness symptoms disrupt involvement in recreational opportunities.
6. Discrimination due to mental illness symptoms prohibits involvement in community activities.
7. Medication has a negative influence on coordination or other skills that are necessary for some recreational activities (e.g., sports).
8. Lacks invitations to recreational activities due to limited social contacts.
9. Unable to pay for or obtain transportation to recreational activities.

__. _____
   _____
__. _____
   _____
__. _____
   _____

LONG-TERM GOALS

1. Increase involvement in recreational activities.
2. Learn about general recreational opportunities.
3. Gain proficiency in the skills that are necessary for involvement in chosen recreational areas.
4. Decrease the effects of severe and persistent mental illness symptoms on recreational activities.

5. Increase assertiveness about the right to be involved in desired recreational areas.
6. Limit side effects of medications, increasing the ability to be involved in physical activities.
7. Develop social contacts with whom to share recreational activities.
8. Obtain funds, transportation, or other prerequisites for recreational activities.

—. _____

_____

—. _____

_____

—. _____

_____

SHORT-TERM OBJECTIVES

THERAPEUTIC INTERVENTIONS

1. Describe the history of recreational involvement. (1, 2)

1. Request that the client describe his/her history of participation in recreational activities.

2. Develop a graphic display, such as a time line, to show the history of the client's recreational involvement, as well as milestones that are related to severe and persistent mental illness (e.g., onset of symptoms, hospitalizations, beginning of treatment).

2. Identify the scope and nature of the effects of the mental illness symptoms on recreational pursuits. (2, 3, 4, 5)

2. Develop a graphic display, such as a time line, to show the history of the client's recreational involvement, as well as milestones that are related to severe and persistent mental illness (e.g., onset of symptoms, hospitalizations, beginning of treatment).

3. Educate the client on the symptoms of his/her mental illness, through informal question-and-answer sessions, or through referral to texts such as _Schizophrenia: The Facts_ by Tsuang and Faraone or _Bipolar_

Disorder: A Guide for Patients and Families by Mondimore.

4. Help the client make the connection between mental illness symptoms and social/recreational problems (e.g., paranoia prohibits involvement in group activities, mania confuses or puts others off).

5. Help the client identify the recreation areas in which he/she has had little experience due to severe and persistent mental illness symptoms.

3. Cooperate with a referral to a physician for a psychotropic medication evaluation. (6)

6. Refer the client for an evaluation by a physician regarding the need for psychotropic medications.

4. Report a decrease in the effects of the mental illness symptoms through the regular use of psychotropic medications. (6, 7, 8)

6. Refer the client for an evaluation by a physician regarding the need for psychotropic medications.

7. Educate the client about the use and the expected benefits of the medication.

8. Monitor the client's medication compliance, effectiveness, and side effects.

5. Report the side effects and effectiveness of the medications to the appropriate professional. (7, 8, 9)

7. Educate the client about the use and the expected benefits of the medication.

8. Monitor the client's medication compliance, effectiveness, and side effects.

9. Acknowledge the manner in which the side effects of the medications may inhibit the client's involvement in some recreational activities (e.g., slowed reaction time decreases motor dexterity); confer with the prescribing physician regarding a possible change in the client's medication regimen.

6. Identify past and current preferences for leisure activities. (10)

10. Refer the client to an activity or recreational therapist for an

assessment of his/her current interests and abilities that are relative to leisure interests.

7. Sample a wide range of leisure activities by participating in a variety of recreational activities. (10, 11, 12)

10. Refer the client to an activity or recreational therapist for an assessment of his/her current interests and abilities that are relative to leisure interests.

11. Contract with the client to pursue a short-term involvement with a variety of activities; emphasize the need to explore several different areas to develop interests.

12. Develop a schedule of activities that samples a broad range of types of activities, settings, length of time, level of involvement, cultural needs, and social contact.

8. Identify preferences for new recreational activities that have been explored. (13)

13. Review the sampling of activities on a regular basis, inquiring about the client's preferences.

9. Identify the emotional barriers to increased involvement in leisure activities. (14, 15)

14. Explore the client's reactions to difficult social experiences in the past; help the client to identify specific emotions.

15. Acknowledge the emotions that may be limiting the client's willingness to be involved in new activities, including fear, embarrassment, or uncertainty.

10. List social/recreational activities that are available within the community. (16, 17)

16. Request that the client develop an inventory of activities that are available in the community. Request that he/she review information from the local newspaper, telephone book, or magazines.

17. Obtain additional resources for the client to review regarding the recreational activities that are available in the community (e.g., brochures from a local tourism board, current events calendars).

11. Obtain financial resources for recreational activities. (18, 19)

18. Assist the client in developing a regular source of income (see the Financial Needs and Employment Problems chapters in this *Planner*).

19. Facilitate the client's access to funds from the agency or from community organizations for assisting people with disabilities; seek out recreational businesses in the community for sponsorship of the client's involvement in recreational activities (e.g., free tickets or supplies).

12. Increase access to remote recreational activities through the use of transportation that is provided by others. (20)

20. Coordinate the use of public transportation or ride sharing with other clients or community members who are attending recreational events.

13. Demonstrate new skills that are useful for participation in recreational activities. (21, 22, 23)

21. Provide a leisure educator or a recreational therapist to teach the client the basic technical skills for participating in leisure activities.

22. Provide the client with access to online services as a way to have increased social contact in a safer setting.

23. Incorporate cooking and meal preparation as a portion of the recreational skills training as an added incentive for the completion of each training session.

14. Attend a support group for individuals with severe and persistent mental illness. (24)

24. Refer the client to a support group for people with severe and persistent mental illness.

15. Implement newly learned social skills that are necessary for recreational involvement with others. (24, 25, 26)

24. Refer the client to a support group for people with severe and persistent mental illness.

25. Refer the client to individual therapy to help him/her learn social skills.

26. Utilize role-playing, behavioral rehearsal, modeling, and role reversal techniques to help the client

understand the use of social skills (e.g., assertiveness, clear communication, handling anger).

16. Caregivers use incidental learning techniques to teach the client social skills. (27)

27. Train the caregivers/staff in the use of incidental learning techniques (e.g., teaching the client social and recreational skills during the course of everyday activities); monitor and reinforce the caregivers' use of incidental learning.

17. Initiate recreational activities during free time. (28, 29)

28. Provide the client with a listing of recreational activities in which he/she has indicated some interest; urge the client to utilize this listing to initiate activity during free times.

29. Provide the client and the caretakers with a chart to monitor and track the involvement that the client has had in various activities. Verbally reinforce the client's involvement in recreational activities.

18. Report feeling more comfortable in new social or recreational activities. (30, 31)

30. Attend recreational activities with the client to provide encouragement and support; allow the client to be in charge of the level of involvement that the clinician maintains.

31. Solicit volunteers from the client's family and peers to attend recreational activities with him/her.

19. Increase the frequency of engagement in activities involving physical exercise and fitness. (32, 33)

32. Refer the client to a physician for a complete physical examination to determine the client's ability to participate in physical activities.

33. Coordinate the client's physical exercise involvement with others who have similar interests, including the nondisabled population, as well as others with severe and persistent mental illness.

20. Increase involvement in social relationships. (34, 35)

34. With the proper release of information, provide information to nondisabled peers about how to best

cope with their friend's severe and persistent mental illness symptoms.

35. Review periodically with the client the successes and difficulties that he/she has experienced in social settings.

21. Utilize relaxation techniques to manage stress while engaged in social/recreational activities. (36)

36. Teach the client relaxation techniques to be used in social situations to reduce stress (e.g., see *The Relaxation and Stress Reduction Workbook,* 6th ed. by Davis, Eshelman, and McKay).

22. Gain freedom from other responsibilities to enjoy recreational activities. (37, 38)

37. Coordinate the provision of respite services to the client who has responsibility for children or other dependent individuals.

38. Incorporate a recreational component into the client's day programming or supported employment program.

23. List the supportive resources that can be called on if abuse or discrimination occurs as social horizons expand. (39)

39. Review the possible situations in which an individual with severe and persistent mental illness might be manipulated or abused. Remind the client of the support system that he/she has and should use if he/she is uncertain about treatment from others.

24. Develop recreational habits that are not associated with substance use or abuse. (40)

40. Emphasize to the client the need for developing social and recreational activities that are not related to the use of mood-altering substances.

__. _____   __. _____
   _____   _____
__. _____   __. _____
   _____   _____
__. _____   __. _____
   _____   _____

DIAGNOSTIC SUGGESTIONS

Axis I:

297.1	Delusional Disorder
295.xx	Schizophrenia
295.10	Schizophrenia, Disorganized Type
295.30	Schizophrenia, Paranoid Type
295.90	Schizophrenia, Undifferentiated Type
295.60	Schizophrenia, Residual Type
295.70	Schizoaffective Disorder
296.3x	Major Depressive Disorder, Recurrent
296.xx	Bipolar I Disorder
296.89	Bipolar II Disorder

_____   _____

_____   _____

Axis II:

301.0	Paranoid Personality Disorder
301.22	Schizotypal Personality Disorder
301.83	Borderline Personality Disorder
301.82	Avoidant Personality Disorder

_____   _____

_____   _____

SELF-DETERMINATION DEFICITS

BEHAVIORAL DEFINITIONS

1. Lacks choice in daily life, school, residence, or vocation.
2. Has limited experience with making decisions.
3. Plans poorly for the near and the distant future, which results in difficult transitions.
4. Responsibilities and opportunities have decreased due to mental impairments.
5. Agencies have been dictating the options/services that are available, limiting the freedom of choice.
6. Lacks skills necessary for living independently.
7. Vocational and/or residential placement have failed due to a lack of appropriate decision-making skills and an inability to adjust to changing situations.
8. Lacks assertiveness, decision-making, and problem-solving skills resulting from caregivers overprotecting the client.
9. Treatment agency structure sets up barriers to the choice of services and providers.
10. Client, family, caregivers, and clinicians lack the knowledge or the training in the concepts of self-determination.

—. _____

_____

—. _____

_____

—. _____

_____

LONG-TERM GOALS

1. Maximize available choices in all aspects of life.
2. Advocate assertively for own needs and preferences.
3. Increase understanding and identification of own needs and preferences.
4. Develop planning and goal-setting skills.
5. Caregivers consistently encourage and reinforce all of the client's movement toward his/her own decision making.
6. Gain access to integrated employment, social, and community opportunities.
7. Treatment agency revises structure to enhance the client's attempts to become more independent.

—. _____

_____

—. _____

_____

—. _____

_____

SHORT-TERM OBJECTIVES

1. Client, caregivers, and family verbalize an understanding of the process and spirit of person-centered planning and self-determination. (1, 2, 3, 4)

THERAPEUTIC INTERVENTIONS

1. Assess the client's understanding of self-determination or person-centered planning ideas.

2. Help the client and caregivers identify examples of self-determination in their own lives as well as in others'; provide personal examples of how the clinician experiences self-determination.

3. Invite the client and his/her family and caregivers to agency trainings on person-centered planning and self-determination.

4. Encourage the client and his/her family and caregivers to discuss the use of self-determination principles relative to the client's treatment, dreams, and desires.

2. Participate in an assessment of the skills that will facilitate self-determination. (5)

3. Develop a plan for a person-centered planning meeting. (6, 7, 8, 9)

5. Assess the client's strengths and weaknesses in self-determination (e.g., autonomy, self-regulation, psychological empowerment, self-realization); share the findings from the client's self-determination assessment, emphasizing his/her strengths and using the results to promote his/her involvement in planning future goals with the support of his/her family.

6. Facilitate the client developing an agenda for a person-centered planning meeting (e.g., what goals the client would like to achieve); provide the client with some examples of possible goals, but pursue his/her input.

7. Assist the client in inviting all of the individuals whom he/she would like to be present during the person-centered planning meeting (e.g., clinicians, family members, peers, advocates, friends); allow the client to choose the members, as well as how they are invited or exempted, and where the meeting is held; review the implications of not inviting a specific individual.

8. Request the client to choose a facilitator for his/her person-centered planning meeting; emphasize that this does not have to be a clinical person.

9. Allow the client to identify "off-limits" topics (i.e., topics that he/she does not wish to be brought up at the person-centered planning meeting). Prompt the client to identify a setting in which he/she would be willing to discuss those topics.

4. Prepare for the person-centered planning meeting by clarifying own goals and barriers to those goals. (10, 11, 12)

10. Assist the client in articulating his/her current daily life, relationships, personal history, preferences, dreams, hopes and fears, community choices, and issues that are related to home, career, and health.

11. Request that the client identify barriers that interfere with his/her stated desires; assist the client in identifying the kinds of support that are needed to attain future goals and dreams.

12. Request that the client identify areas in which he/she would like to experience improvement (e.g., living situation, work setting, relationships).

5. Participate in a person-centered planning meeting. (13, 14)

13. Facilitator or client call the person-centered planning meeting to order, focusing the participants on the client and his/her desires and needs; participants should direct their comments to the client, rather than the clinician or the facilitator.

14. Ask the client to answer first, then the rest of the participants, in posing questions such as "Who is __?", "What are __'s strengths and problems?", "What supports, accommodations, or barriers exist?" and/or "What shall we put in the action plan for goals/objectives?"

6. Identify short- and long-term hopes, dreams, and desires. (15, 16)

15. Assist the client in making a list of his/her short- and long-term goals. Request that the client identify his/her favorite three; ensure that continuity exists between short-term and long-term goals and that those goals are objectively observable and obtainable in a reasonable amount of time.

16. Assist the client in identifying and creating conditions that will facilitate the realization of his/her goals and desires (e.g., expand and deepen friendships, increase community participation, exercise more control and choice in life, and develop competencies); identify creative solutions for breaking the existing barriers to identified goals.

7. Increase involvement in chosen recreational, social, employment, financial, and residential activities. (17, 18)

17. Explore the client's desires to participate in a wide range of possible activities (e.g., social contacts, independent living, volunteer or work placement, service groups, church, or recreational events) that promote community integration and the development of self-determination skills.

18. Arrange for all significant people in the client's life (e.g., family, advocates, community members, staff, agency personnel) to brainstorm creative options for expansion of the client's personal choices and to commit to assisting the client in attaining the identified goals.

8. Demonstrate the ability to make choices that are safe, responsible, informed, and not harmful to self or others. (17, 19, 20)

17. Explore the client's desires to participate in a wide range of possible activities (e.g., social contacts, independent living, volunteer or work placement, service groups, church, or recreational events) that promote community integration and the development of self-determination skills.

19. Assess the client's potential for making adverse choices; help the client understand the risk of the choices that may result in physical and/or mental harm.

20. Weigh the assessed risk-of-harm level against the client's right to make his/her own choices; factor in the likelihood of short- or long-term harm, physical or psychological harm, direct or indirect harm, and predictable or unpredictable harm to himself/herself or others to obtain a reasonable degree of freedom of choice (e.g., total independence with unrestricted choice or limited independence with restricted options).

9. Choose service providers based on own preferences, needs, and financial resources. (21, 22, 23)

21. Remind the client (or guardian) that he/she has a choice about the services provided, who provides them, and where he/she receives these services.

22. Develop a listing or a network of providers for the client (or guardian) to choose from, which may include the clinician's own services.

23. Provide the client with the cost of each individual service/provider who is available and appropriate for meeting his/her needs; allow the client (or guardian) to choose whatever services and providers that they see fit within their financial resources.

10. Service providers verbalize a recognition that the client has a choice of providers and must be given respectful, service-oriented treatment. (24)

24. Focus the service providers on the need to provide customer service, and emphasize that the client has a choice of providers available (help the provider adopt a "We need them!" philosophy, rather than "They need us.").

11. Advocate for self, representing own best interest and exercising choices. (25, 26, 27)

25. Help the client identify actual examples from his/her life when he/she has used decision-making skills such as gathering information, weighing pros and cons, consulting with others, and so forth.

26. Teach the client techniques for assertive self-advocacy, (e.g., see *The Self-Advocacy Manual for Consumers* by the Michigan Protection and Advocacy Service, Inc.; or *The Self-Advocacy Workbook* by Gardner); promote self-advocacy and leadership by providing practice opportunities whenever possible (e.g., with counselors, personal care support personnel, and residential supervisors).

27. Teach the client the difference between passive, assertive, and aggressive behaviors; model assertive, aggressive, and passive responses to the same situation, and request that the client identify the most effective style.

12. Implement problem-solving techniques to resolve daily-life issues. (28)

28. Teach the client problem-solving techniques (e.g., see *Thinking It Through: Teaching a Problem-Solving Strategy for Community Living* by Foxx and Bittle); use role-playing, modeling, and journaling to reinforce these techniques.

13. Express preferences and choices in all aspects of personal life. (26, 29, 30, 31)

26. Teach the client techniques for assertive self-advocacy, (e.g., see *The Self-Advocacy Manual for Consumers* by the Michigan Protection and Advocacy Service, Inc., or *The Self-Advocacy Workbook* by Gardner); promote self-advocacy and leadership by providing practice opportunities whenever possible (e.g., with counselors, personal care support personnel, and residential supervisors).

29. Assess the client's responses to various activities and situations to

better understand his/her preferences (e.g., approach, verbaliza-
tions, gestures, affect).

30. Stress to the family, caregivers,
and support staff that the client
should be provided opportunities
to choose in all areas of his/her
life (e.g., leisure, shopping, meal-
time, lifestyle, employment).

31. Provide many learning opportunities and plan for self-determination
skill generalization by expanding
the range of situations to which the
client responds, and by providing
similarity between learning
stimuli and the client's natural
environment.

14. Review own behavior and assess
whether it is focused on goal
attainment. (32, 33)

32. Review with the client his/her
decisions, and encourage him/her
to evaluate his/her own behavior
to determine if it is compatible
with the identified goals; assist
the client in changing his/her behavior to obtain goals, as needed.

33. Discuss with the client the rein-
forcers that he/she desires, pointing
out that they can be independently
attainable, contingent on the occur-
rence of his/her own predeter-
mined target behaviors.

15. Develop cooperative relationships
with peers, both with and without
mental illness. (34, 35, 36)

34. Teach the client social skills
through didactic presentation and
role-playing (e.g., basic conversational skills, self-assertion, hon-
esty, truthfulness, and how to
handle teasing) (see the Social
Skills Deficits chapter in this
Planner).

35. Arrange for the client to utilize
social skills in situations that
he/she has identified as desirable;
reinforce the client for taking risks
in participating in social situations

with people who have disabilities and with those who do not.

36. With proper authorization to release information, provide feedback to the family and (non-mentally ill) peers about how best to approach the client and his/her needs (e.g., equality, respect, reciprocity of friendship).

16. Increase participation in community-based opportunities for social, recreation, and vocational activities. (37, 38)

37. Teach the client about the availability, use of, and skills to access community resources (see the Independent Activities of Daily Living [IADL] chapter in this *Planner*).

38. Assist the client in obtaining employment, via a supported employment referral, or assisting with the preparation of a resume, job applications, and so forth (see the Employment Problems chapter in this *Planner*).

17. Family members support and reinforce the client in making his/her own decisions. (39, 40, 41)

39. Assist family members in identifying the specific steps to promote the client's decision making, problem solving, goal setting and attainment, as well as his/her self-awareness and knowledge in the home.

40. Demonstrate to the family the many opportunities throughout the day that the client can use for exerting choices and preferences (e.g., meal choices, schedule for the day, clothing choices); encourage the family to foster independence by helping only when needed, permitting the client to maximize his/her abilities.

41. Emphasize with the family that the freedom to make choices, even harmful ones, is a freedom that most people value; encour-

age the family to allow the client to assume responsibility for his/her own actions and the natural consequences, both positive and negative, that result.

—. _____   —. _____
_____   _____
—. _____   —. _____
_____   _____
—. _____   —. _____
_____   _____

DIAGNOSTIC SUGGESTIONS

Axis I: 297.1   Delusional Disorder
295.xx   Schizophrenia
295.10   Schizophrenia, Disorganized Type
295.20   Schizophrenia, Catatonic Type
295.90   Schizophrenia, Undifferentiated Type
295.30   Schizophrenia, Paranoid Type
295.70   Schizoaffective Disorder
296.xx   Bipolar I Disorder
296.89   Bipolar II Disorder

_____   _____
_____   _____

SEXUALITY CONCERNS

BEHAVIORAL DEFINITIONS

1. Has a history of sexual victimization due to the vulnerability that is caused by severe and persistent mental illness symptoms.
2. Reports bizarre sexual thoughts due to hallucinations, delusions, or other severe and persistent mental illness symptoms.
3. Engages in behavior that is high-risk for sexually transmitted diseases (STDs) due to a lack of understanding about healthy sexual behavior.
4. Engages in impulsive sexual acting out or hypersexuality.
5. Experiences sexual dysfunction due to the side effects of long-term psychotropic medication use.
6. Has medical problems that are related to STDs.
7. Obtains inadequate prenatal care due to homelessness, confusion, or other effects of mental illness symptoms.
8. Experiences conflicts in sexual or romantic relationships due to bizarre behavior or other symptoms.

—. _____
_____
—. _____
_____
—. _____
_____

LONG-TERM GOALS

1. Increase resistance to sexual victimization.
2. Understand the effects of sexual behavior and increase the use of safer-sex practices.

3. Obtain the appropriate medical care that is related to the sexual behavior (e.g., prenatal care, birth control, STD treatment).

4. Decrease the severe and persistent mental illness symptoms that precipitate sexual acting out.

5. Return to a normal libido and sexual functioning relative to the medication usage.

6. Normalize sexual or romantic relationship that is less affected by the symptoms of mental illness.

—. _____

_____

—. _____

_____

—. _____

_____

SHORT-TERM OBJECTIVES

1. Identify the possible areas of sexuality concerns. (1)

2. Verbalize the degree of comfort regarding discussing sexuality issues. (2)

3. Describe the details of sexuality concerns. (3, 4, 5, 6)

THERAPEUTIC INTERVENTIONS

1. Explore the client's history and medical records of sexual abuse, sexual dysfunction, deviant sexual practices, or vulnerability to sexual victimization.

2. Present to the client inquiries into sexuality issues in a tentative, open manner, due to the highly personal and emotional nature of such issues; emphasize the voluntary nature of working on these issues, and that he/she is in control of how quickly or intensely these issues are addressed.

3. Request that the client identify the details of his/her history of sexual difficulties, dysfunction, or confusion.

4. With the proper consent to release information, obtain additional information about sexuality concerns

from the client's spouse, partner, or other family members.

5. Assist the client in preparing a time line reviewing his/her history of sexual involvement; relate this history to his/her struggles with mental illness.

6. Focus the client on differentiating between the reality of the experience and the possible altered perception of reality due to severe and persistent mental illness symptoms; assess the client's reality testing.

4. Disclose the history of sexual abuse. (7, 8)

7. Educate the client about the definition of sexual abuse.

8. Ask the client to describe his/her history of sexual abuse.

5. Demonstrate a reduced emotional response to prior sexual abuse. (9, 10, 11)

9. Review the common emotional, self-esteem, and relationship effects of sexual abuse with the client.

10. Assign readings on surviving sexual abuse (e.g., *The Courage to Heal: A Guide for Women Survivors of Child Sexual Abuse* by Bass and Davis; *Reach for the Rainbow: Advanced Healing for Survivors of Sexual Abuse* by Finney; or assignments from *The Courage to Heal Workbook: For Men and Women Survivors of Child Sexual Abuse* by Davis) to assist the client in processing and understanding his/her feelings that are related to sexual abuse.

11. Refer the client for ongoing psychotherapy with a therapist who is knowledgeable about sexual conflicts and chronic mental illness.

6. Take steps to protect self from a continuation of current sexual victimization. (12, 13, 14, 15)

12. Ask the client about specific current situations in which he/she may be experiencing sexual assault or abuse; report sexual vic-

timization to the police or to an adult protective services agency, in accordance with agency guidelines and local legal requirements.

13. Advocate for the client to obtain the needed supports that will remove him/her from an abusive situation (e.g., domestic violence shelter, protection order).

14. Assist the client in stabilizing financial and residential needs to decrease the likelihood of having to be dependent on a sexually or physically abusive partner (see the Homelessness and Financial Needs chapters in this *Planner*).

15. Educate the client about self-defense strategies, such as those described in *Self-Defense: Steps to Success* by Nelson.

7. Terminate sexually abusive or otherwise inappropriate behaviors toward others. (16)

16. Provide feedback to the client on his/her sexually inappropriate, and possibly illegal, behavior and refer the client to a sexual offender treatment group, if needed.

8. Verbalize an increased knowledge about human sexuality. (17, 18)

17. Educate the client about human sexuality through videotapes, books, and other literature (e.g., *All About Sex: A Family Resource on Sex and Sexuality* by Moglia and Knowles; or *Sexual Health: Questions You Have . . . Answers You Need* by Reitano and Ebel).

18. Refer the client to a sex education group.

9. Take psychotropic medications consistently to decrease severe and persistent mental illness symptoms. (19, 20)

19. Refer the client to a physician or a psychiatrist for an evaluation of the need for psychotropic medication.

20. Educate the client about the use, expected benefits, and possible side effects of psychotropic medications; monitor his/her compliance,

medication effectiveness, and side-effects, reporting significant developments to medical staff.

10. Report an improved self-image as a result of improved activities of daily living (ADLs) or personal appearance. (21, 22)

21. Advocate for the client, with a psychiatrist, for the use of medications that reduce the likelihood of extrapyramidal side effects (EPSs).

22. Assist the client in increasing ADLs (see the Activities of Daily Living [ADL] and Independent Activities of Daily Living [IADL] chapters in this *Planner*).

11. Report an improvement in social and romantic relationships. (23, 24)

23. Refer the client to a support group for mentally ill adults.

24. Teach the client social skills that can be applied to a range of intimate relationships (see the Social Skills Deficits chapter in this *Planner*).

12. Partner reports a decrease in tension within the relationship and within the family unit. (4, 25, 26, 27, 28)

4. With the proper consent to release information, obtain additional information about sexuality concerns from the client's spouse, partner, or other family members.

25. Educate the client's spouse/partner about mental illness symptoms and their impact on intimacy.

26. Assist the client's spouse/partner in resolving family needs that are not related directly to the client's mental illness symptoms (e.g., day care needs for their children, transportation needs, medical help, etc.), but that are increasing the tension level within the marriage.

27. Engage the client's partner in an active role in the client's treatment (e.g., attending treatment meetings, providing feedback to the clinicians, managing medications) as allowed by the client.

28. Refer the client and his/her partner for conjoint therapy that is

related to ongoing problem areas, or to "inoculate" the relationship from future troubles.

13. Identify sexual dysfunction concerns. (4, 29)

4. With the proper consent to release information, obtain additional information about sexuality concerns from the client's spouse, partner, or other family members.

29. Review typical sexual needs that may have been neglected due to mental illness symptoms; ask specifically about sexual dysfunction symptoms.

14. Resolve medical issues that inhibit sexual functioning. (30, 31, 32, 33)

30. Review the sexual side effects of the medications with the client and the medical staff so that he/she can make an informed decision about whether to use them.

31. Refer the client for a complete medical evaluation that is especially focused on possible biochemical causes for sexual dysfunction; coordinate the recommended follow-up, including prescribed lab tests, new medications, or specialty evaluations.

32. Review sexual dysfunction concerns with the prescribing physician. Advocate with the physician for a psychotropic medication regimen that minimizes the impact on sexual libido and sexual functioning.

33. Assess the client carefully for decompensation, interpreting the sexual dysfunction as a precursor or a signal for crisis.

15. Decrease the likelihood of contracting STDs. (34, 35)

34. Educate the client about STDs and how to avoid them (e.g., abstinence, use of condoms); suggest reading material on STDs

(e.g., *Sexually Transmitted Diseases: A Physician Tells You What You Need to Know* by Marr).

35. Provide the client with free condoms or refer him/her to an agency that provides them; teach the client about proper and timely use.

16. Cooperate with an assessment and treatment for STDs. (36, 37)

36. Refer the client to a public health facility or to a physician to test for or treat acquired immune deficiency syndrome (AIDS) and other STDs.

37. Refer the client who tests positive for the human immunodeficiency virus (HIV-positive) to an appropriate support group.

17. List the pros and cons of parenthood. (38, 39)

38. Review the possible motivations that are related to parenthood, which may be prominent with mentally ill individuals (e.g., a redefinition of the client's self-concept from a "mentally ill individual" to a "parent," or a greater desire to maintain his/her psychological health).

39. Focus the client on the stressors that are related to parenthood (e.g., financial burdens, increased responsibility) that may exacerbate mental illness symptoms.

18. Use contraception consistently. (35, 40, 41)

35. Provide the client with free condoms or refer him/her to an agency that provides them; teach the client about proper and timely use.

40. Teach the client about the correct and effective use of condoms, birth control pills, and other contraceptives.

41. Refer the client for birth control measures that are less likely to fail due to human error (e.g., Depo-Provera shots).

19. Verbalize a plan of reaction to possible pregnancy. (11, 42, 43)

11. Refer the client for ongoing psychotherapy with a therapist who is knowledgeable about sexual conflicts and chronic mental illness symptoms.

42. Provide the client with information regarding options that are available for reacting to pregnancy (e.g., abortion, release for adoption, keeping the baby).

43. Educate the client about, and emphasize the critical need for, discontinuing alcohol or street drug use if it is possible that the client is pregnant; inform the client's prescribing physician immediately if the client suspects that she might be pregnant.

20. Verbalize an acceptance of self regardless of sexual identity. (11, 44, 45, 46)

11. Refer the client for ongoing psychotherapy with a therapist who is knowledgeable about sexual conflicts and chronic mental illness symptoms.

44. Assist the client in identifying atypical sexual behavior, which is related to psychosis, mania, or other severe and persistent mental illness symptoms, as opposed to his/her typical sexual behavior or sexual orientation.

45. Validate the client's experience of additional stigmatization or discrimination that he/she may have experienced because of being mentally ill *and* gay/lesbian. Acknowledge that the stressors may, indeed, exacerbate the symptoms; affirm the client's worth, regardless of his/her sexual identity.

46. Refer the client to a support group for those who are struggling with sexual orientation issues and mental illness concerns.

___. _____   ___. _____
      _____   _____
___. _____   ___. _____
      _____   _____
___. _____   ___. _____
      _____   _____

DIAGNOSTIC SUGGESTIONS

Axis I:	297.1	Delusional Disorder
	295.xx	Schizophrenia
	295.70	Schizoaffective Disorder
	296.xx	Bipolar I Disorder
	296.89	Bipolar II Disorder
	293.xx	Psychotic Disorder Due to . . . *[General Medical Condition]*
	292.xx	Substance-Induced Psychotic Disorder
	302.71	Hypoactive Sexual Desire Disorder
	302.79	Sexual Aversion Disorder
	302.72	Sexual Arousal Disorder
	302.7x	Orgasmic Disorders
	302.70	Sexual Dysfunction NOS
	302.9	Sexual Disorder NOS
	V61.1	Sexual Abuse of Adult
	995.83	Sexual Abuse of Adult, Victim

_____   _____

_____   _____

SOCIAL ANXIETY

BEHAVIORAL DEFINITIONS

1. Overall pattern of social anxiety, shyness, or timidity that presents itself in most social situations.
2. Hypersensitivity to the criticism or disapproval of others.
3. No close friends or confidants outside of first-degree relatives.
4. Avoidance of situations that require a degree of interpersonal contact.
5. Reluctant involvement in social situations out of fear of saying or doing something foolish or of becoming emotional in front of others.
6. Debilitating performance anxiety and/or avoidance of required social performance demands.
7. Increased heart rate, sweating, dry mouth, muscle tension, and shakiness in social situations.

—. _____

_____

—. _____

_____

—. _____

_____

LONG-TERM GOALS

1. Interact socially without undue fear or anxiety.
2. Participate in social performance requirements without undue fear or anxiety.
3. Develop the essential social skills that will enhance the quality of relationship life.

4. Develop the ability to form relationships that will enhance recovery support system.
5. Reach a personal balance between solitary time and interpersonal interaction with others.

—. _____

_____

—. _____

_____

—. _____

_____

SHORT-TERM OBJECTIVES

THERAPEUTIC INTERVENTIONS

1. Describe the history and nature of social fears and avoidance. (1, 2, 3)

1. Focus on developing a level of trust with the client. Provide support and empathy to encourage the client to feel safe in expressing his/her social anxiety.

2. Assess the client's frequency, intensity, duration, and history of social fears and avoidance (e.g., *The Anxiety Disorders Interview Schedule for the DSM-IV* by Brown, DiNardo, and Barlow).

3. Assess the nature of any stimulus, thoughts, or situations that precipitate the client's social fear and/or avoidance.

2. Complete psychological tests designed to assess the nature and severity of social anxiety and avoidance. (4)

4. Administer a measure of social anxiety to further assess the depth and breadth of social fears and avoidance (e.g., *The Social Interaction Anxiety Scale* and/or *Social Phobia Scale* by Mattick and Clarke).

3. Differentiate between symptoms that are related to anxiety versus those that are related to severe and

2. Assess the client's frequency, intensity, duration, and history of social fears and avoidance

persistent mental illness.
(2, 3, 5, 6, 7)

(e.g., *The Anxiety Disorders Interview Schedule for the DSM-IV* by Brown, DiNardo, and Barlow).

3. Assess the nature of any stimulus, thoughts, or situations that precipitate the client's social fear and/or avoidance.

5. Help the client differentiate symptoms that are a direct effect of his/her severe and persistent mental illness (e.g., a product of delusion), as opposed to a separate diagnosis of an anxiety disorder.

6. Acknowledge that both real and delusional experiences can cause anxiety, providing support to the client.

7. Utilizing a description of anxiety symptoms such as that found in Bourne's *The Anxiety and Phobia Workbook*; help the client to identify with a specific diagnostic classification.

▽ 4. Cooperate with an evaluation by a physician for psychotropic medication. (8, 9)

8. Arrange for the client to be evaluated for a prescription of psychotropic medications. ▽

9. Monitor the client for prescription compliance, side effects, and overall effectiveness of the medication; consult with the prescribing physician at regular intervals. ▽

▽ 5. Participate in small group therapy for social anxiety, or individual therapy if the group is unavailable. (10)

10. Enroll the client in a small (closed enrollment) group for social anxiety (see Turk, Heimberg and Hope), or individual therapy if a group cannot be formed. ▽

▽ 6. Verbalize an accurate understanding of the vicious cycle of

11. Educate the client about how social anxiety derives from cognitive

---

▽indicates that the Objective/Intervention is consistent with those found in evidence-based treatments.

social anxiety and avoidance. (11, 12)

biases that overestimate negative evaluation by others, undervalue the self, distress, and often lead to unnecessary avoidance. ▽

12. Assign the client to read chapters of books or treatment manuals on social anxiety that reinforce in-session education on the cycle of social anxiety and avoidance, and the rationale for treatment (e.g., *Overcoming Shyness and Social Phobia* by Rapee; or *Overcoming Social Anxiety and Shyness* by Butler). ▽

▽ 7. Verbalize an understanding of the rationale for treatment of social anxiety. (13, 14)

13. Educate the client about how cognitive restructuring and exposure serve as an arena to desensitize learned fear, build social skills and confidence, and reality-test biased thoughts. ▽

14. Assign the client to read about cognitive restructuring and exposure-based therapy in chapters of books or treatment manuals on social anxiety (e.g., *Managing Social Anxiety by* Hope, Heimberg, Juster, and Turk; or *Dying of Embarrassment* by Markaway, Carmin, Pollard, and Flynn). ▽

▽ 8. Learn and implement calming and coping strategies to manage anxiety symptoms during moments of social anxiety. (15, 16)

15. Teach the client calming and attentional focusing skills (e.g., staying focused externally and on behavioral goals, muscular relaxation, evenly paced diaphragmatic breathing, ride the wave of anxiety) to manage social anxiety symptoms. ▽

16. Assign the client to read about calming and coping strategies in books or treatment manuals on social anxiety (e.g., *Overcoming Shyness and Social Phobia* by Rapee). ▽

▽ 9. Identify, challenge, and replace biased, fearful self-talk with reality-based, positive self-talk. (17, 18, 19)

17. Explore the client's schema and self-talk that mediate his/her social fear response, challenge the biases; assist him/her in generating appraisals that correct for the biases and build confidence. ▽

18. Assign the client to read about cognitive restructuring in books or treatment manuals on social anxiety (e.g., *The Shyness and Social Anxiety Workbook* by Antony and Swinson). ▽

19. Assign the client a homework exercise in which he/she identifies fearful self-talk and creates reality-based alternatives; review and reinforce success, providing corrective feedback for failure (see "Restoring Socialization Comfort" in *Adult Psychotherapy Homework Planner*, 2nd ed. by Jongsma, *The Shyness and Social Anxiety Workbook* by Antony and Swinson, or *Overcoming Shyness and Social Phobia* by Rapee). ▽

▽ 10. Undergo gradual repeated exposure to feared social situations within individual or group therapy sessions and review with group members and therapist. (20, 21, 22)

20. Direct and assist the client in construction of a hierarchy of anxiety-producing situations associated with the phobic response. ▽

21. Select initial *in vivo* or role-played exposures that have a high likelihood of being a successful experience for the client; do cognitive restructuring within and after the exposure, use behavioral strategies (e.g., modeling, rehearsal, social reinforcement) to facilitate the exposure; review with the client and group members, if done in group (see *Social Anxiety Disorder* by Turk, Heimberg, and Hope). ▽

22. Assign the client to read about exposure in books or treatment

manuals on social anxiety (e.g., *The Shyness and Social Anxiety Workbook* by Antony and Swinson; or *Overcoming Shyness and Social Phobia* by Rapee). ▽

▽ 11. Undergo gradual repeated exposure to feared social situations outside of individual or group therapy sessions. (23)

23. Assign the client a homework exercise in which he/she does an exposure exercise and records responses (or assign "Gradually Reducing Your Phobic Fear" in *Adult Psychotherapy Homework Planner*, 2nd ed. by Jongsma; also see *The Shyness and Social Anxiety Workbook* by Antony and Swinson; or *Overcoming Shyness and Social Phobia* by Rapee); review and reinforce success, providing corrective feedback toward improvement. ▽

▽ 12. Learn and implement social skills to reduce anxiety and build confidence in social interactions. (24, 25)

24. Use instruction, modeling, and role-playing to build the client's general social and/or communication skills (see *Social Effectiveness Therapy* by Turner, Beidel, and Cooley). ▽

25. Assign the client to read about general social and/or communication skills in books or treatment manuals on building social skills (e.g., *Your Perfect Right* by Alberti and Emmons; or *Conversationally Speaking* by Garner). ▽

▽ 13. Implement relapse prevention strategies for managing possible future anxiety symptoms. (26, 27, 28, 29)

26. Educate the client about the distinction between a lapse and relapse, associating a lapse with an initial and reversible return of symptoms, fear, or urges to avoid and relapse with the decision to return to fearful and avoidant patterns. ▽

27. Identify and rehearse with the client the management of future situations or circumstances in which lapses could occur. ▽

28. Instruct the client to routinely use strategies learned in therapy (e.g., using cognitive restructuring, social skills, and exposure) while building social interactions and relationships. ▽

29. Develop a "coping card" on which coping strategies and other important information (e.g., "pace your breathing," "focus on the task at hand," "you can manage it," and "it will go away") are written for the client's later use. ▽

14. Explore past experiences that may be the source of low self-esteem and social anxiety currently. (30, 31)

30. Probe childhood experiences of criticism, abandonment, or abuse that would foster low self-esteem and shame; process these.

31. Assign the client to read a book on shame (e.g., *Healing the Shame That Binds You* by Bradshaw or *Facing Shame* by Fossum and Mason), and process key ideas.

15. Verbally describe the defense mechanisms used to avoid close relationships. (32)

32. Assist the client in identifying defense mechanisms that keep others at a distance and prevent him/her from developing trusting relationships; identify ways to minimize defensiveness.

16. Return for a follow-up session to track progress, reinforce gains, and problem-solve barriers. (33)

33. Schedule a follow-up or booster session for the client one to three months after therapy ends.

—. _____

_____

—. _____

_____

—. _____

_____

—. _____

_____

—. _____

_____

—. _____

_____

DIAGNOSTIC SUGGESTIONS

Axis I:	300.23	Social Anxiety Disorder (Social Phobia)
	300.4	Dysthymic Disorder
	296.xx	Major Depressive Disorder
	300.7	Body Dysmorphic Disorder
	_____	_____
	_____	_____
Axis II:	301.82	Avoidant Personality Disorder
	301.0	Paranoid Personality Disorder
	301.22	Schizotypal Personality Disorder
	_____	_____
	_____	_____

SOCIAL SKILLS DEFICITS

BEHAVIORAL DEFINITIONS

1. Demonstrates repeated bizarre or other inappropriate social behaviors.
2. Has a history of repeated broken or conflicted relationships due to personal deficiencies in problem solving, maintaining a trusting relationship, or choosing abusive/dysfunctional partners/friends.
3. Exhibits a pattern of social shyness, anxiety, or timidity.
4. Displays rude, angry, oppositional, or demanding behaviors toward peers and others.
5. Reveals an inability to establish, nurture, and maintain meaningful interpersonal relationships due to a failure to listen, support, communicate needs, or negotiate differences of opinion.
6. Estranged from others due to the negative effects of psychotic symptoms (i.e., hallucinations, delusions, manic phases) on social interactions.
7. Complains of loneliness, lost relationships, and a lack of friends or a social network to provide support during crises.
8. Shows a lack of assertiveness, difficulty resisting peer pressure, or a deficiency in expressing needs or saying "no."
9. Lacks experience with or an understanding of the social aspects of recreational/leisure activities.

—. _____
_____

—. _____
_____

—. _____
_____

LONG-TERM GOALS

1. Establish or reestablish mutually satisfying, important interpersonal relationships.
2. Understand how chronic mental illness symptoms impact social skills and relationships.
3. Accept the need for and the usefulness of increasing social skills abilities.
4. Develop basic social skills techniques such as communicating needs, making requests, reading body language, and establishing eye contact.
5. Learn advanced social skill techniques such as assertiveness, active listening, and negotiation.
6. Family, friends, and caregivers develop realistic expectations about the client's social capabilities.

—. _____

_____

_____

—. _____

_____

_____

—. _____

_____

SHORT-TERM OBJECTIVES	THERAPEUTIC INTERVENTIONS
1. Describe current social network. (1, 2)	1. Assist the client in preparing a list of all important relationships, including friends, family, and treatment providers; inquire about expected relationships that are absent.
	2. Develop a family genogram to assist the client in identifying important relationships in the family.
2. Describe various social interactions with friends, family, acquaintances, and others, identifying positives and negatives of those interactions. (3)	3. Thoroughly assess social skill strengths and weaknesses across several settings ranging from low to high in the demand for social skill.
3. Participate in an interview focused on assessing social skills	4. Conduct a semi-structured interview of social skills with the client

and allow a friend or family member to be interview, if needed. (4, 5)

and a person(s) familiar with him or her facilitated by the use of a standardized instrument such as the Social Behavior Schedule or the Social Adjustment Scale.

5. Differentiate among social skill deficits that are due to interference of existing skills by social anxiety, and social skills deficits that are symptoms of a more severe mental disorder (e.g., negative symptom of schizophrenia, manic behavior) and adapt treatment plan to address (see the Social Anxiety chapter or other chapters in this *Planner* relevant to the disorder).

4. Cooperate with a cognitive assessment. (6)

6. Assess the client's cognitive ability via psychological testing such as the *Weschler Adult Intelligence Scale,* 3rd ed. (WAIS-III) or *The Wide Range Achievement Test,* 3rd ed. (WRAT-3), and evaluate the implications for social skills learning.

▽ 5. Take the antipsychotic medication consistently as prescribed. (7, 8, 9, 10)

7. Educate the client about the expected or the common symptoms of his/her mental illness, which impact upon social relationships (i.e., manic behaviors or negative symptoms of schizophrenia). ▽

8. Arrange for a psychiatric evaluation to assess the need for antipsychotic or other psychotropic medication, and arrange a prescription, if appropriate. ▽

9. Monitor the client's use of the medications, their effectiveness, side effects, and compliance; intervene as needed to help solve any problems. ▽

▽ indicates that the Objective/Intervention is consistent with those found in evidence-based treatments.

▽ 6. Verbalize an understanding of the reasons for learning new and improving existing social skills. (11)

▽ 7. Participate in individual or group therapy focused on strengthening social skills. (12)

▽ 8. Learn and implement assertive communication skills. (13, 14)

▽ 9. Identify basic body language signals and state their meaning. (15, 16)

10. Assist the client in recognizing the positive impact of consistent use of the psychiatric medications on social interactions. ▽

11. Provide a rationale for social skills training that communicates the benefits of improved social interactions and decreased negative social actions. ▽

12. Provide or refer the client to individual or, preferably, group social skills training that employs cognitive behavioral strategies (e.g., education, modeling, role-play, practice, reinforcement, and generalization) to teach skills. ▽

13. Assign the client reading material from books or treatment manuals consistent with the social skill being taught to facilitate his/her advancement through therapy (e.g., *Your Perfect Right* by Alberti and Emmons for assertiveness skills; *Conversationally Speaking* by Garner for conversational skills). ▽

14. Use education, modeling, role-playing, practice, reinforcement, and generalization strategies to teach relevant assertive skills, or refer to an assertiveness training workshop that uses like methods. ▽

15. Assist the client in identifying different body language messages from appropriate media sources (e.g., preselected photographs from magazines, family photos). ▽

16. Use education, modeling, role-playing, practice, reinforcement, and generalization strategies to teach the client how to accurately interpret body language signals. ▽

▽ 10. Increase the frequency of speaking with appropriate eye contact in social situations. (17, 18)

17. Discuss the client's lack of eye contact, its consequences, and the benefits of improvement; engage the client in improving his/her eye contact. ▽

18. Use education, modeling, role-playing, practice, reinforcement, and generalization strategies to teach the client use of eye contact when speaking with others. ▽

▽ 11. Learn and implement conversational skills. (19, 20, 21, 22)

19. Give the client homework of developing a brief conversation list of topics in which he/she is interested, as well as topics in which others seem to be interested. ▽

20. Use role-playing to have the client practice asking questions about areas of interest while modeling eye contact, noninterruptive listening, and assertiveness in the process. ▽

21. Assign the client to practice using his/her new conversational skills in a few social situations; review successes and difficulties, gradually increasing the number and complexity of situations over time. ▽

22. Refer the client to a self-help or peer-led support group for individuals with chronic mental illness to provide a supportive environment and to continue the practice of conversation skills. ▽

▽ 12. Learn and implement calming and coping strategies to manage anxiety symptoms during moments of social anxiety. (23)

23. Teach the client calming and attentional focusing skills (e.g., staying focused externally and on behavioral goals, muscular relaxation, evenly paced diaphragmatic breathing, ride the wave of anxiety) to manage social anxiety symptoms. ▽

▽ 13. Identify, challenge, and replace negative self-talk with accurate positive self-talk. (24, 25)

24. Use cognitive therapy techniques to explore self-talk that interferes with successful social skill development, challenge the biases; assist the client in generating alternative appraisals that correct biases and build confidence. ▽

25. Assign the client a homework exercise in which he/she identifies fearful self-talk and creates reality-based alternatives; review and reinforce success, providing corrective feedback for failure (see "Restoring Socialization Comfort" in *Adult Psychotherapy Homework Planner*, 2nd ed. by Jongsma). ▽

▽ 14. Verbalize an understanding of the impact of psychotic symptoms on social interactions. (26, 27, 28)

26. Monitor and give feedback to the client about areas in which mental illness symptoms may affect his/her thought process. ▽

27. Assist the client in developing support from others by identifying trusted individuals who can provide feedback about the mental illness symptoms' effects on thoughts (e.g., delusions) and behavior (e.g., impulsiveness). ▽

28. Assign the client homework of asking for feedback from others in selected social situations; process the homework with the client. ▽

▽ 15. Report instances of verbally accepting and acknowledging praise from others. (29)

29. Assign the client to be aware of and graciously acknowledge (without discounting) praise and compliments from others. ▽

▽ 16. Invite others to join in a group activity. (30)

30. Role-play the client approaching others to ask them to be involved in a group activity. ▽

▽ 17. List group activities that would be enjoyable to share with family/ friends. (31)

31. Assist the client in identifying mutually satisfying social activities for himself/herself and

▼ 18. Participate in community- or agency-sponsored social/recreational activities. (32)

19. Share instances of experiencing social discrimination based on mental illness. (33, 34)

20. Practice making self-affirming statements daily. (35)

21. Family members express their emotions related to the client's social skills deficits and mental illness symptoms. (36, 37)

22. Family members increase positive support of the client to reduce stress and to decrease the exacerbation of the primary symptoms. (38, 39)

friends/family members; assign engagement in these activities and review the experiences. ▼

32. Encourage and facilitate the client's involvement in community-based or agency-sponsored social/recreational opportunities (e.g., bowling, exercise groups, church groups). ▼

33. Reframe instances of discrimination toward the client in community involvement as a fault of the discriminating individual or group, while acknowledging the hurt that the client may experience.

34. Help the client identify previous rejections and process the pain that is related to these rejections.

35. Use a positive self-affirmation technique (i.e., the client writes from 6 to 10 positive statements about himself on 3-by-5-inch cards and reviews them several times per day) to increase the client's focus on his/her positive characteristics that may draw others toward him/her.

36. Encourage the family members to identify and vent about the client's past behavior and symptoms.

37. Coordinate a family therapy session to allow the family to kindly express concerns, emotions, and expectations directly to client.

38. After obtaining the proper release of information, answer family questions about the client's mental illness symptoms and abilities.

39. Refer the client's family members to a community-based support group for loved ones of chronically mentally ill individuals.

23. Identify important relationships that have been lost and that could possibly be reconciled. (40, 41)

40. Review the client's list of important relationships, processing which lost relationships could be salvaged, developed, or resurrected.

41. Assist the client in identifying those who have been hurt in these previous relationships; urge the client to agree to apologize to these people.

24. Apologize/make amends for previous behavior that has offended others. (42)

42. Coordinate a conjoint therapy session for the client making an apology/making amends.

__. _____   __. _____
   _____   _____

__. _____   __. _____
   _____   _____

__. _____   __. _____
   _____   _____

DIAGNOSTIC SUGGESTIONS

Axis I:	297.1	Delusional Disorder
	295.xx	Schizophrenia
	295.10	Schizophrenia, Disorganized Type
	295.70	Schizoaffective Disorder
	296.xx	Bipolar I Disorder
	296.89	Bipolar II Disorder
	V61.9	Relational Problem Related to a Mental Disorder
	V62.81	Relational Problem NOS
	_____	_____
	_____	_____

SPECIFIC FEARS AND AVOIDANCE

BEHAVIORAL DEFINITIONS

1. Describes a persistent and unreasonable fear of a specific object or situation that promotes avoidance behaviors because an encounter with the phobic stimulus provokes an immediate anxiety response.
2. Avoids the phobic stimulus/feared environment or endures it with distress, resulting in interference of normal routines.
3. Acknowledges a persistence of fear despite recognition that the fear is unreasonable.
4. Demonstrates no evidence of a panic disorder.

—. _____
   _____
   _____
—. _____
   _____
   _____
—. _____
   _____

LONG-TERM GOALS

1. Reduce fear of the specific stimulus object or situation that previously provoked phobic anxiety.
2. Reduce phobic avoidance of the specific object or situation, leading to comfort and independence in moving around in public environment.
3. Eliminate interference in normal routines and remove distress from feared object or situation.

—. _____
   _____
—. _____
   _____
—. _____
   _____

SHORT-TERM OBJECTIVES

1. Describe the history and nature of specific fears and avoidance. (1, 2, 3)

2. Complete psychological tests designed to assess the nature and severity of specific fears and avoidance. (4)

3. Differentiate between symptoms that are related to anxiety versus those that are related to severe and persistent mental illness. (2, 3, 5, 6, 7)

THERAPEUTIC INTERVENTIONS

1. Focus on developing a level of trust with the client; provide support and empathy to encourage the client to feel safe in expressing his/her phobia.

2. Assess the client's frequency, intensity, duration, and history of phobic symptoms, fear, and avoidance (e.g., *The Anxiety Disorders Interview Schedule for the DSM-IV* by Brown, DiNardo, and Barlow).

3. Assess the nature of any stimulus, thoughts, or situations that precipitate the client's specific fears and avoidance.

4. Administer a client-report measure (e.g., from *Measures for Specific Phobia* by Antony) to further assess the depth and breadth of phobic responses.

2. Assess the client's frequency, intensity, duration, and history of phobic symptoms, fear, and avoidance (e.g., *The Anxiety Disorders Interview Schedule for the DSM-IV* by Brown, DiNardo, and Barlow).

3. Assess the nature of any stimulus, thoughts, or situations that precipitate the client's specific fears and avoidance.

5. Help the client differentiate symptoms that are a direct effect of his/her severe and persistent mental illness (e.g., a product of delusion), as opposed to a separate diagnosis of an anxiety disorder.

6. Acknowledge that both real and delusional experiences can cause anxiety, providing support to the client.

7. Utilizing a description of anxiety symptoms such as that found in Bourne's *The Anxiety and Phobia Workbook,* helps the client to identify with a specific diagnostic classification.

▽ 4. Cooperate with an evaluation by a physician for psychotropic medication. (8, 9)

8. Arrange for the client to be evaluated for a prescription of psychotropic medications. ▽

9. Monitor the client for prescription compliance, side effects, and overall effectiveness of the medication; consult with the prescribing physician at regular intervals. ▽

▽ 5. Verbalize an accurate understanding of information about phobias and their treatment. (10, 11, 12)

10. Educate the client about how phobias are very common and a natural but misplaced expression of our fight or flight response, not a sign of weakness, but cause unnecessary distress and disability. ▽

11. Educate the client about how phobic fear is maintained by a phobic cycle of unwarranted fear and avoidance that precludes positive, corrective experiences with the

---

▽ indicates that the Objective/Intervention is consistent with those found in evidence-based treatments.

feared object or situation, and how treatment breaks the cycle by encouraging these experiences (see *Mastering Your Fears and Phobias: Therapist Guide* by Craske, Antony and Barlow; or *Specific Phobias* by Bruce and Sanderson). ▽

12. Assign the client to read psychoeducational chapters of books or treatment manuals on specific phobias (e.g., *Mastering Your Fears and Phobias: Workbook* by Antony, Craske, and Barlow; or *The Anxiety and Phobia Workbook* by Bourne). ▽

▽ 6. Verbalize an understanding of the cognitive, physiological, and behavioral components of anxiety and its treatment. (12, 13, 14)

12. Assign the client to read psychoeducational chapters of books or treatment manuals on specific phobias (e.g., *Mastering Your Fears and Phobias: Workbook* by Antony, Craske, and Barlow; or *The Anxiety and Phobia Workbook* by Bourne). ▽

13. Discuss how phobias involve perceiving unrealistic threats, bodily expressions of fear, and avoidance of what is threatening that interact to maintain the problem (see *Mastering Your Fears and Phobias: Therapist Guide* by Craske, Antony, and Barlow; or *Specific Phobias* by Bruce and Sanderson). ▽

14. Discuss how exposure serves as an arena to desensitize learned fear, build confidence, and feel safer by building a new history of success experiences (see *Mastering Your Fears and Phobias: Therapist Guide* by Craske, Antony, and Barlow; or *Specific Phobias* by Bruce and Sanderson). ▽

▽ 7. Learn and implement calming skills to reduce and manage

15. Teach the client anxiety management skills (e.g., staying focused

anxiety symptoms that may emerge during encounters with phobic objects or situations. (15, 16, 17, 18)

on behavioral goals, muscular relaxation, evenly paced diaphragmatic breathing, positive self-talk) to address anxiety symptoms that may emerge during encounters with phobic objects or situations. ▽

16. Assign the client to read psychoeducational chapters of books or treatment manuals describing calming strategies (e.g., *Mastering Your Fears and Phobias: Workbook* by Antony, Craske, and Barlow). ▽

17. Assign the client a homework exercise in which he/she practices daily calming skills; review and reinforce success, providing corrective feedback for failure. ▽

18. Use biofeedback techniques to facilitate the client's success at learning calming skills. ▽

▽ 8. Learn and implement applied tension skills. (19, 20)

19. Teach the client applied tension in which he/she tenses neck and upper torso muscles to curtail blood flow out of the brain to help prevent fainting during encounters with phobic objects or situations involving blood, injection, or injury (see "Applied tension, exposure in vivo, and tension-only in the treatment of blood phobia" in *Behaviour Research and Therapy* by Ost, Fellenius, and Sterner). ▽

20. Assign the client a homework exercise in which he/she practices daily applied tension skills; review and reinforce success, providing corrective feedback for failure. ▽

▽ 9. Identify, challenge, and replace biased, fearful self-talk with positive, realistic, and empowering self-talk. (21, 22, 23, 24)

21. Explore the client's schema and self-talk that mediate his/her fear response; challenge the biases; assist him/her in replacing the

distorted messages with reality-based, positive self-talk. ▽

22. Assign the client to read about cognitive restructuring in books or treatment manuals on panic disorder and agoraphobia (e.g., *Mastering Your Fears and Phobias: Workbook* by Antony, Craske, and Barlow; or *The Anxiety and Phobia Workbook* by Bourne). ▽

23. Assign the client a homework exercise in which he/she identifies fearful self-talk and creates reality-based alternatives (or assign "Journal and Replace Self-Defeating Thoughts" in *Adult Psychotherapy Homework Planner,* 2nd ed. by Jongsma); review and reinforce success, providing corrective feedback for failure. ▽

24. Use behavioral techniques (e.g., modeling, corrective feedback, imaginal rehearsal, social reinforcement) to train the client in positive self-talk that prepares him/her to endure anxiety symptoms without serious consequences. ▽

▽ 10. Undergo repeated exposure to feared or avoided phobic objects or situations. (25, 26, 27, 28)

25. Direct and assist the client in construction of a hierarchy of anxiety-producing situations associated with the phobic response. ▽

26. Select initial exposures that have a high likelihood of being a successful experience for the client; develop a plan for managing the symptoms and rehearse the plan. ▽

27. Assign the client to read about situational exposure in books or treatment manuals on specific phobias (e.g., *Mastering Your Fears and Phobias: Workbook*

by Antony, Craske, and Barlow;
or *Living with Fear* by Marks). ▽

28. Assign the client a homework exercise in which he/she does situational exposures and records responses (see "Gradually Reducing Your Phobic Fear" in *Adult Psychotherapy Homework Planner,* 2nd ed. by Jongsma); *Mastering Your Fears and Phobias: Workbook* by Antony, Craske, and Barlow; or *Living with Fear* by Marks); review and reinforce success or provide corrective feedback toward improvement. ▽

▽ 11. Implement relapse prevention strategies for managing possible future anxiety symptoms. (29, 30, 31, 32)

29. Educate the client about the distinction between a lapse and relapse, associating a lapse with a temporary and reversible return of symptoms, fear, or urges to avoid, and relapse with the decision to return to fearful and avoidant patterns. ▽

30. Identify and rehearse with the client the management of future situations or circumstances in which lapses could occur. ▽

31. Instruct the client to routinely use strategies learned in therapy (e.g., cognitive restructuring, exposure), building them into his/her life as much as possible. ▽

32. Develop a "coping card" on which coping strategies and other important information (e.g., "You're safe," "pace your breathing," "focus on the task at hand," "you can manage it," "stay in the situation," "let the anxiety pass") are written for the client's later use. ▽

12. Verbalize the costs and benefits of remaining fearful and avoidant. (33)

33. Probe for the presence of secondary gain that reinforces the client's phobic actions through escape or avoidance mechanisms.

13. Verbalize the separate realities of the irrationally feared object or situation and the emotionally painful experience from the past that has been evoked by the phobic stimulus. (34, 35)

14. Commit self to not allowing phobic fear to take control of life and lead to a consistent avoidance of normal responsibilities and activities. (36, 37)

15. Return for a follow-up session to track progress, reinforce gains, and problem-solve barriers. (38)

34. Clarify and differentiate between the client's current irrational fear and past emotional pain.

35. Encourage the client's sharing of feelings associated with past traumas through active listening, positive regard, and questioning.

36. Support the client in following through with work, family, and social activities rather than escaping or avoiding them.

37. Ask the client to list several ways his/her life will be more satisfying or fulfilling as he/she manages his/her symptoms of panic and continues normal responsibilities.

38. Schedule a booster session for the client one to three months after therapy ends.

___. _____

___. _____

___. _____

___. _____

___. _____

___. _____

DIAGNOSTIC SUGGESTIONS

Axis I: 300.29   Specific Phobia

_____   _____

_____   _____

SUICIDAL IDEATION

BEHAVIORAL DEFINITIONS

1. Reports recurrent thoughts or preoccupations with death.
2. Acknowledges auditory command hallucinations that direct harm to himself/herself.
3. Verbalizes recurrent ongoing suicidal ideation without any specific plans.
4. Describes ongoing suicidal ideation with a specific plan.
5. Has made a recent suicide attempt.
6. Has a history of suicide attempts that have required hospitalization or other direct intervention.
7. Has a positive family history for suicide or affective disorder.
8. Demonstrates extreme impulsivity due to mania, psychosis, or other severe and persistent mental illness symptoms.
9. Reports a significant increase in depressive symptoms (e.g., a bleak, hopeless attitude toward life), coupled with a recent increase in severe stressors (e.g., loss of a loved one, relationship problems, loss of a job/home).

—. _____
   _____
—. _____
   _____
—. _____
   _____

LONG-TERM GOALS

1. Stabilize the current suicidal crisis.
2. Terminate suicidal ideation.
3. Reestablish reality orientation.
4. Improve coping skills for crisis stressors.

5. Decrease severe stressors.
6. Reestablish a sense of hope for self and for the future.
7. Decrease affective disorder or other severe and persistent mental illness symptoms, returning to highest previous level of functioning.

—. _____
   _____
   _____

—. _____
   _____
   _____

—. _____
   _____

SHORT-TERM OBJECTIVES

1. Verbalize the current level of suicidal intent. (1, 2, 3, 4, 5)

THERAPEUTIC INTERVENTIONS

1. Question the client directly and openly about the presence of suicidal ideation.

2. Perform a risk assessment of the suicidal ideation (see *The Suicide and Homicide Risk Assessment and Prevention Treatment Planner* by Klott and Jongsma), including the nature of the client's suicidal statement, specific plans, access to the means of suicide, and the degree of hope for the future. Focus on his/her statements rather than (flattened) affect, which may be influenced by other symptoms of his/her mental illness.

3. Arrange for psychological testing, including a test specifically designed to assess suicide lethality (e.g., the *Suicide Probability Scale* or the *Beck Scale for Suicide Ideation*).

4. Request feedback from family members, friends, or caregivers about the client's suicidal ideation and symptom intensity.

5. Obtain clinical supervision or feedback from clinical peers regarding a necessary safety reaction to the client's current suicidal status.

2. Cooperate with a hospital and/or residential care if the urge for suicide is not controllable. (6, 7)

6. Obtain immediate emergency medical care for any suicide attempt.

7. Coordinate an admission to a psychiatric hospital or a crisis residential program which has a 24-hour, trained staff; petition the appropriate court or legal entity to involuntarily admit the client to a psychiatric unit, if needed.

3. Cooperate with a crisis care plan that includes 24-hour supervision by friends and/or family members. (8)

8. Develop and implement a crisis care plan, including supervision from caretakers, friends, and family; obtain an agreement from the client about his/her willingness to proceed with the crisis care plan.

4. Family/caregivers decrease lethal means that are available to the client. (9, 10)

9. Advise the family/caregivers to remove lethal means from the client's access (i.e., take away firearms, knives, poisons, or other chemicals).

10. Recommend that the family/caregivers limit the amount of available medication to a less-than-lethal or harmful dose; dispense daily if necessary (see the Independent Activities of Daily Living [IADL] or Medication Management chapters in this *Planner*).

5. Verbalize a commitment to a suicide prevention contract. (11)

11. Write out a suicide prevention contract, including the commitment to contact the clinician or a 24-hour, professionally staffed crisis hotline. Explain, verbally and in writing, where the client

or the caregivers should call or go to if the suicidal ideation persists or increases.

6. Verbalize hopeful statements regarding the future. (12)

12. Provide verbal reinforcement to the client for a more positive focus, hopeful statements, and so on.

7. Agree to structure time with specific tasks and goals for the immediate future that confirm a desire to live. (13, 14)

13. Direct the client in developing structure to his/her time, scheduling the next several hours or days.

14. Remind the client to focus on the portion of himself/herself that wants to go on living; point out that the client's interaction with the clinician is evidence that a part of him/her wants to live.

8. Verbalize an understanding that suicide is not a constructive solution to current stressors. (15, 16, 17, 18)

15. Normalize the client's thoughts of suicide in the context of current problem areas; validate the connection between suicidal thoughts and emotional pain.

16. Talk openly and honestly about the client's suicidal concerns, focusing on suicide as being a permanent solution (with devastating side effects) to what is often a temporary problem or emotional state.

17. Discourage the client from simply disregarding or denying suicidal ideation, reminding him/her that this approach generally increases the suicidal thoughts.

18. Acknowledge the fact that the client is ultimately in control of his/her suicidal activity, reinforcing the idea of suicide as an inadequate solution to stressors that the client temporarily views as intolerable.

9. Caretakers, friends, and family members provide support and supervision to the client. (8, 19, 20, 21)

8. Develop and implement a crisis care plan, including supervision from caretakers, friends, and family; obtain an agreement from

the client about his/her willingness to proceed with the crisis care plan.

19. Provide the client's caretakers, friends, and family members with information about available treatment options; give feedback to family members based on their concerns.

20. With the appropriate permission to release information (or without permission if the crisis meets the legal requirement for breaking confidentiality to preserve life), give the client's caretakers, friends, and family members information about his/her specific suicidal ideation/ concerns.

21. Direct the family or the caretakers to structure the environment to reduce the level of stimulation to the agitated or psychotic client and to reassure him/her of their caring.

10. Participate in an evaluation by a physician as to the need for medication to treat depression or psychosis and take medications as prescribed. (22, 23, 24)

22. Refer the client to a physician or a psychiatrist for an evaluation of the need for psychiatric medication.

23. Educate the client about the use and the expected benefits of psychotropic medications; monitor his/her medication compliance and effectiveness.

24. Review the potential side effects of the medications with the client and report any significant incidents of side effects to the medical staff.

11. Identify the stressors that led to decompensation and suicidal ideation. (25)

25. Request that the client identify life circumstances that have contributed to suicidal ideation (e.g., the loss of a job or a relationship, problems getting along with others, hallucinations/delusions).

12. Process the emotions that are related to the stressors that contribute to suicidal ideation. (26, 27)

26. Inquire about feelings of
hopelessness, anger, frustration,
or sadness, which may be
contributing to suicidal ideation;
encourage the client to vent these
and other emotions in a positive
manner.

27. Encourage the client to identify
the hallucinations and delusions
as a symptom of his/her mental
illness, reminding him/her that
the emotional reaction that
he/she experiences due to the
hallucinations/delusions is not
reality-based.

13. Verbalize a willingness to tolerate the pain of passing negative
emotions. (28, 29)

28. Assist the client in labeling the
suicidal behavior as an avoidance
of emotional pain; focus the client
on the passing nature of his/her
emotions, and the probability of
not having the negative emotions
at some point in the future.

29. Assist the client in externalizing
suicidal ideation, emphasizing the
use of suicidal impulses as a
"warning sign" that other issues
need to be addressed.

14. Verbalize a distinction between
psychotic hallucinations/
delusions and reality.
(27, 30, 31, 32)

27. Encourage the client to identify
the hallucinations and delusions
as a symptom of his/her mental
illness, reminding him/her that
the emotional reaction that
he/she experiences due to the
hallucinations/delusions is not
reality-based.

30. Provide directives to the client in
clear, straightforward terms,
avoiding philosophical discus-
sions or "why" questions.

31. Assist the client in identifying the
hallucinations and the delusions
that prompt suicidal gestures.

32. Explore coping skills and other interventions (e.g., reducing external stressors, implementing distraction techniques, seeking out reality checking with caregivers), which will assist in decreasing psychotic thinking (see the Psychosis chapter in this *Planner*).

15. Report an increase in healthy thinking patterns replacing suicidal ideation. (33, 34)

33. Help the client identify healthy coping practices that support more optimistic, upbeat thinking patterns (e.g., expressing emotions, social involvement, hobbies, or exercise).

34. Monitor the client more closely for suicidal activity if his/her mood suddenly shifts from depressed and withdrawn to serene and at ease with previously overwhelming problems (e.g., he/she has decided to pursue a suicide attempt rather than to fight the stressors).

16. Identify specific, positive reasons to go on living. (35, 36, 37)

35. When the client is in a stable period, request that he/she write a letter to himself/herself regarding how positive and healthy his/her life can be. Read this with the client when he/she has decompensated to a suicidal state.

36. Focus the client on the positive aspects of his/her life; ask him/her to provide a list of reasons to go on living.

37. Request that the client take the *Reasons for Staying Alive When You Are Thinking of Killing Yourself: Reasons for Living Scale* by Linehan and Goodstein.

17. Attend and participate in support and advocacy groups with other seriously mentally ill people. (38)

38. Refer the client to a support group or advocacy group for individuals with mental illness.

18. Acknowledge substance abuse as a precipitating factor in decompensation and suicidal ideation. (39)

39. Assess the client for substance abuse and refer him/her to a substance abuse treatment program if necessary (see the Chemical Dependence chapter in this *Planner*).

19. Implement problem-solving skills to resolve stressful conflicts. (40)

40. Teach and reinforce problem-solving skills through modeling and didactic training (e.g., focus on the positive, utilize negotiation, evaluate the pros and cons of alternatives, practice assertiveness).

20. Demonstrate improved social skills that can be used to build relationships and to reduce isolation. (41)

41. Using modeling, role-playing, and behavioral rehearsal to teach the client personal social skills or refer him/her to social skills training (see the Social Skills Deficits chapter in this *Planner*).

21. Keep in contact with the caregivers and the therapists through crises. (42)

42. Monitor the client more closely at possible crisis intervals (e.g., change in clinician, periods of loss).

22. Agree to the terms of a long-term relapse prevention plan. (43, 44)

43. Formulate a written, long-term plan with the client and his/her family for dealing with stressors/symptoms contributing to suicidal ideation, as well as specific plans for monitoring and supporting him/her. Coordinate this plan with all necessary supports or clinicians, gradually tapering contact with the client to a maintenance level.

44. Make personalized crisis cards, including a brief description of relapse prevention techniques, encouragement, and crisis contact numbers, providing these cards to the client.

23. Decrease the use of suicidal statements and gestures for secondary gain. (45, 46)

45. Point out to the client the powerful responses that a suicidal gesture can cause in others; assist the client in listing healthy ways to get his/her need for attention and affirmation of caring met.

46. With the proper release, develop a specialized treatment plan that can be distributed to other agencies that might be involved with a suicide attempt (e.g., local emergency room); focus this plan on how to decrease a secondary gain for suicidal gestures.

___. _____   ___. _____
    _____   _____
___. _____   ___. _____
    _____   _____
___. _____   ___. _____
    _____   _____

DIAGNOSTIC SUGGESTIONS

Axis I:	295.xx	Schizophrenia
	295.10	Schizophrenia, Disorganized Type
	295.20	Schizophrenia, Catatonic Type
	295.90	Schizophrenia, Undifferentiated Type
	295.30	Schizophrenia, Paranoid Type
	295.70	Schizoaffective Disorder
	296.xx	Bipolar I Disorder
	296.89	Bipolar II Disorder
	297.1	Delusional Disorder
	292.xx	Substance-Induced Psychotic Disorder
	298.9	Psychotic Disorder NOS

_____   _____

_____   _____

Appendix A

BIBLIOTHERAPY SUGGESTIONS

General

Many references are made throughout the chapters to a therapeutic home-work resource that was developed by the authors as a corollary to *The Complete Adult Psychotherapy Treatment Planner,* 4th ed. (Jongsma, A. E. and Peterson, L. M.). This frequently cited homework resource book is:

Jongsma, A. E. (2006). *Adult Psychotherapy Homework Planner,* 2nd ed. Hoboken, NJ: Wiley.

Activities of Daily Living (ADL)

American College of Sports Medicine. (2003). *ACSM Fitness Book.* Champaign, IL: Human Kinetics.

Aslett, D. (1999). *The Cleaning Encyclopedia: Your A to Z Illustrated Guide to Cleaning Like the Pros.* New York: Dell.

Bittman, M. (2006). *How to Cook Everything.* Hoboken, NJ: Wiley.

Editors of Good Housekeeping. (2001). *The Good Housekeeping Illustrated Cookbook.* New York: Hearst Books.

Editors of the University of California, Berkeley wellness letter. (1995). *The New Wellness Encyclopedia.* New York: Houghton-Mifflin.

Pinkham, M., and Burg, D. (1994). *Mary Ellen's Complete Home Reference Book.* New York: Three Rivers Press.

Sharkey, B., and Gaskill, S. (2006). *Fitness and Health,* 6th ed. Champaign, IL: Human Kinetics.

Taintor, J., and Taintor, M. (1999). *The Complete Guide to Better Dental Care.* New York: Checkmark Books.

Aging

Beresford, L. (1993). *The Hospice Handbook.* New York: Little, Brown and Company.

Carter, R., and Golant, S. (1999). *Helping Someone with Mental Illness: A Compassionate Guide for Family, Friends, and Caregivers.* New York: Three Rivers Books.

Cassel, C. (Ed.). (2000). *The Practical Guide to Aging: What Everyone Needs to Know.* New York: New York University Press.

Cleveland, J. (1998). *Simplifying Life as a Senior Citizen.* New York: St. Martin's Griffin.

Hay, J. (1996). *Alzheimer's and Dementia: Questions You Have . . . Answers You Need.* Allentown, PA: People's Medical Society.

Helm, A. (Ed.). (1995). *E-Z Legal Advisor.* Deerfield Beach, FL: E-Z Legal Books.

Lebow, G., Kane, B., and Lebow, I. (1999). *Coping with Your Difficult Older Parent: A Guide for Stressed-Out Children.* New York: Avon Books.

Mueser, K. (1994). *Coping with Schizophrenia: A Guide for Families.* Oakland, CA: New Harbinger.

Quinn, B. (2000). *The Depression Sourcebook,* 2nd ed. New York: McGraw-Hill.

Torrey, E. (2006). *Surviving Schizophrenia: A Manual for Families, Consumers and Providers,* 5th ed. New York: HarperCollins.

Anger Management

Copeland, M. (2001). *The Depression Workbook,* 2nd ed. Oakland, CA: New Harbinger.

Davis, M., Eshelman, E., and McKay, M. (2008). *The Relaxation and Stress Reduction Workbook,* 6th ed. Oakland, CA: New Harbinger.

Deffenbacher, J. L., and McKay, M. (2000). *Overcoming Situational and General Anger: Client Manual (Best Practices for Therapy).* Oakland, CA: New Harbinger.

McKay, M., and Rogers, P. (2000). *The Anger Control Workbook.* Oakland, CA: New Harbinger.

Rosellini, G., and Worden, M. (1997). *Of Course You're Angry.* Center City, MN: Hazelden Foundation.

Rubin, T. (1998). *The Angry Book.* New York: Touchstone.

Smedes, L. (2007). *Forgive and Forget: Healing the Hurts We Don't Deserve.* New York: HarperOne.

Weisinger, H. (1985). *Dr. Weisinger's Anger Workout Book.* New York: Quill.

Williams, R., and Williams, V. (1993). *Anger Kills: 17 Strategies for Controlling the Hostility That Can Harm Your Health.* New York: Harper.

Woolis, R. (2003). *When Someone You Love Has a Mental Illness: A Handbook for Family, Friends, and Caregivers.* New York: Penguin.

Anxiety

Beck, A., Emery, G., and Greenberg, R. (2005). *Anxiety Disorders and Phobias: A Cognitive Perspective.* New York: Basic Books.

Bourne, E. (2005). *The Anxiety and Phobia Workbook,* 4th ed. Oakland, CA: New Harbinger.

Bourne, E. J., and Garano, L. (2003). *Coping with Anxiety: 10 Simple Ways to Relieve Anxiety, Fear, and Worry.* Oakland, CA: New Harbinger.

Burns, D. D. (1999). *Ten Days to Self-Esteem.* New York: HarperCollins.

Craske, M. G., and Barlow, D. H. (2006). *Mastery of Your Anxiety and Worry: Workbook,* 2nd ed. New York: Oxford University Press.

Davis, M., Eshelman, E., and McKay, M. (2008). *The Relaxation and Stress Reduction Workbook,* 6th ed. Oakland, CA: New Harbinger.

Flannery, R. (1995). *Post-Traumatic Stress Disorder: The Victim's Guide to Healing and Recovery.* New York: Crossroads.

Hayes, S. C. (2005). *Get Out of Your Mind and Into Your Life: The New Acceptance and Commitment Therapy.* Oakland, CA: New Harbinger.

Leahy, R. L. (2006). *The Worry Cure: Seven Steps to Stop Worry from Stopping You.* New York: Three Rivers Press.

Zinbarg, R. E., Craske, M. G., and Barlow, D. H. (2006). *Mastery of Your Anxiety and Worry: Therapist Guide,* 2nd ed. New York: Oxford University Press.

Borderline Personality

Fruzzetti, A. E., and Linehan, M. M. (2003). *The High Conflict Couple: A Dialectical Behavior Therapy Guide to Finding Peace, Intimacy, and Validation.* Oakland, CA: New Harbinger.

Herman, J. L. (1997). *Trauma and Recovery.* New York: Basic Books.

Kreisman, J., and Straus, H. (1991). *I Hate You—Don't Leave Me.* New York: Avon Press.

Marra, T. (2004). *Depressed and Anxious: The Dialectical Behavior Therapy Workbook for Overcoming Depression and Anxiety.* Oakland, CA: New Harbinger.

Miller, D. (2005). *Women Who Hurt Themselves: A Book of Hope and Understanding,* 10th anniversary ed. New York: Basic Books.

Reiland, R. (2004). *Get Me Out of Here: My Recovery from Borderline Personality Disorder.* Center City, MN: Hazelden Foundation.

Spadlin, S. E. (2003). *Don't Let Your Emotions Run Your Life: How Dialectical Behavior Therapy Can Put You in Control.* Oakland, CA: New Harbinger.

Chemical Dependence

Alberti, R. E., and Emmons, M. L. (2001). *Your Perfect Right: Assertiveness and Equality in Your Life and Relationships,* 8th ed. Atascadero, CA: Impact.

Alcoholics Anonymous. (2001). *Alcoholics Anonymous,* 4th ed. New York: Alcoholics Anonymous World Services.

Alcoholics Anonymous. (2002). *Twelve-Step and Twelve Traditions.* New York: Alcoholics Anonymous World Services.

Beattie, M. (1992). *Codependent No More.* Center City, MN: Hazelden Foundation.

Denning, P., Little, J., and Glickman, A. (2003). *Over the Influence: The Harm Reduction Guide for Managing Drugs and Alcohol.* New York: Guilford Press.

Fanning, P., and O'Neill, J. (1996). *The Addiction Workbook.* Oakland, CA: New Harbinger.

Friends in Recovery. (1995). *The 12 Steps—A Way Out.* Curtis, WA: RPI.

Garner, A. (1997). *Conversationally Speaking: Tested New Ways to Increase Your Personal and Social Effectiveness.* New York: McGraw-Hill.

Grateful Members. (1994). *The Twelve Steps for Everyone . . . Who Really Wants Them.* Center City, MN: Hazelden Foundation.

Marlatt, G. A. (2002). *Harm Reduction: Pragmatic Strategies for Managing High-Risk Behaviors.* New York: Guilford Press.

Miller, W. R., and Munoz, R. F. (2004). *Controlling Your Drinking: Tools to Make Moderation Work for You.* New York: Guilford Press.

Miller, W. R., and Rollnick, S. (2002). *Motivational Interviewing: Preparing People for Change,* 2nd ed. New York: Guilford Press.

Mooney, A., Eisenberg, A., and Eisenberg, H. (1992). *The Recovery Book.* New York: Workman.

Rosellini, G., and Worden, M. (1997). *Of Course You're Angry.* Center City, MN: Hazelden Foundation.

Depression

Addis, M. E., and Martell, C. R. (2004). *Overcoming Depression One Step at a Time: The New Behavioral Activation Approach to Getting Your Life Back.* Oakland, CA: New Harbinger.

Appleton, W. (2000). *Prozac and the New Antidepressants.* New York: Plume.

Bieling, P. J., Antony, M. M., and Beck, A. T. (2003). *Ending the Depression Cycle: A Step-By-Step Guide for Preventing Relapse.* Oakland, CA: New Harbinger.

Bower, S., and Bower, G. (2004). *Asserting Yourself: A Practical Guide for Positive Change.* New York: Da Capo Press.

Burns, D. D. (1999). *Feeling Good: The New Mood Therapy.* New York: HarperCollins.

Burns, D. D. (1999). *The Feeling Good Handbook.* New York: Plume.

Burns, D. D. (1999). *Ten Days to Self-Esteem.* New York: HarperCollins.

Copeland, M. (2002). *The Depression Workbook.* Oakland, CA: New Harbinger.

Gilson, M., and Freemen, A. (2004). *Overcoming Depression: A Cognitive Therapy Approach for Taming the Depression Beast: Client Workbook.* New York: Oxford University Press.

Golant, M., and Golant, S. (2007). *What to Do When Someone You Love Is Depressed: A Practical and Helpful Guide.* New York: Henry Holt.

Greenberger, D., and Padesky, C. (1995). *Mind over Mood: Change How You Feel by Changing the Way You Think.* New York: Guilford Press.

Hayes, S. C. (2005). *Get Out of Your Mind and Into Your Life: The New Acceptance and Commitment Therapy.* Oakland, CA: New Harbinger.

Helmstetter, S. (1990). *What to Say When You Talk to Yourself.* New York: Pocket Books.

Leith, L. M. (1998). *Exercising Your Way to Better Mental Health.* Morgantown, WV: Fitness Information Techology.

Lewinsohn, P. (1992). *Control Your Depression.* New York: Fireside.

Marsh, D., and Dickens, R. (1997). *Troubled Journey: Coming to Terms with the Mental Illness of a Sibling or Parent.* New York: Tarcher/Putnam.

Miklowitz, D. J. (2002) *Bipolar Disorder Survival Guide: What You and Your Family Need to Know.* New York: Guilford Press.

Pettit, J. W., Joiner, T. E., and Rehm, L. P. (2005). *The Interpersonal Solution to Depression: A Workbook for Changing How You Feel by Changing How You Relate.* Oakland, CA: New Harbinger.

Segal, Z. V., Williams, J. M. G., and Teasdale, J. D. (2001). *Mindfulness-Based Cognitive Therapy for Depression: A New Approach to Preventing Relapse.* New York: Guilford Press.

Weissman, M. M. (2005). *Mastering Depression through Interpersonal Psychotherapy: Patient Workbook.* New York: Oxford University Press.

Employment Problems

Bolles, R. (2007). *What Color Is Your Parachute? 2008.* Berkeley, CA: Ten Speed Press.

Fein, R. (1999). *101 Quick Tips for a Dynamite Resume.* Manassas Park, VA: Impact Publications.

Lindenfield, G. (2001). *Assert Yourself.* New York: HarperThorsons.

McGraw-Hill Editors. (2005). *Resumes for the First Time Job Hunter (Includes Sample Cover Letters),* 3rd ed. New York: McGraw-Hill.

Morgan, D. (1998). *10 Minute Guide to Job Interviews.* New York: Arco Books.

Pfeiffer, R. (2003). *The Real Solution Assertiveness Workbook.* New York: Growth.

Family Conflicts

Brown, E. M. (1989). *My Parent's Keeper: Adult Children of the Emotionally Disturbed.* Oakland, CA: New Harbinger.

Carter, R., and Golant, S. (1999). *Helping Someone with Mental Illness: A Compassionate Guide for Family, Friends, and Caregivers.* New York: Three Rivers Books.

Court, B., and Nelson, G. (1996). *Bipolar Puzzle Solution: A Mental Health Client's Perspective.* New York: Brunner-Rutledge.

Esser, A. H., and Lacey, S. D. (1989). *Mental Illness: A Homecare Guide*. New York: Wiley.

Hatfield, A. B., and Lefley, H. P. (1993). *Surviving Mental Illness: Stress, Coping, and Adaptation*. New York: Guilford Press.

Johnson, J. T. (2007). *Hidden Victims, Hidden Healers: An Eight-Stage Healing Process for Families and Friends of the Mentally Ill*. Charleston, SC: BookSurge.

Marsh, D. T., and Dickens, R. (1998). *How to Cope with Mental Illness in Your Family: A Self-Care Guide for Siblings, Offspring, and Parents*. New York: Tarcher/Putnam.

Medina, J. (1998). *Depression: How It Happens—How It's Healed*. Oakland, CA: New Harbinger.

Miller, W. R. (1999). *Enhancing Motivation for Change in Substance Abuse Treatment*. Rockville, MD: The Center.

Mueser, K. (1994). *Coping with Schizophrenia: A Guide for Families*. Oakland, CA: New Harbinger.

National Alliance on Mental Illness. www.nami.org.

Otto, M., Reilly-Harrington, N., Knauz, R. O., Heinin, A., Kogan, J. N., and Sachs, G. S. (2008). *Living with Bipolar Disorder*. Cambridge, MA: Oxford University Press.

Quinn, B. (2000). *The Depression Sourcebook*, 2nd ed. New York: McGraw-Hill.

Secunda, V. (1998). *When Madness Comes Home: Help and Hope for the Children, Siblings, and Partners of the Mentally Ill*. New York: Hyperion.

Torrey, E. (2006). *Surviving Schizophrenia: A Manual for Families, Consumers, and Providers*, 5th ed. New York: HarperCollins.

Tsuang, M., and Faraone, S. (1997). *Schizophrenia: The Facts*. New York: Oxford University Press.

Woolis, R. (2003). *When Someone You Love Has a Mental Illness: A Handbook for Family, Friends, and Caregivers*. New York: Penguin.

Financial Needs

Bierman, T., and Masten, D. (1998). *The Fix Your Credit Workbook*. New York: St. Martin's Griffin.

Bosley, M. and Gurwitz, A. (1993). *How to Get Every Penny You're Entitled to from Social Security*. New York: Perigee Books.

Gelb, E. (1995). *Personal Budget Planner: A Guide for Financial Success*. Woodmere, NY: Career Advancement Center.

Grief and Loss

James, J., and Friedman, R. (1998). *The Grief Recovery Handbook: The Action Program for Moving Beyond Death, Divorce, and Other Losses*. New York: HarperCollins.

Kubler-Ross, E., and Kessler, D. (2007). *On Grief and Grieving*. New York: Scribner.

Kushner, H. (2004). *When Bad Things Happen to Good People*. New York: Anchor.

Lafond, V. (2002). *Grieving Mental Illness: A Guide for Patients and Their Caregivers.* Toronto, Ontario, Canada: University of Toronto Press.

Smedes, L. (2000). *How Can It Be All Right When Everything Is All Wrong?* Colorado Springs, CO: Shaw Books.

Smedes, L. (2007). *Forgive and Forget: Healing the Hurts We Don't Deserve.* New York: HarperOne.

Zonnebelt-Smeenge, S. J. and De Vries, R. C. (1998). *Getting to the other Side of Grief.* Grand Rapids, MI: Baker Books.

Health Issues

Roizen, M. F., and Oz, M. (2006). *You: The Smart Patient.* New York: Free Press.

Zakarian, B. (1996). *The Activist Cancer Patient: How to Take Charge of Your Treatment.* Hoboken, NJ: Wiley.

Homelessness

Aslett, D. (1999). *The Cleaning Encyclopedia: Your A to Z Illustrated Guide to Cleaning Like the Pros.* New York: Dell.

Barrett, P. (1998). *Too Busy To Clean? Over 500 Tips and Techniques to Make Housecleaning Easier.* Pownal, VT: Storey Books.

Pinkham, M., and Burg, D. (1994). *Mary Ellen's Complete Home Reference Book.* New York: Three Rivers Press.

Portman, J. and Stewart, M. (2007). *Renters' Rights.* Berkley, CA: Nolo.

Independent Activities of Daily Living (IADL)

Avdul, D., and Avdul, S. (2004). *Real Life 101: A Guide to Stuff that Actually Matters.* Manhattan Beach, CA: Galt Industries.

Bierman, T., and Masten, D. (1998). *The Fix Your Credit Workbook.* New York: St. Martin's Griffin.

Bowers, J. (2001). *On Your Own for the First Time.* Utica, NY: Pyramid.

Gelb, E. (1995). *Personal Budget Planner: A Guide for Financial Success.* Woodmere, NY: Career Advancement Center.

Intimate Relationship Conflicts

Carter, R., and Golant, S. (1999). *Helping Someone with Mental Illness: A Compassionate Guide for Family, Friends, and Caregivers.* New York: Three Rivers Books.

Colgrove, M., Bloomfield, H., and McWilliams, P. (1991). *How to Survive the Loss of a Love.* Los Angeles: Prelude Press.

Comfort, A., and Marcus, E. (1991). *The New Joy of Sex.* New York: Crown.

Court, B., and Nelson, G. (1996). *Bipolar Puzzle Solution: A Mental Health Client's Perspective.* New York: Brunner/Rutledge.

Gorman, J. (1998). *The Essential Guide to Mental Health.* New York: St. Martin's Griffin.

Joslin, K. (1994). *Positive Parenting From A to Z.* New York: Fawcett Columbine.

Kaplan, H. (1987). *The Illustrated Manual of Sex Therapy,* 2nd ed. Bristol, PA: Brunner/Mazel.

Medina, J. (1998). *Depression: How It Happens—How It's Healed.* Oakland, CA: New Harbinger.

Mondimore, F. (2006). *Bipolar Disorder: A Guide for Patients and Families,* 2nd ed. Baltimore: Johns Hopkins University Press.

Mueser, K. (1994). *Coping With Schizophrenia: A Guide For Families.* Oakland, CA: New Harbinger.

Phelan, T. (2004). *1-2-3 Magic: Effective Discipline for Children 2–12,* 3rd ed. Glen Ellyn, IL: Child Management.

Quinn, B. (2000). *The Depression Sourcebook,* 2nd ed. New York: McGraw-Hill.

Roberts, A., and Padgett-Yawn, B. (Eds.). (1998). *The Reader's Digest Guide to Love and Sex.* Pleasantville, NY: Reader's Digest Association.

Sinclair Institute. (1991). *Better Sex Videos. Vol. 1: Better Sexual Techniques, Volume 3: Making Sex Fun, Volume 8: You Can Last Longer: Solutions for Ejaculatory Control.* Available from Sinclair Institute, P.O. Box 8865, Chapel Hill, NC 27515. (800) 955–0888, Ext. 8NET2, or http://www.bettersex.com.

Torrey, E. (2006). *Surviving Schizophrenia: A Manual for Families, Consumers, and Providers,* 5th ed. New York: HarperCollins.

Tsuang, M., and Faraone, S. (1997). *Schizophrenia: The Facts.* New York: Oxford University Press.

Woolis, R. (2003). *When Someone You Love Has a Mental Illness: A Handbook for Family, Friends, and Caregivers.* New York: Penguin.

Legal Concerns

Bergman, P., and Berman-Barett, S. (1999). *The Criminal Law Handbook: Know Your Rights, Survive the System.* Berkeley, CA: Nolo Press.

Carnes, P. (2001). *Out of the Shadows: Understanding Sexual Addiction.* Center City, MN: Hazelden Foundation.

Ventura, J. (2002). *The Will Kit.* Chicago: Dearborn Financial.

Mania or Hypomania

Basco, M. R. (2005). *The Bipolar Workbook: Tools for Controlling Your Mood Swings.* New York: Guilford Press.

Court, R., and Nelson, G. (1996). *Bipolar Puzzle Solution: A Mental Health Client's Perspective.* New York: Brunner-Rutledge.

Davis, M., Eshelman, E., and McKay, M. (2008). *The Relaxation and Stress Reduction Workbook,* 6th ed. Oakland, CA: New Harbinger.

Gorman, J. (1998). *The Essential Guide to Mental Health.* New York: St. Martin's Griffin.

Hauri, P., and Linde, S. (1996). *No More Sleepless Nights: A Proven Guide to Conquering Insomnia.* New York: Wiley.

Miklowitz, D. J. (2002). *The Bipolar Disorder Survival Guide: What You and Your Family Need to Know.* New York: Guilford Press.

Miller, W. R. (1999). *Enhancing Motivation for Change in Substance Abuse Treatment.* Rockville, MD: The Center.

Mondimore, F. (2006). *Bipolar Disorder: A Guide for Patients and Families,* 2nd ed. Baltimore: Johns Hopkins University Press.

Torrey, E. (2006). *Surviving Schizophrenia: A Manual for Families, Consumers, and Providers,* 5th ed. New York: HarperCollins.

Zammit, G., and Zanca, J. (1998). *Good Nights: How to Stop Sleep Deprivation, Overcome Insomnia, and Get the Sleep You Need.* Kansas City, MO: Andrews McMeel.

Medication Management

Gorman, J. (2007). *The Essential Guide to Psychiatric Drugs.* New York: St. Martin's Griffin.

McFarlane, W. R. (2002). *Multifamily Groups in the Treatment of Severe Psychiatric Disorders.* New York: Guilford Press.

Miklowitz, D. J., and Goldstein, M. J. (1997). *Bipolar Disorder: A Family-Focused Treatment Approach.* New York: Guilford Press.

Obsessive-Compulsive Disorder (OCD)

Baer, L. (2000). *Getting Control: Overcoming Your Obsessions and Compulsions,* rev. ed. New York: Plume.

Bourne, E. (2005). *The Anxiety and Phobia Workbook,* 4th ed. Oakland, CA: New Harbinger.

Foa, E. B., and Wilson, R. (2001). *Stop Obsessing! How to Overcome Your Obsessions and Compulsions,* rev. ed. New York: Bantam Books.

Hyman, B. M., and Pedrick, C. (2005). *The OCD Workbook: Your Guide to Breaking Free from Obsessive-Compulsive Disorder,* 2nd ed. Oakland, CA: New Harbinger.

Munford, P. (2004). *Overcoming Compulsive Checking: Free Your Mind from OCD.* Oakland, CA: New Harbinger.

Munford, P. (2005). *Overcoming Compulsive Washing: Free Your Mind from OCD.* Oakland, CA: New Harbinger.

Neziroglu, F., Bubrick, J., and Yaryura-Tobias, J. A. (2004). *Overcoming Compulsive Hoarding: Why You Save and How You Can Stop.* Oakland, CA: New Harbinger.

Penzel, F. (2000). *Obsessive-Compulsive Disorders: A Complete Guide to Getting Well and Staying Well.* New York: Oxford University Press.

Purdon, C., and Clark, D. A. (2005). *Overcoming Obsessive Thoughts: How to Gain Control of Your OCD.* Oakland, CA: New Harbinger.

Schwartz J. M. (1997). *Brain Lock: Free Yourself from Obsessive-Compulsive Behavior.* New York: Regan Books.

Steketee, G. S. (1999). *Overcoming Obsessive Compulsive Disorder (Client Manual).* Oakland, CA: New Harbinger.

Steketee, G. S., and White, K. (1990). *When Once Is Not Enough: Help for Obsessive Compulsives.* Oakland, CA: New Harbinger.

Panic/Agoraphobia

Antony, M. M., and McCabe, R. E. (2004). *10 Simple Solutions to Panic.* Oakland, CA: New Harbinger.

Bourne, E. (2005). *The Anxiety and Phobia Workbook,* 4th ed. Oakland, CA: New Harbinger.

Clum, G. (1990). *Coping with Panic.* Pacific Grove, CA: Brooks/Cole.

Craske, M. G., and Barlow, D. H. (2006). *Mastery of Your Anxiety and Panic: Workbook.* New York: Oxford University Press.

Marks, I. M. (2001). *Living With Fear,* 2nd ed. London: McGraw-Hill.

Wilson, R. R. (1996). *Don't Panic: Taking Control of Anxiety Attacks,* 2nd ed. New York: Harper & Row.

Paranoia

Alberti, R. E., and Emmons, M. L. (2008). *Your Perfect Right.* Atascadero, CA: Impact.

Burns, D. D. (1999). *The Feeling Good Handbook.* New York: Plume.

Cudney, M., and Hardy, R. (1993). *Self-Defeating Behaviors.* San Francisco: Harper-Collins.

Davis, M., Eshelman, E., and McKay, M. (2008). *The Relaxation and Stress Reduction Workbook,* 6th ed. Oakland, CA: New Harbinger.

Garner, A. (1997). *Conversationally Speaking,* 3rd ed. Chicago, Contemporary Books.

National Alliance on Mental Illness. www.nami.org.

Ross, J. (1994). *Triumph over Fear.* New York: Bantam Books.

Parenting

Carter, R., and Golant, S. (1999). *Helping Someone with Mental Illness: A Compassionate Guide for Family, Friends, and Caregivers.* New York: Three Rivers Books.

Cline, F., and Fay, J. (1992). *Parenting Teens with Love and Logic: Preparing Adolescents for Responsible Adulthood.* Colorado Springs, CO: Pinion Press.

Court, B., and Nelson, G. (1996). *Bipolar Puzzle Solution: A Mental Health Client's Perspective.* New York: Brunner/Rutledge.

Davis, M., Eshelman, E., and McKay, M. (2008). *The Relaxation and Stress Reduction Workbook,* 6th ed. Oakland, CA: New Harbinger.

Dobson, J. (1992). *The New Dare to Discipline.* Wheaton, IL: Tyndale House.

Gorman, J. (1998). *The Essential Guide to Mental Health.* New York: St. Martin's Griffin.

Joslin, K. (1994). *Positive Parenting From A to Z.* New York: Fawcett Columbine.

Larson, D. (Ed.). (1990). *Mayo Clinic Family Health Book.* New York: William Morrow.

McKay, M., Fanning, P., Paleg, K., and Landis, D. (1996). *When Your Anger Hurts Your Kids: A Parent's Guide.* Oakland, CA: New Harbinger.

Miller, S. (1995). *When Parents Have Problems: A Book for Teens and Older Children with an Abusive, Alcoholic, or Mentally Ill Parent.* Springfield. IL: Charles C Thomas.

Mondimore, F. (2006). *Bipolar Disorder: A Guide for Patients and Families,* 2nd ed. Baltimore: Johns Hopkins University Press.

Mueser, K. (1994). *Coping With Schizophrenia: A Guide For Families.* Oakland, CA: New Harbinger.

Phelan, T. (1995). *1-2-3 Magic: Effective Discipline for Children 2–12,* 2nd ed. Glen Ellyn, IL: Child Management.

Quinn, B. (2000). *The Depression Sourcebook,* 2nd ed. New York: McGraw-Hill.

Torrey, E. (2006). *Surviving Schizophrenia: A Manual for Families, Consumers and Providers,* 5th ed. New York: HarperCollins.

Tsuang, M., and Faraone, S. (1997). *Schizophrenia: The Facts.* New York: Oxford University Press.

Posttraumatic Stress Disorder (PTSD)

Allen, J. (2004). *Coping with Trauma: A Guide to Self-Understanding.* Washington, DC: American Psychiatric Press.

Foa, E. B., Davidson, J. R. T., and Frances, A. (1999). The Expert Consensus Guideline Series: Treatment of Posttraumatic Stress Disorder. *Journal of Clinical Psychiatry,* 60 (16). Also available online at: http://www.psychguides.com/ptsdhe.pdf.

Follette, V. M., and Pistorello, J. (2007). *Finding Life Beyond Trauma.* Oakland, CA: New Harbinger.

Follette, V. M., and Ruzek, J. I. (2007). *Cognitive-Behavioral Therapies for Trauma,* 2nd ed. New York: Guilford Press.

Leith, L. M. (1998). *Exercising Your Way to Better Mental Health.* Morgantown, WV: Fitness Information Techology.

Matsakis, A. (1996). *I Can't Get Over It: A Handbook for Trauma Survivors,* 2nd ed. Oakland, CA: New Harbinger.

Rothbaum, B., and Foa, E. (2004). *Reclaiming Your Life After Rape: Cognitive-Behavioral Therapy for Posttraumatic Stress Disorder—Client Workbook.* New York: Oxford University Press.

Rothbaum, B., Foa, E., and Humbree, E. (2007). *Reclaiming Your Life from a Traumatic Experience: A Prolonged Exposure Treatment Program Workbook.* New York: Oxford University Press.

Smyth, L. (1999). *Overcoming Post-Traumatic Stress Disorder: A Cognitive-Behavioral Exposure-Based Protocol for the Treatment of PTSD and the Other Anxiety Disorders.* Oakland, CA: New Harbinger.

Walser, R. D., and Westrup, D. (2007). *Acceptance and Commitment Therapy for the Treatment of Post-Traumatic Stress Disorder: A Practitioner's Guide to Using Mindfulness and Acceptance Strategies.* Oakland, CA: New Harbinger.

Williams, M. B., and Poijula, S. (2002). *The PTSD Workbook: Simple, Effective Techniques for Overcoming Traumatic Stress Symptoms.* Oakland, CA: New Harbinger.

Psychosis

Carter, R., and Golant, S. (1999). *Helping Someone with Mental Illness: A Compassionate Guide for Family, Friends, and Caregivers.* New York: Three Rivers Books.

Court, B., and Nelson, G. (1996). *Bipolar Puzzle Solution: A Mental Health Client's Perspective.* New York: Brunner/Rutledge.

Mueser, K. (1994). *Coping With Schizophrenia: A Guide for Families.* Oakland, CA: New Harbinger.

National Alliance on Mental Illness. www.nami.org.

Torrey, E. (2006). *Surviving Schizophrenia: A Manual for Families, Consumers, and Providers,* 5th ed. New York: HarperCollins.

Recreational Deficits

American College of Sports Medicine. (1998). *The ACSM Fitness Book.* Champaign, IL: Human Kinetics.

Davis, M., Eshelman, E., and McKay, M. (2008). *The Relaxation and Stress Reduction Workbook,* 6th ed. Oakland, CA: New Harbinger.

Helmstetter, S. (1990). *What to Say When You Talk to Yourself.* New York: Pocket Books.

Mondimore, F. (2006). *Bipolar Disorder: A Guide for Patients and Families,* 2nd ed. Baltimore: Johns Hopkins University Press.

Sharkey, B. (2006). *Fitness and Health,* 6th ed. Champaign, IL: Human Kinetics.

Tsuang, M., and Faraone, S. (1997). *Schizophrenia: The Facts.* New York: Oxford University Press.

Self-Determination Deficits

Foxx, R., and Bittle, R. (1989). *Thinking It Through: Teaching a Problem-Solving Strategy for Community Living.* Champaign, IL: Research Press.

Gardner, N. E. S. (1980). *The Self-Advocacy Workbook.* Lawrence, KS: Kansas Center for Mental Retardation and Human Development.

Michigan Protection and Advocacy Service, Inc. (1998). *The Self-Advocacy Manual for Consumers.* Lansing MI: MPAS. www.mpas.org.

Pearpoint, J. (1993). *PATH: A Workbook for Planning Positive Possible Futures.* Toronto, Ontario, Canada: Inclusion Press.

Sexuality Concerns

Bass, E., and Davis, L. (1994). *The Courage to Heal: A Guide for Women Survivors of Child Sexual Abuse,* 3rd ed. San Francisco: HarperCollins.

Davis, L. (1990). *The Courage to Heal Workbook: For Men and Women Survivors of Child Sexual Abuse.* San Francisco: HarperCollins.

Esser, A., and Lacey, S. (1989). *Mental Illness: A Homecare Guide.* New York: Wiley.

Finney, L. (1992). *Reach for the Rainbow: Advanced Healing for Survivors of Sexual Abuse.* New York: Perigee Books.

Helmer, D. (1999). *Let's Talk About When Your Mom or Dad Is Unhappy.* Center City, MN: Hazelden Foundation.

Marr, L. (2007). *Sexually Transmitted Diseases: A Physician Tells You What You Need to Know,* 2nd ed. Baltimore: Johns Hopkins University Press.

Moglia, R., and Knowles, J. (Planned Parenthood). (1997). *All About Sex: A Family Resource on Sex and Sexuality.* Westminster, MD: Random House.

Nelson, J. (1991). *Self-Defense: Steps to Success.* Champaign, IL: Leisure Press.

Reitano, M., and Ebel, C. (1999). *Sexual Health: Questions You Have . . . Answers You Need.* Allentown, PA: People's Medical Society.

Strong, S. (1996). *Strong on Defense.* New York: Pocket Books.

Social Anxiety

Alberti, R. E., and Emmons, M. L. (2001). *Your Perfect Right: Assertiveness and Equality in Your Life and Relationships,* 8th ed. Atascadero, CA: Impact.

Antony, M. M., and Swinson, R. P. (2000). *The Shyness and Social Anxiety Workbook: Proven, Step-By-Step Techniques for Overcoming Your Fear.* Oakland, CA: New Harbinger.

Bourne, E. (2005). *The Anxiety and Phobia Workbook,* 4th ed. Oakland, CA: New Harbinger.

Butler, G. (1999). *Overcoming Social Anxiety and Shyness: A Self-Help Guide Using Cognitive Behavioral Techniques.* London: Robinson.

Desberg, P. (1996). *No More Butterflies: Overcoming Shyness, Stage Fright, Interview Anxiety, and Fear of Public Speaking.* Oakland, CA: New Harbinger.

Ellis, A. and Harper, R. (1975). *A Guide to Rational Living.* Chatsworth, CA: Wilshire.

Garner, A. (1997). *Conversationally Speaking: Tested New Ways to Increase Your Personal and Social Effectiveness.* New York: McGraw-Hill.

Markway, B. G., Carmin, C. N., Pollard, C. A., and Flynn, T. (1992). *Dying of Embarrassment: Help for Social Anxiety and Phobia.* Oakland, CA: New Harbinger.

Rapee, R. M. (1998). *Overcoming Shyness and Social Phobia: A Step-By-Step Guide.* Northvale, NJ: Aronson.

Schneier, F., and Welkowitz, L. (1996). *The Hidden Face of Shyness: Understanding and Overcoming Social Anxiety.* New York: Avon Books.

Soifer, S., Zgourides, G. D., Himle, J., and Pickering, N. L. (2001). *Shy Bladder Syndrome: Your Step-By-Step Guide to Overcoming Paruresis.* Oakland, CA: New Harbinger.

Stein, M. B., and Walker, J. R. (2001). *Triumph over Shyness: Conquering Shyness and Social Anxiety.* New York: McGraw-Hill.

Steiner, C. (1997). *Achieving Emotional Literacy: A Personal Program to Improve Your Emotional Intelligence.* New York: Avon Books.

Social Skills Deficits

Alberti, R. E., and Emmons, M. L. (2001). *Your Perfect Right: Assertiveness and Equality in Your Life and Relationships,* 8th ed. Atascadero, CA: Impact.

Garner, A. (1997). *Conversationally Speaking: Tested New Ways to Increase Your Personal and Social Effectiveness.* New York: McGraw-Hill.

Lindenfield, G. (2001). *Assert Yourself.* New York: HarperThorsons.

Pfeiffer, R. (2003). *The Real Solution Assertiveness Workbook.* New York: Growth.

Specific Fears and Avoidance

Antony, M. M., Craske, M. G., and Barlow, D. H. (2006). *Mastering Your Fears and Phobias: Workbook,* 2nd ed. New York: Oxford University Press.

Antony, M. M., and McCabe, R. E. (2006). *Overcoming Animal and Insect Phobias: How to Conquer Fear of Dogs, Snakes, Rodents, Bees, Spiders, and More.* Oakland, CA: New Harbinger.

Antony, M. M., and Rowa, K. (2007). *Overcoming Fear of Heights: How to Conquer Acrophobia and Live a Life without Limits.* Oakland, CA: New Harbinger.

Antony, M. M., and Watling, M. A. (2006). *Overcoming Medical Phobias: How to Conquer Fear of Blood, Needles, Doctors, and Dentists.* Oakland, CA: New Harbinger.

Bourne, E. (1998). *Overcoming Specific Phobias—Client Manual: A Hierarchy and Exposure-Based Protocol for the Treatment of All Specific Phobias.* Oakland, CA: New Harbinger.

Bourne, E. (2005). *The Anxiety and Phobia Workbook,* 4th ed. Oakland, CA: New Harbinger.

Suicidal Ideation

Klott, J., and Jongsma, A. E. (2004) *The Suicide and Homicide Risk Assessment and Prevention Treatment Planner.* Hoboken, NJ: Wiley.

Linehan, M., and Goodstein, J. (1983). "Reasons for staying alive when you are thinking of killing yourself: The Reasons for Living Scale." *Journal of Consulting and Clinical Psychology, 51,* 276–286.

Appendix B

REFERENCES FOR
EVIDENCE-BASED CHAPTERS

Anger Management

Deffenbacher, J. L., Dahlen, E. R., Lynch, R. S., Morris, C. D., and Gowensmith, W. N. (2000). An application of Beck's cognitive therapy to general anger reduction. *Cognitive Therapy and Research, 24,* 687–689.

Deffenbacher, J. L., Oetting, E. R., Huff, M. E., Cornell, G. R., and Dallagher, C. J., et al. (1996). Evaluation of two cognitive-behavioral approaches to general anger reduction. *Cognitive Therapy and Research, 20,* 551–573.

Deffenbacher, J. L., Story, D., Brandon, A., Hogg, J., and Hazaleus, S. (1988). Cognitive and cognitive relaxation treatment of anger. *Cognitive Therapy and Research, 12,* 167–184.

DiGiuseppe, R., and Tafrate, R. C. (2003). Anger treatment for adults: A meta-analytic review. *Clinical Psychology: Science and Practice, 10,* 70–84.

Feindler, E., and Ecton, R. (1986). *Adolescent Anger Control: Cognitive-Behavioral Techniques.* New York: Pergamon Press.

Meichenbaum, D. (1985). *Stress Inoculation Training.* New York: Pergamon Press.

Meichenbaum, D. (1993). Stress inoculation training: A twenty-year update. In R. L. Woolfolk and P. M. Lehrer (Eds.), *Principles and Practices of Stress Management.* New York: Guilford Press.

Meichenbaum, D. (2001). *Treatment of Individuals with Anger Control Problems and Aggressive Behaviors: A Clinical Handbook.* Clearwater, FL: Institute Press.

Novaco, R. (1975). *Anger Control: The Development and Evaluation of an Experimental Treatment.* Lexington, MA: Lexington Books.

Novaco, R. (1976). The functions and regulation of the arousal of anger. *American Journal of Psychiatry, 133,* 1124–1128.

Novaco, R. (1977). A stress inoculation approach to anger management in the training of law enforcement officers. *American Journal of Community Psychology, 5,* 327–346.

Anxiety

Barlow, D. H., Raffa, S. D., and Cohen, E. M. (2002). Psychosocial treatments for panic disorders, phobias, and generalized anxiety disorder. In P. E. Nathan and J. M. Gorman (Eds.), *A Guide to Treatments that Work,* 2nd ed. (pp. 301–335). New York: Oxford University Press.

Beck, A. T., and Emory, G. (1990). *Anxiety Disorders and Phobias: A Cognitive Perspective.* New York: Basic Books.

Bernstein, D. A., and Borkovec, T. D. (1973). *Progressive Relaxation Training.* Champaign, IL: Research Press.

Brown, T. A., DiNardo, P. A., and Barlow, D. H. (2006). *Anxiety Disorders Interview Schedule Adult Version (ADIS-IV): Client Interview Schedule.* New York: Oxford University Press.

Brown, T. A., O'Leary, T., and Barlow, D. H. (2001). Generalized anxiety disorder. In D. H. Barlow (Ed.), *Clinical Handbook of Psychological Disorders: A Step-by-Step Treatment Manual,* 3rd ed. (pp. 154–208). New York: Guilford Press.

Chambless, D. L., Baker, M. J., Baucom, D., Beutler, L. E., Calhoun, K. S., Crits-Christoph, P., et al. (1998). Update on Empirically Validated Therapies: Pt. II. *Clinical Psychologist, 51*(1), 3–16.

Chambless, D. L., and Ollendick, T. H. (2001). Empirically supported psychological interventions: Controversies and evidence. *Annual Review of Psychology, 52,* 685–716.

Haley, J. (1984). *Ordeal Therapy.* San Francisco: Jossey-Bass.

Meyer, T. J., Miller, M. L., Metzger, R. L., and Borkovec, T. D. (1990). Development and validation of the Penn State Worry Questionnaire. *Behaviour Research and Therapy, 28,* 487–495.

Rygh, J. L., and Sanderson, W. C. (2004). *Treating GAD: Evidence-Based Strategies, Tools, and Techniques.* New York: Guilford Press.

Zinbarg, R. E., Craske, M. G., and Barlow, D. H. (2006). *Mastery of Your Anxiety and Worry: Therapist Guide,* 2nd ed. New York: Oxford University Press.

Borderline Personality

Beck, A. T., Rush, A. J., Shaw, B. F., and Emery, G. (1979). *Cognitive Therapy of Depression.* New York: Guilford Press.

Freeman, A. (2002). Cognitive behavioral therapy for severe personality disorders. In S. G. Hofmann and M. C. Tompson (Eds.), *Treating Chronic and Severe Mental Disorders: A Handbook of Empirically Supported Interventions* (pp. 382–402). New York: Guilford Press.

Linehan, M. M. (1993). *Cognitive-Behavioral Treatment of Borderline Personality Disorder.* New York: Guilford Press.

Linehan, M. M. (1993). *Skills Training Manual for Treating Borderline Personality Disorder.* New York: Guilford Press.

Linehan, M. M., Armstrong, H., Suarez, A., Allmon, D., and Heard, H. (1991). Cogni-tive-behavioral treatment of chronically parasuicidal borderline patients. *Archives of General Psychiatry, 48,* 1060–1064.

Linehan, M. M., Cochran, B. N., and Kehrer, C. A. (2001). Dialectical Behavior Therapy for Borderline Personality Disorder. In D. H. Barlow (Ed.), *Clinical Handbook of Psychological Disorders: A Step-by-Step Treatment Manual,* 3rd ed. New York: Guilford Press.

Linehan, M. M., Dimeff, L. A., and Koerner, K. (2007). *Dialectical Behavior Therapy in Clinical Practice: Applications across Disorders and Settings.* New York: Guilford Press.

Linehan, M. M., Heard, H. L., and Armstrong, H. E. (1993). Naturalistic follow-up of a behavioral treatment for chronically parasuicidal borderline patients. *Archives of General Psychiatry, 50,* 971–974.

Linehan, M. M., Schmidt, H., Dimeff, L. A., Craft, J. C., Kanter, J., and Comtois, K. A. (1999). Dialectical behavior therapy for patients with borderline personality disorder and drug-dependence. *American Journal on Addiction, 8*(4), 279–292.

Linehan, M. M., Tutek, D., Heard, H., and Armstrong, H. (1992). Interpersonal outcome of cognitive behavioral treatment for chronically suicidal borderline patients. *American Journal of Psychiatry, 151*(12), 1771–1775.

Resick, P. A., and Calhoun, K. S. (2001). Posttraumatic stress disorder. In D. H. Barlow (Ed.), *Clinical Handbook of Psychological Disorders: A Step-by-Step Treatment Manual,* 3rd ed. New York: Guilford Press.

Safer, D. L., Telch, C. F., and Agras, W. S. (2001). *American Journal of Psychiatry, 158(*4), 632–634.

Whitehurst, T., Ridolfi, M. E., and Gunderson, J. (2002). Multiple family group treatment for borderline personality disorder. In S. G. Hofmann and M. C. Tompson (Eds.), *Treating Chronic and Severe Mental Disorders: A Handbook of Empirically Supported Interventions* (pp. 343–363). New York: Guilford Press.

Chemical Dependence

Abbot, P. J., Weller, S. B., Delaney, H. D., and Moore, B. A. (1998). Community rein-forcement approach in the treatment of opiate addicts. *American Journal of Drug and Alcohol Abuse, 24*(1), 17–30.

Drake, R. E., McHugo, G., and Noordsy, D. L. 1993). Treatment of alcoholism among schizophrenic outpatients: Four-year outcomes. *American Journal of Psychiatry, 150,* 328–329.

Epstein, E. E., and McGrady, B. S. (1998). Behavioral couples treatment of alcohol and drug use disorders: Current status and innovations. *Clinical Psychology Review, 18,* 689–711.

Finney, J. W., and Moos, R. H. (2002). Psychosocial treatments for alcohol use disorders. In P. E. Nathan and J. M. Gorman (Eds.), *A Guide to Treatments That Work* (Vol. II). New York: Oxford University Press.

Marlatt, G. A., and Gordon, J. R. (1985). *Relapse Prevention: Maintenance Strategies in the Treatment of Addictive Behaviors.* New York: Guilford Press.

McCrady, B. S. (2001). Alcohol use disorders. In D. H. Barlow (Ed.), *Clinical Handbook of Psychological Disorders,* 3rd ed. New York: Guilford Press.

Miller, W. R., Andrews, N. R., Wilbourne, P., and Bennett, M. E. (1998). A wealth of alternatives: Effective treatments for alcohol problems. In W. R. Miller and N. Heather (Eds.), *Treating Addictive Behaviors,* 2nd ed. (pp. 203–216). New York: Plenum Press.

Miller, W. R., and Rollnick, S. (2002). *Motivational Interviewing: Preparing People for Change,* 2nd ed. New York: Guilford Press.

Mueser, K. T., Noordsy, D. L., Drake, R. E., and Fox, L. (2003). *Integrated Treatment for Dual Disorders: A Guide to Effective Practice.* New York: Guilford Press.

O'Farrell, T. J., Choquette, K. A., and Cutter, H. S. G. (1998). Couples relapse prevention sessions after Behavioral Marital Therapy for male alcoholics: Outcomes during the three years after starting treatment. *Journal of Studies on Alcohol, 59,* 357–370.

O'Farrell, T. J., Choquette, K. A., Cutter H. S. G., Brown, E. D., and McCourt, W. F. (1993). Behavioral Marital Therapy with and without additional couples relapse prevention sessions for alcoholics and their wives. *Journal of Studies on Alcohol, 54,* 652–666.

Ouimette, P. C., Finney, J. W., and Moos, R. H. (1997). Twelve step and cognitive-behavioral treatment for substance abuse: A comparison of treatment effectiveness. *Journal of Consulting and Clinical Psychology, 65,* 230–240.

Prochaska, J. O., DiClemente, C. C., and Norcross, J. C. (1992). In search of how people change: Applications to addictive behavior. *American Psychologist, 47*(9), 1102–1114.

Project, MATCH Research Group. (1997). Matching alcoholism treatments to client heterogeneity: Project MATCH posttreatment drinking outcomes. *Journal of Studies on Alcohol, 58,* 7–29.

Smith, J. E., Meyers, R. J., and Delaney, H. D. (1998). The community reinforcement approach with homeless alcohol-dependent individuals. *Journal of Consulting and Clinical Psychology, 66,* 541–548.

Depression

Beck, A. T., Rush, A. J., Shaw, B. F., and Emery, G. (1979). *Cognitive Therapy of Depression.* New York: Guilford Press.

Beck, A. T., Steer, R. A. (1988). *Beck Hopelessness Scale.* San Antonio, TX: Psychological Corporation.

Beck, A. T., Steer, R. A., and Brown, G. K. (1996). *Beck Depression Inventory Manual,* 2nd ed. San Antonio, TX: Psychological Corporation.

Beck, J. S. (1995). *Cognitive Therapy: Basics and Beyond.* New York: Guilford Press.

Bowman, D., Scogin, F., and Lyrene, B. (1995). The efficacy of self-examination and cognitive bibliotherapy in the treatment of mild to moderate depression. *Psychotherapy Research, 5,* 131–140.

Klerman, G. L., Weissman, M. M., Rounasacille, B. J., and Chevron, E. S. (1984). *Interpersonal Psychotherapy of Depression.* New York: Basic Books.

Leith, L. M. (1998). *Exercising Your Way to Better Mental Health.* Morgantown, WV: Fitness Information Techology.

Lewinsohn, P. M. (1974). A behavioural approach to depression. In R. J. Friedman and Katz (Eds.), *The Psychology of Depression.* Washington, DC: Winston.

Lewinsohn, P. M., Antonuccio, D. O., Steinmetz, J. L., and Teri, L. (1984). *The Coping with Depression Course: A Psychoeducational Intervention for Unipolar Depression.* Eugene, OR: Castalia.

Nezu, A. M., Nezu, C. M., and Perri, M. G. (1989). *Problem-Solving Therapy for Depression: Theory, Research, and Clinical Guidelines.* New York: Wiley.

Scogin, F., Jamison, C., and Gochneaur, K. (1989). Comparative efficacy of cognitive and behavioral bibliotherapy for mildly and moderately depressed adults. *Journal of Consulting and Clinical Psychology, 57,* 403–407.

Weissman, M. M., Markowitz, J. C., and Klerman, G. L. (2000). *Comprehensive Guide to Interpersonal Psychotherapy.* New York: Basic Books.

Zimmerman, M., Coryell, W., Corenthal, C., and Wilson, S. (1986). A self-report scale to diagnose major depressive disorder. *Archives of General Psychiatry, 43,* 1076–1081.

Employment Problems

Becker, D. R., and Drake, R. E. (2003). *A Working Life for People with Severe Mental Illness.* New York: Oxford University Press.

Bond, G. R. (2004). Supported employment: Evidence for an evidence-based practice. *Psychiatric Rehabilitation Journal, 27,* 345–359.

Fein, R. (1999). *101 Quick Tips for a Dynamite Resume.* Manassas Park, VA: Impact Publications.

Salyers, M. P., Becker, D. R., Drake, R. E., Torrey, W. C., and Wyzik, P. F. (2004). Ten-year follow-up of clients in a supported employment program. *Psychiatric Services, 55,* 302–308.

Family Conflicts

Bebbington, P., and Kuipers, L. (1994). The predictive utility of expressed emotion in schizophrenia: An aggregate analysis. *Psychological Medicine, 24,* 707–718.

Falloon, I. R. H. (2002). Cognitive-behavioral family and educational interventions for schizophrenic disorders. In S. G. Hofmann and M. G. Thompson (Eds.), *Treating Chronic and Severe Mental Disorders* (pp. 3–17). New York: Guilford Press.

Falloon, I. R. H., Boyd, J., and McGill, C. (1984). *Family Care of Schizophrenia.* New York: Guilford Press.

Falloon, I. R. H., and Penderson, J. (1985). Family management in the prevention of morbidity of schizophrenia: The adjustment of the family unit. *Archives of General Psychiatry, 147,* 156–163.

Hogarty, G. E., Anderson, C. M., Reiss, D. J., Kornblith, S. J., Greenwald, D. P., Javna, C. D., et al. (1986). Family psychoeducation, social skills training, and maintenance chemotherapy in the aftercare treatment of schizophrenia: Pt. I. One-year effects of a controlled study on relapse and expressed emotion. *Archives of General Psychiatry, 34,* 633–642.

Hogarty, G. E., Anderson, C. M., Reiss, D. J., Kornblith, S. J., Greenwald, D. P., Ulrich, R. F., et al. (1991). Family psychoeducation, social skills training, and maintenance chemotherapy in the aftercare treatment of schizophrenia: Pt. II. Two-year effects of a controlled study on relapse and adjustment. *Archives of General Psychiatry, 48,* 340–347.

Hogarty, G. E., Greenwald D., Ulrich, R. F., Kornblith, S. J., DiBarry, A. L., Cooley, S., et al. (1997). Three-year trials of personal therapy among schizophrenic patients living with or independent of family: Pt. II. Effects on adjustment of patients. *American Journal of Psychiatry, 154*(11), 1514–1524.

Hogarty, G. E. Kornblith, S. J., Greenwald, D., DiBarry, A. L., Cooley, S., Ulrich, R., et al. (1997). Three-year trials of personal therapy among schizophrenic patients living with or independent of family: Pt. I. Description of study and effects on relapse rates. *American Journal of Psychiatry, 154*(11), 1504–1513.

Leff, J. (1994). Working with families of schizophrenic consumers. *British Journal of Psychiatry, 164*(Suppl. 23), 71–76.

Leff, J., Berkowitz, R., Shavit, N., Strachan, A., Glass, I., and Vaughn, C. (1989). A trial of family therapy v. a relatives group for schizophrenia. *British Journal of Psychiatry, 154,* 58–66.

Leff, J., Berkowitz, R., Shavit, N., Strachan, A., Glass, I., and Vaughn, C. (1990). A trial of family therapy v. a relatives group for schizophrenia: Two-year follow-up. *British Journal of Psychiatry, 157,* 571–577.

McFarlane, W. R. (2002). Empirical studies of outcome in multifamily groups. In W. R. McFarlane (Ed.), *Multifamily Groups in the Treatment of Severe Psychiatric Disorders* (pp. 49–70). New York: Guilford Press.

McFarlane, W. R., Dixon, L., Lukens, E., and Lucksted, A. (2003). Family psychoeducation and schizophrenia: A review of the literature. *Journal of Marital and Family Therapy, 29,* 223–245.

McFarlane, W. R., Lukens, E., Link, B., Dushay, R., Deakins, S. A., Newmark, M., et al. (1995). Multiple-family groups and psychoeducation in the treatment of schizophrenia. *Archives of General Psychiatry, 52,* 679–687.

Miklowitz, D. (2001). Bipolar disorder. In D. H. Barlow (Ed.), *Clinical Handbook of Psychological Disorders: A Step-by-Step Treatment Manual,* 3rd ed. New York: Guilford Press.

Miklowitz, D. J., George, E. L., Richards, J. A., Simoneau, T. L., and Suddath, R. L. (2003). A randomized study of family-focused psychoeducation and pharmacotherapy in the outconsumer management of bipolar disorder. *Archives of General Psychiatry, 60,* 904–912.

Miklowitz, D. J., and Goldstein, M. J. (1997). *Bipolar Disorder: A Family-Focused Treatment Approach.* New York: Guilford Press.

Miklowitz, D. J., and Hooley, J. M. (1998). Developing family psychoeducational treatments for patients with bipolar and other severe psychiatric disorders. *Journal of Marital and Family Therapy, 24*(4), 419–435.

Miklowitz, D. J., Simoneau, T. L., George, E. L., Richards, J. A., Kalbag, A., Sachs-Ericcson, N., et al. (2000). Family-focused treatment of bipolar disorder: One-year effects of a psychoeducational program in conjunction with pharmacotherapy. *Biological Psychiatry, 48,* 582–592.

Miller, W. R. (1999). *Enhancing Motivation for Change in Substance Abuse Treatment.* Rockville, MD: The Center.

Otto, M., Reilly-Harrington, N., Knauz, R. O., Heinin, A., Kogan, J. N., and Sachs, G. S. (2008). *Living with Bipolar Disorder.* Cambridge, MA: Oxford University Press.

Rea, M. M., Tompson, M. C., Miklowitz, D. G., Goldstein, M. J., Hwang, S., and Mintz, J. (2003). Family focused treatment versus individual treatment for bipolar disorder: Results of a randomized clinical trial. *Journal of Consulting and Clinical Psychology, 71*(3), 482–492.

Sensky, T., Turkington, D., Kingdon, D., Scott, J. L., Scott, J., Siddle, R., et al. (2000). A randomised controlled trial of cognitive behavioural therapy for persistent symptoms in schizophrenia resistant to medication. *Archives of General Psychiatry, 57,* 165–172.

Tarrier, N., Kinney, C., McCarthy, E., Humphreys, L., Wittowski, A., and Morris, J. (2000). Two-year follow-up of cognitive behaviour therapy and supportive counseling in the treatment of persistent symptoms in chronic schizophrenia. *Journal of Consulting and Clinical Psychology, 68,* 917–922.

Tarrier, N., Kinney, C., McCarthy, E., Wittkowski, A., Yusupoff, Y., Gledhill, A., et al. (2001). The cognitive-behavioural treatment of persistent symptoms in chronic schizophrenia: Are some types of psychotic symptoms more responsive to cognitive-behaviour therapy? *Behavioural and Cognitive Psychotherapy, 29,* 45–56.

Tarrier, N., Wells, A., and Haddock, G. (1998). *Treating Complex Cases: The Cognitive Behavioural Therapy Approach.* Chichester, West Sussex, England: Wiley.

Tarrier, N., Wittkowski, A., Kinney, C., McCarthy, E., Morris, J., and Humphreys, L. (1999). The durability of the effects of cognitive behaviour therapy in the treatment of chronic schizophrenia: Twelve months follow-up. *British Journal of Psychiatry, 174,* 500–504.

Tarrier, N., Yusupoff, L., Kinney, C., McCarthy, E., Gledhill, A., Haddock, G., et al. (1998). A randomised controlled trial of intensive cognitive behaviour therapy for chronic schizophrenia. *British Medical Journal, 317,* 303–307.

Mania or Hypomania

Falloon, I. R. G., Boyd, J. L., and McGill, C. W. (1984). *Family Care of Schizophrenia: A Problem-Solving Approach to the Treatment of Mental Illness.* New York: Guilford Press.

Hooley, and Teasdale. *Perceived Criticism Scale.*

Miklowitz, D. (2001). Bipolar Disorder. In D. H. Barlow (Ed.), *Clinical Handbook of Psychological Disorders: A Step-by-Step Treatment Manual,* 3rd ed. New York: Guilford Press.

Miklowitz, D. J., George, E. L., Richards, J. A., Simoneau, T. L., and Suddath, R. L. (2003). A randomized study of family-focused psychoeducation and pharmacotherapy in the outpatient management of bipolar disorder. *Archives of General Psychiatry, 60,* 904–912.

Miklowitz, D. J., and Goldstein, M. J. (1997). *Bipolar Disorder: A Family-Focused Treatment Approach.* New York: Guilford Press.

Miklowitz, D. J., and Hooley, J. M. (1998). Developing family psychoeducational treatments for patients with bipolar and other severe psychiatric disorders. *Journal of Marital and Family Therapy, 24*(4), 419–435.

Miklowitz, D. J., and Simoneau, T. L., George, E. L., Richards, J. A., Kalbag, A., Sachs-Ericcson, N., et al. (2000). Family-focused treatment of bipolar disorder: One-year effects of a psychoeducational program in conjunction with pharmacotherapy. *Biological Psychiatry, 48,* 582–592.

Miller, W. R. (1999). *Enhancing Motivation for Change in Substance Abuse Treatment.* Rockville, MD: The Center.

Otto, M., and Reilly-Harrington, N. (2002). Cognitive behavioral therapy for the management of bipolar disorder. In S. G. Hofmann and M. C. Tompson (Eds.), *Treating Chronic and Severe Mental Disorders: A Handbook of Empirically Supported Interventions.* New York: Guilford Press.

Perry, A., Tarrier, N., Morris, R., McCarthy, E., and Limb, K. (1999). Randomised controlled trial of efficacy of teaching patients with bipolar disorder to identify early symptoms of relapse and obtain treatment. *British Medical Journal, 318,* 149–153.

Rea, M. M., Tompson, M., Miklowitz, D. J., Goldstein, M. J., Hwang, S., and Mintz, J. (2003). Family focused treatment vs. individual treatment for bipolar disorder: Results of a randomized clinical trial. *Journal of Consulting and Clinical Psychology, 71,* 482–492.

Simoneau, T. L., Miklowitz, D. J., Richards, J. A., Saleem, R., and George, E. L. (1999). Bipolar disorder and family communication: Effects of a psychoeducational treatment program. *Journal of Abnormal Psychology, 108,* 588–597.

Wendel, J. S., Miklowitz, D. J., Richards J. A., and George E. L. (2000). Expressed emotion and attributions in the relatives of bipolar patients: an analysis of problem-solving interactions. *Journal of Abnormal Psychology, 109,* 792–796.

Medication Management

Azrin, N. H., and Teichner, G. (1998). Evaluation of an instructional program for improving medication compliance for chronically mentally ill outpatients. *Behaviour Research and Therapy, 36,* 849–861.

Blackwell, B. (1997). *Treatment Compliance and the Therapeutic Alliance.* Amsterdam: Harwood Academic.

Boczkowski, J., Zeichner, A., and DeSanto, N. (1985). Neuroleptic compliance among chronic schizophrenic outpatients: An intervention outcome report. *Journal of Consulting and Clinical Psychology, 53,* 666–671.

Cramer, J. A., and Rosenheck, R. (1999). Enhancing medication compliance for people with serious mental illness. *The Journal of Nervous and Mental Disease, 87,* 53–55.

Kelly, G. R., and Scott, J. E. (1990). Medication compliance and health education among outpatients with chronic mental disorders. *Medical Care, 28,* 1181–1197.

Kemp, R., Hayward, P., Applewhaite, G., Everitt, B., and David A. (1996). Compliance therapy in psychotic patients: randomised controlled trial. *British Medical Journal, 312,* 345–349.

Kemp, R., Kirov, G., Everitt, B., Hayward, P., and David, A. (1998). Randomised controlled trial of compliance therapy: 18-month follow-up. *British Journal of Psychiatry, 172,* 413–419.

McFarlane, W. R. (2002). *Multifamily Groups in the Treatment of Severe Psychiatric Disorders.* New York: Guilford Press.

Miklowitz, D. J., and Goldstein, M. J. (1997). *Bipolar Disorder: A Family-Focused Treatment Approach.* New York: Guilford Press.

Miller, W. R., and Rollnick, S. (2002). *Motivational Interviewing: Preparing People for Change,* 2nd ed. New York: Guilford Press.

Nosè M., Barbui C., Gray R., and Tansella, M. (2003). Clinical interventions for treatment non-adherence in psychoses: meta-analysis. *British Journal of Psychiatry, 183,* 197–206.

O'Donnell, C., Donohoe, G., Sharkey, L., Owens, N., Migone, M., Harries, R., et al. (2003). Compliance therapy: A randomised controlled trial in schizophrenia. *British Medical Journal, 327,* 834.

Zuckoff, A., and Daley, D. (1999). *Improving Treatment Compliance: Counseling and Systems Strategies for Substance Abuse and Dual Disorders.* Center City, MN: Hazelden Foundation.

Obsessive-Compulsive Disorder (OCD)

Brown, T. A., DiNardo, P. A., and Barlow, D. H. (2006). *Anxiety Disorders Interview Schedule Adult Version (ADIS-IV): Client Interview Schedule.* New York: Oxford University Press.

Foa, E. B., and Franklin, M. E. (2001). Obsessive-compulsive disorder. In D. H. Barlow (Ed.), *Clinical Handbook of Psychological Disorders: A Step-by-Step Treatment Manual,* 3rd ed. New York: Guilford Press.

Franklin, R., March, J., and Foa, E. (2002). Obsessive-compulsive disorder. In M. Hersen (Ed.), *Clinical Behavior Therapy: Adults and Children.* Hoboken, NJ: Wiley.

Goodman, W. K., Price, L. H., Rasmussen, S. A., Mazure, C., Delgado, P., Heninger, G. R., et al. (1989). The Yale-Brown Obsessive-Compulsive Scale II. Validity. *Archives of General Psychiatry, 46,* 1012–1016.

Goodman, W. K., Price, L. H., Rasmussen, S. A., Mazure, C., Fleishmann, R. L., Hill, C. L. et al. (1989). The Yale-Brown Obsessive-Compulsive Scale I. Development, use, and reliability. *Archives of General Psychiatry, 46,* 1006–1011.

Hiss, H., Foa, E. B., and Kozak, M. J. (1994). A relapse prevention program for treatment of obsessive compulsive disorder. *Journal of Consulting and Clinical Psychology, 62,* 801–808.

Kozak, M., and Foa, E. B. (2004). *Mastery of Obsessive-Compulsive Disorder: A Cognitive Behavioral Approach.* San Antonio, TX: Psychological Corporation.

McGinn, L. and Sanderson, W. C. (1999). *Treatment of Obsessive-Compulsive Disorder.* Northvale, NJ: Aronson.

Riggs, D. S., and Foa, E. B. (1993). Obsessive-compulsive disorder. In D. H. Barlow (Ed.), *Clinical Handbook of Psychological Disorders,* 2nd ed. New York: Guilford Press.

Salkovskis, P. M., and Kirk, J. (1997). Obsessive-compulsive disorder. In D. M. Clark and C. G. Fairburn (Eds.), *Science and Practice of Cognitive Behaviour Therapy.* Oxford, England: Oxford University Press.

Steketee, G. (1993). *Treatment of Obsessive Compulsive Disorder.* New York: Guilford Press.

Turner, S. M., and Beidel, D. C. (1988). *Treating Obsessive-Compulsive Disorder.* New York: Pergamon.

Panic/Agoraphobia

Barlow, D. H., Craske, M. G., Cerny, J. A., and Klosko, J. S. (1989). Behavioral treatment of panic disorder. *Behavior Therapy, 20,* 261–282.

Brown, T. A., DiNardo, P. A., and Barlow, D. H. (2006). *Anxiety Disorders Interview Schedule Adult Version (ADIS-IV): Client Interview Schedule.* New York: Oxford University Press.

Chambless, D. L., Baker, M. J., Baucom, D., Beutler, L. E., Calhoun, K. S., Crits-Christoph, P., et al. (1998). Update on Empirically Validated Therapies: Pt. II. *Clinical Psychologist, 51*(1), 3–16.

Chambless, D. L., Caputo, G. C., Jasin, S. E., Gracel, E. J., and Williams, C. (1985). The mobility inventory for agoraphobia. *Behaviour Research and Therapy, 23,* 35–44.

Chambless, D. L., and Ollendick, T. H. (2001). Empirically supported psychological interventions: Controversies and evidence. *Annual Review of Psychology, 52,* 685–716.

Clark, D. M., Salkovskis, P. M., Hackman, A., Middleton, H., Anastasiades, P., and Gelder, M. (1994). A comparison of cognitive therapy, applied relaxation, and imipramine in the treatment of panic disorder. *British Journal of Psychiatry, 164,* 759–769.

Craske, M. G., and Barlow, D. H. (2006). *Mastery of Your Anxiety and Panic: Therapist Guide.* New York: Oxford University Press.

Craske, M. G., and Barlow, D. H. (2000). *Mastery of Your Anxiety and Panic (MAP-3): Agoraphobia Supplement.* San Antonio, TX: Graywind/Psychological Corporation.

Febbraro, G. A. R. (2005). An investigation into the effectiveness of bibliotherapy and minimal contact interventions in the treatment of panic attacks. *Journal of Clinical Psychology, 61,* 763–779.

Nathan, P. E., and Gorman, J. M. (Eds.). (2002). *A Guide to Treatments That Work* (Vol. II). New York: Oxford University Press.

Reiss, Peterson, and Gursky. *The Anxiety Sensitivity Index.*

Reiss, S., Peterson, R. A., Gursky, D. M., and McNally, R. J. (1986). Anxiety sensitivity, anxiety frequency, and the prediction of fearfulness. *Behaviour Research and Therapy, 24,* 1–8.

Paranoia

Bebbington, P., and Kuipers, L. (1994). The predictive utility of expressed emotion in schizophrenia: An aggregate analysis. *Psychological Medicine, 24,* 707–718.

Falloon, I. R. H. (2002). Cognitive-behavioral family and educational interventions for schizophrenic disorders. In S. G. Hofmann and M. G. Thompson (Eds.), *Treating Chronic and Severe Mental Disorders* (pp. 3–17). New York: Guilford Press.

Falloon, I. R. H., Boyd, J., and McGill, C. (1984). *Family Care of Schizophrenia.* New York: Guilford Press.

Falloon, I. R. H., and Penderson, J. (1985). Family management in the prevention of morbidity of schizophrenia: The adjustment of the family unit. *Archives of General Psychiatry, 147,* 156–163.

Hogarty, G. E. (2002). *Personal Therapy: A Guide to the Individual Treatment of Schizophrenia and Related Disorders.* New York: Guilford Press.

Hogarty, G. E., Anderson, C. M., Reiss, D. J., Kornblith, S. J., Greenwald, D. P., Javna, C. D., et al. (1986). Family psychoeducation, social skills training, and maintenance chemotherapy in the aftercare treatment of schizophrenia: Pt. I. One-year effects of a controlled study on relapse and expressed emotion. *Archives of General Psychiatry, 34,* 633–642.

Hogarty, G. E., Anderson, C. M., Reiss, D. J., Kornblith, S. J., Greenwald, D. P., Ulrich, R. F., et al. (1991). Family psychoeducation, social skills training, and maintenance chemotherapy in the aftercare treatment of schizophrenia: Pt. II. Two-year effects of a controlled study on relapse and adjustment. *Archives of General Psychiatry, 48,* 340–347.

Hogarty, G. E., Greenwald D., Ulrich, R. F., Kornblith, S. J., DiBarry, A. L., Cooley, et al. (1997). Three-year trials of personal therapy among schizophrenic patients living with or independent of family: Pt. II. Effects on adjustment of patients. *American Journal of Psychiatry, 154*(11), 1514–1524.

Hogarty, G. E. Kornblith, S. J., Greenwald, D., DiBarry, A. L., Cooley, S., Ulrich, R., et al. (1997). Three-year trials of personal therapy among schizophrenic patients living with or independent of family: Pt. I. Description of study and effects on relapse rates. *American Journal of Psychiatry, 154*(11), 1504–1513.

Kuipers, E., Garety, P., Fowler, D., Chisholm, D., Freeman, D., Dunn, G., et al. (1998). London-East Anglia randomized controlled trial of cognitive-behavioural therapy for psychosis: Pt. III. Follow-up and economic evaluation at 18 months. *British Journal of Psychiatry, 173,* 61–68.

Kuipers, E., Garety, P., Fowler, D., Dunn, G., Bebbington, P., Freeman, D., et al. (1997). London-East Anglia randomised controlled trial of cognitive-behavioural therapy for psychosis: Pt. I. Effects of the treatment phase. *British Journal of Psychiatry, 171,* 319–327.

Leff, J. (1994). Working with families of schizophrenic consumers. *British Journal of Psychiatry, 164*(Suppl. 23), 71–76.

Leff, J., Berkowitz, R., Shavit, N., Strachan, A., Glass, I., and Vaughn, C. (1989). A trial of family therapy v. a relatives group for schizophrenia. *British Journal of Psychiatry, 154,* 58–66.

Leff, J., Berkowitz, R., Shavit, N., Strachan, A., Glass, I., and Vaughn, C. (1990). A trial of family therapy v. a relatives group for schizophrenia: Two-year follow-up. *British Journal of Psychiatry, 157,* 571–577.

Lehman, A. F., Steinwachs, D. M., Buchanan, R., Carpenter, W. T., Dixon, L. B., Fahey, M., et al. (1998). Translating research into practice: The Schizophrenia Consumer Outcomes Research Team (PORT) treatment recommendations. *Schizophrenia Bulletin, 24,* 1–10.

Lewis, S., Tarrier, N., Haddock, G., Bentall, R., Kinderman, P., Kingdon, P., and the SOCRATES Group. (in press). A randomised trial of cognitive behaviour therapy in early schizophrenia and related disorders. *British Journal of Psychiatry.*

McFarlane, W. R. (2002). Empirical studies of outcome in multifamily groups. In W. R. McFarlane (Ed.), *Multifamily Groups in the Treatment of Severe Psychiatric Disorders* (pp. 49–70). New York: Guilford Press.

McFarlane, W. R., Dixon, L., Lukens, E., and Lucksted, A. (2003). Family psychoeducation and schizophrenia: A review of the literature. *Journal of Marital and Family Therapy.* 29, 223–245.

McFarlane, W. R., Lukens, E., Link, B., Dushay, R., Deakins, S. A., Newmark, M., et al. (1995). Multiple-family groups and psychoeducation in the treatment of schizophrenia. *Archives of General Psychiatry, 52,* 679–687.

Miklowitz, D. J., George, E., L., Richards, J. A., Simoneau, T. L., and Suddath, R. L. (2003). A randomized study of family-focused psychoeducation and pharmacotherapy in the outconsumer management of bipolar disorder. *Archives of General Psychiatry, 60,* 904–912.

Miklowitz, D. J., and Goldstein, M. J. (1997). *Bipolar Disorder: A Family Focused Approach.* New York: Guilford Press.

Rea, M. M., Tompson, M. C., Miklowitz, D. G., Goldstein, M. J., Hwang, S., and Mintz, J. (2003). Family focused treatment versus individual treatment for bipolar disorder:

Results of a randomized clinical trial. *Journal of Consulting and Clinical Psychology, 71*(3), 482–492.

Sensky, T., Turkington, D., Kingdon, D., Scott, J. L., Scott, J., Siddle, R., et al. (2000). A randomised controlled trial of cognitive behavioural therapy for persistent symptoms in schizophrenia resistant to medication. *Archives of General Psychiatry, 57,* 165–172.

Tarrier, N. (2002). "The use of coping strategies and self-regulation in the treatment of psychosis," In A. P. Morrison, (Ed.), *A Casebook of Cognitive Therapy for Psychosis,* edited by New York: Taylor & Francis.

Tarrier, N., Kinney, C., McCarthy, E., Humphreys, L., Wittowski, A., and Morris, J. (2000). Two-year follow-up of cognitive behaviour therapy and supportive counseling in the treatment of persistent symptoms in chronic schizophrenia. *Journal of Consulting and Clinical Psychology, 68,* 917–922.

Tarrier, N., Kinney, C., McCarthy, E., Wittkowski, A., Yusupoff, Y., Gledhill, A., et al. (2001). The cognitive-behavioural treatment of persistent symptoms in chronic schizophrenia: Are some types of psychotic symptoms more responsive to cognitive-behaviour therapy? *Behavioural and Cognitive Psychotherapy, 29,* 45–56.

Tarrier, N., Wells, A., and Haddock, G. (1998). *Treating Complex Cases: The Cognitive Behavioural Therapy Approach.* Chichester, West Sussex, England: Wiley.

Tarrier, N., Wittkowski, A., Kinney, C., McCarthy, E., Morris, J., and Humphreys, L. (1999). The durability of the effects of cognitive behaviour therapy in the treatment of chronic schizophrenia: Twelve months follow-up. *British Journal of Psychiatry, 174,* 500–504.

Tarrier, N., Yusupoff, L., Kinney, C., McCarthy, E., Gledhill, A., Haddock, G., et al. (1998). A randomised controlled trial of intensive cognitive behaviour therapy for chronic schizophrenia. *British Medical Journal, 317,* 303–307.

Posttraumatic Stress Disorder (PTSD)

Brown, T. A., DiNardo, P. A., and Barlow, D. H. (2006). *Anxiety Disorders Interview Schedule for the DSM-IV.* New York: Oxford University Press.

Bryant, R. A., and Harvey, A. G. (2000). *Acute Stress Disorder: A Handbook of Theory, Assessment, and Treatment.* Washington, DC: American Psychological Association.

Dunmore, E., Clark, D. M., and Ehlers, A. (2001). A prospective investigation of the role of cognitive factors in persistent Posttraumatic Stress Disorder (PTSD) after physical or sexual assault. *Behaviour Research and Therapy, 39,* 1063–1084.

Ehlers, A., and Clark, D. M. (2000). A cognitive model of posttraumatic stress disorder. *Behaviour Research and Therapy, 38,* 319–345.

Falsetti, S. A., and Resnick, H. S. (2001). Posttraumatic stress disorder. In W. J. Lyddon and J. V. Jones Jr. (Eds.), *Empirically Supported Cognitive Therapies: Current and Future Applications* (pp. 182–99). New York: Springer.

Foa, E. B., Dancu, C. V., Hembree, E. A., Jaycox, L. H., Meadows, E. A., and Street, G. (1999). A comparison of exposure therapy, stress inoculation training and their combination for reducing posttraumatic stress disorder in female assault victims. *Journal of Consulting and Clinical Psychology, 67,* 194–200.

Foa, E. B., Hembree, E. A, and Rothbaum, B. O. (2007). *Prolonged Exposure Therapy for PTSD: Emotional Processing of Traumatic Experiences, Therapists Guide.* New York: Oxford University Press.

Foa, E. B., Keane, T. M., and Friedman, M. J. (2004). *Effective Treatments for PTSD: Practice Guidelines from the International Society for Traumatic Stress Studies.* New York: Guilford Press.

Foa, E. B., and Rothbaum, B. O. (1998). *Treating the Trauma of Rape: Cognitive-Behavioral Therapy for PTSD.* New York: Guilford Press.

Foy, D. W. (Ed.). (1992). *Treating PTSD: Cognitive Behavioral Strategies.* New York: Guilford Press.

Marks, I., Lovell, K., Noshirvani, H., Livanou, M., and Thrasher, S. (1998). Treatment of post-traumatic stress disorder by exposure and/or cognitive restructuring: A controlled study. *Archives of General Psychiatry, 55,* 317–325.

McNally, R. J. (2003). *Remembering Trauma.* Cambridge, MA: Harvard University Press.

Meichenbaum, D. A. (1995). *Clinical Handbook/Practical Therapist Manual for Assessing and Treating Adults with Post-Traumatic Stress Disorder (PTSD).* Clearwater, FL: Institute Press.

Najavits, L. M. (2002). *Seeking Safety: A Treatment Manual for PTSD and Substance Abuse.* New York: Guilford Press.

Padesky, C. A., Candido, D., Cohen, A., Gluhoski, V., McGinn, L. K., Sisti, M., et al. (2002). *Academy of Cognitive Therapy's Trauma Task Force Report.* Available online at: http://academyofct.org.

Resick, P. A., and Calhoun, K. S. (2001). Posttraumatic stress disorder. In D. H. Barlow (Ed.), *Clinical Handbook of Psychological Disorders: A Step-by-Step Treatment Manual,* 3rd ed. New York: Guilford Press.

Resick, P. A., and Schnicke, M. K. (1996). *Cognitive Processing Therapy for Rape Victims: A Treatment Manual.* Newbury Park, CA: Sage.

Rothbaum, B. O., Astin, M. C., and Marsteller, F. (2005). Prolonged Exposure vs Eye Movement Desensitization and Reprocessing (EMDR) for PTSD Rape Victims. *Journal of Traumatic Stress, 18*(6), 607–616.

Wilson, J. P., Friedman, M. J., and Lindy, J. D. (Eds.). (2001). *Treating Psychological Trauma and PTSD.* New York: Guilford Press.

Wilson, J. P., and Keane, T. M. (Eds.). (1997). *Assessing Psychological Trauma and PTSD.* New York, NY: Guilford Press.

Yule, W. (Ed.). (1999). *Post-Traumatic Stress Disorders: Concepts and Therapy.* New York: Wiley.

Psychosis

Bebbington, P., and Kuipers, L. (1994). The predictive utility of expressed emotion in schizophrenia: An aggregate analysis. *Psychological Medicine, 24,* 707–718.

Falloon, I. R. H. (2002). Cognitive-behavioral family and educational interventions for schizophrenic disorders. In S. G. Hofmann and M. G. Thompson (Eds.), *Treating Chronic and Severe Mental Disorders* (pp. 3–17). New York: Guilford Press.

Falloon, I. R. H., Boyd, J., and McGill, C. (1984). *Family Care of Schizophrenia.* New York: Guilford Press.

Falloon, I. R. H., and Penderson, J. (1985). Family management in the prevention of morbidity of schizophrenia: The adjustment of the family unit. *Archives of General Psychiatry, 147,* 156–163.

Hogarty, G. E. (2002). *Personal Therapy: A Guide to the Individual Treatment of Schizophrenia and Related Disorders.* New York: Guilford Press.

Hogarty, G. E., Anderson, C. M., Reiss, D. J., Kornblith, S. J., Greenwald, D. P., Javna, C. D., et al. (1986). Family psychoeducation, social skills training, and maintenance chemotherapy in the aftercare treatment of schizophrenia: Pt. I. One-year effects of a controlled study on relapse and expressed emotion. *Archives of General Psychiatry, 34,* 633–642.

Hogarty, G. E., Anderson, C. M., Reiss, D. J., Kornblith, S. J., Greenwald, D. P., Ulrich, R. F., et al. (1991). Family psychoeducation, social skills training, and maintenance chemotherapy in the aftercare treatment of schizophrenia: Pt. II. Two-year effects of a controlled study on relapse and adjustment. *Archives of General Psychiatry, 48,* 340–347.

Hogarty, G. E., Greenwald D., Ulrich, R. F., Kornblith, S. J., DiBarry, A. L., Cooley, S., et al. (1997). Three-year trials of personal therapy among schizophrenic patients living with or independent of family: Pt. II. Effects on adjustment of patients. *American Journal of Psychiatry, 154*(11), 1514–1524.

Hogarty, G. E. Kornblith, S. J., Greenwald, D., DiBarry, A. L., Cooley, S., Ulrich, R., et al. (1997). Three-year trials of personal therapy among schizophrenic patients living with or independent of family: Pt. I. Description of study and effects on relapse rates. *American Journal of Psychiatry, 154*(11), 1504–1513.

Kuipers, E., Garety, P., Fowler, D., Chisholm, D., Freeman, D., Dunn, G., et al. (1998). London-East Anglia randomized controlled trial of cognitive-behavioural therapy for psychosis: Pt. III. Follow-up and economic evaluation at 18 months. *British Journal of Psychiatry, 173,* 61–68.

Kuipers, E., Garety, P., Fowler, D., Dunn, G., Bebbington, P., Freeman, D., et al. (1997). London-East Anglia randomised controlled trial of cognitive-behavioural therapy for psychosis: Pt. I. Effects of the treatment phase. *British Journal of Psychiatry, 171,* 319–327.

Leff, J. (1994). Working with families of schizophrenic consumers. *British Journal of Psychiatry, 164*(Suppl. 23), 71–76.

Leff, J., Berkowitz, R., Shavit, N., Strachan, A., Glass, I., and Vaughn, C. (1989). A trial of family therapy v. a relatives group for schizophrenia. *British Journal of Psychiatry, 154,* 58–66.

Leff, J., Berkowitz, R., Shavit, N., Strachan, A., Glass, I., and Vaughn, C. (1990). A trial of family therapy v. a relatives group for schizophrenia: Two-year follow-up. *British Journal of Psychiatry, 157,* 571–577.

Lehman, A. F., Steinwachs, D. M., Buchanan, R., Carpenter, W. T., Dixon, L. B., Fahey, M., et al. (1998). Translating research into practice: The Schizophrenia Consumer Outcomes Research Team (PORT) treatment recommendations. *Schizophrenia Bulletin, 24,* 1–10.

Lewis, S., Tarrier, N., Haddock, G., Bentall, R., Kinderman, P., Kingdon, P., and the SOCRATES Group. (in press). A randomised trial of cognitive behaviour therapy in early schizophrenia and related disorders. *British Journal of Psychiatry.*

McFarlane, W. R. (2002). Empirical studies of outcome in multifamily groups. In W. R. McFarlane (Ed.), *Multifamily Groups in the Treatment of Severe Psychiatric Disorders* (pp. 49–70). New York: Guilford Press.

McFarlane, W. R., Dixon, L., Lukens, E., and Lucksted, A. (2003). Family psychoeducation and schizophrenia: A review of the literature. *Journal of Marital and Family Therapy, 29,* 223–245.

McFarlane, W. R., Lukens, E., Link, B., Dushay, R., Deakins, S. A., Newmark, M., et al. (1995). Multiple-family groups and psychoeducation in the treatment of schizophrenia. *Archives of General Psychiatry, 52,* 679–687.

Miklowitz, D. J., George, E. L., Richards, J. A., Simoneau, T. L., and Suddath, R. L. (2003). A randomized study of family-focused psychoeducation and pharmacotherapy in the outconsumer management of bipolar disorder. *Archives of General Psychiatry, 60,* 904–912.

Miklowitz, D. J., and Goldstein, M. J. (1997). *Bipolar Disorder: A Family Focused Approach.* New York: Guilford Press.

Rea, M. M., Tompson, M. C., Miklowitz, D. G., Goldstein, M. J., Hwang, S., and Mintz, J. (2003). Family focused treatment versus individual treatment for bipolar disorder: Results of a randomized clinical trial. *Journal of Consulting and Clinical Psychology, 71*(3), 482–492.

Sensky, T., Turkington, D., Kingdon, D., Scott, J. L., Scott, J., Siddle, R., et al. (2000). A randomised controlled trial of cognitive behavioural therapy for persistent symptoms in schizophrenia resistant to medication. *Archives of General Psychiatry, 57,* 165–172.

Tarrier, N., Kinney, C., McCarthy, E., Humphreys, L., Wittowski, A., and Morris, J. (2000). Two year follow-up of cognitive behaviour therapy and supportive counseling in the treatment of persistent symptoms in chronic schizophrenia. *Journal of Consulting and Clinical Psychology, 68,* 917–922.

Tarrier, N., Kinney, C., McCarthy, E., Wittkowski, A., Yusupoff, Y., Gledhill, A., et al. (2001). The cognitive-behavioural treatment of persistent symptoms in chronic schizophrenia: Are some types of psychotic symptoms more responsive to cognitive-behaviour therapy? *Behavioural and Cognitive Psychotherapy, 29,* 45–56.

Tarrier, N., Wells, A., and Haddock, G. (1998). *Treating Complex Cases: The Cognitive Behavioural Therapy Approach.* Chichester, West Sussex, England: Wiley.

Tarrier, N., Wittkowski, A., Kinney, C., McCarthy, E., Morris, J., and Humphreys, L. (1999). The durability of the effects of cognitive behaviour therapy in the treatment of chronic schizophrenia: Twelve months follow-up. *British Journal of Psychiatry, 174,* 500–504.

Tarrier, N., Yusupoff, L., Kinney, C., McCarthy, E., Gledhill, A., Haddock, G., et al. (1998). A randomised controlled trial of intensive cognitive behaviour therapy for chronic schizophrenia. *British Medical Journal, 317,* 303–307.

Social Anxiety

Antony, M. M., and Swinson, R. P. (2000). *Phobic Disorders and Panic in Adults: A Guide to Assessment and Treatment.* Washington, DC: American Psychological Association.

Beidel, D. C., and Turner, S. M. (1998). *Shy Children, Phobic Adults: Nature and Treatment of Social Phobia.* Washington, DC: American Psychological Association.

Brown, T. A., DiNardo, P. A., and Barlow, D. H. (2006). *Anxiety Disorders Interview Schedule Adult Version (ADIS-IV): Client Interview Schedule.* New York: Oxford University Press.

Bruce, T. J., and Saeed, S. A. (1999). Social anxiety disorder: A common, underrecognized mental disorder. *American Family Physician, 60*(8), 2311–2320.

Chambless, D. L, Baker, M. J., Baucom, D., Beutler, L. E., Calhoun, K. S., Crits-Christoph, P., et al. (1998). Update on empirically validated therapies: Pt. II. *Clinical Psychologist, 51*(1), 3–16.

Chambless, D. L., and Ollendick, T. H. (2001). Empirically supported psychological interventions: Controversies and evidence. *Annual Review of Psychology, 52,* 685–716.

Clark, D. M., and Wells, A. (1995). A cognitive model of social phobia. In R. G. Heimberg M. R. Liebowitz (Eds.), *Social Phobia: Diagnosis, Assessment, and Treatment* (pp. 69–93). New York: Guilford Press.

Crozier, W. R., and Alden, L. E. (2001). *International Handbook of Social Anxiety: Concepts, Research and Interventions Relating to the Self and Shyness.* New York: Wiley.

Heimberg, R. G., and Becker, R. E. (2002). *Cognitive-Behavioral Group Therapy for Social Phobia: Basic Mechanisms and Clinical Strategies.* New York: Guilford Press.

Heimberg, R. G., Liebowitz, M. R., Hope, D. A., and Schneier, F. R. (Eds.). (1995). *Social Phobia: Diagnosis, Assessment, and Treatment.* New York: Guilford Press.

Hofmann, S. G., and DiBartolo, P. M. (2001). *From Social Anxiety to Social Phobia: Multiple Perspectives.* Needham Heights, MA: Allyn & Bacon.

Hope, D. A., Heimberg, R. G., Juster, H. R., and Turk, C. L. (2000). *Managing Social Anxiety.* Boulder, CO: Graywind.

Mattick, R. P., and Clarke, J. C. (1998). Development and validation of measures of social phobia scrutiny fear and social interaction anxiety. *Behaviour Research and Therapy, 36,* 455–470.

Mattick and Clarke. *The Social Interaction Anxiety Scale and or Social Phobia Scale.*

Nathan, P. E., and Gorman, J. M. (Eds.). (2002). *A Guide to Treatments That Work (Vol. II).* New York: Oxford University Press.

Rapee, R. M., and Sanderson, W. C. (1998). *Social Phobia: Clinical Application of Evidence-Based Psychotherapy.* Northvale, NJ: Aronson.

Schelver, S. R., and Gutsch, K. U. (1983). The effects of self-administered cognitive therapy on social-evaluative anxiety. *Journal of Clinical Psychology, 39,* 658–666.

Schmidt, L. A., and Schulkin, J. (Eds.). (1999). *Extreme Fear, Shyness, and Social Phobia: Origins, Biological Mechanisms, and Clinical Outcomes.* New York: Oxford University Press.

Scholing, A., Emmelcamp, P., and Van Oppen, P. (1996). Cognitive Behavioral Treatment of Social Phobia. In V. B. Van Hasselt and M. Hersen (Eds.), *Sourcebook of Psychological Treatment Manuals for Adult Disorders.* New York: Plenum.

Stein, M. B. (Ed.). (1995). *Social Phobia: Clinical and Research Perspectives.* Washington, DC: American Psychiatric Press.

Turk, C., Heimberg, R. G., and Hope, D. A. (2001). Social anxiety disorder. In D. H. Barlow (Ed.), *Clinical Handbook of Psychological Disorders,* 3rd ed. New York: Guilford Press.

Turner, S. M., Beidel, D. C., and Cooley, M. (1997). *Social Effectiveness Therapy: A Program for Overcoming Social Anxiety and Phobia.* Toronto, Ontario, Canada: Multi-Health Systems (Telephone: 416-424-1700, Fax: 416-424-1736).

Social Skills Deficits

Bellack, A., Mueser, K., Gingerich, S., and Agresta, J. (2004). *Social Skills Training for Schizophrenia: A Step-by-Step Guide.* New York: Guilford Press.

Chambon, O., and Marie-Cardine, M. (1998). An evaluation of social skills training modules with schizophrenia inpatients in France. *International Review of Psychiatry, 10,* 26–29.

Eckman, T. A., Wirshing, W. C., Marder, S. R., Liberman, R. P., Johnston-Cronk, K., Zimmerman, K., et al. (1992). Technique for training schizophrenic patients in illness self-management: A controlled trial. *American Journal of Psychiatry, 149,* 1549–1555.

Heinssen, R. K., Liberman, R. P., and Kopelowicz, A. (2000). Psychosocial skills training for schizophrenia: Lessons from the laboratory. *Schizophrenia Bulletin, 26,* 21–46.

Liberman, R. P., Derisi, W. J., and Meuser, K. T. (2001). *Social Skills Training for Psychiatric Patients.* Needham Heights, MA: Allyn and Bacon.

Liberman, R. P., Wallace, C. J., Blackwell, G., MacKain, S., and Eckman, T. A. (1992). Training social and independent living skills: Applications and impact in chronic schizophrenia. In J. Cottraux, P. Legeron, and E. Mollard (Eds.), *Which Psychotherapies in Year 2000?* (pp. 65–90). Amsterdam: Swets & Zeitlinger.

Marder, S. R., Wirshing, W. C., Mintz, J., McKenzie, J., Johnston, K., Eckman, T. A., et al. (1996). Two-year outcome of social skills training and group psychotherapy for outpatients with schizophrenia. *American Journal of Psychiatry, 153,* 1585–1592.

Penn, D. L., and Mueser, K. T. (1996). Research update on the psychosocial treatment of schizophrenia, *American Journal of Psychiatry,* 153, 607–617.

Sayers, M. D., Bellack, A. S., Wade, J. H., Bennett, M. E., and Fong, P. (1995). An empirical method for assessing social problem solving in schizophrenia. *Behavior Modification, 19,* 267–289.

Wallace, C. J., Liberman, R. P., MacKain, S. J., Blackwell, G., and Eckman, T. A. (1992). Effectiveness and replicability of modules for teaching social and instrumental skills to the severely mentally ill. *American Journal of Psychiatry, 149,* 654–658.

Wykes, T., and Sturt, E. (1986). The measurement of social behaviour in psychiatric patients: An assessment of the reliability and validity of the S. S. schedule. *British Journal of Psychiatry, 148,* 1–11.

Specific Fears and Avoidance

Antony, M. M. (2001). Measures for specific phobia. In M. M. Antony, S. M. Orsillo, and I. Roemer (Eds.), *Practitioner's Guide to Empirically-Based Measures of Anxiety.* New York: Kluwer Academic/Plenum Press.

Brown, T. A., DiNardo, P. A., and Barlow, D. H. (2006). *Anxiety Disorders Interview Schedule Adult Version (ADIS-IV): Client Interview Schedule.* New York: Oxford University Press.

Bruce, T., and Sanderson, W. (1998*). Specific Phobias: Clinical Applications of Evidence-Based Psychotherapy.* Northvale, NJ: Aronson.

Craske, M. G., Antony, M. M., and Barlow, D. H. (2006). *Mastering Your Fears and Phobias: Therapist Guide,* 2nd ed. New York: Oxford University Press.

Marks, I. (1978). *Living with Fear.* New York: McGraw Hill.

Ost, L. G., Fellenius, J., and Sterner, U. (1991). Applied tension, exposure in vivo, and tension-only in the treatment of blood phobia. *Behaviour Research and Therapy, 29*(6), 561–574.

Appendix C

INDEX OF *DSM-IV-TR* CODES
ASSOCIATED WITH
PRESENTING PROBLEMS

Printed in the United States of America
ED-05-24-12